CW00969582

Collins

Measurements
& Conversions

William Collins' dream of knowledge for all began with the publication of his first book in 1819. A self-educated mill worker, he not only enriched millions of lives, but also founded a flourishing publishing house. Today, staying true to this spirit, Collins books are packed with inspiration, innovation, and practical expertise. They place you at the centre of a world of possibility and give you exactly what you need to explore it.

Collins. Do more.

Collins

Measurements
& Conversions

Collins

HarperCollins Publishers
Westerhill Road, Bishopbriggs,
Glasgow G64 2QT

www.collins.co.uk

A Diagram book created by Diagram Visual Information Limited of
195 Kentish Town Road, London NW5 2JU

First published 2005

© Diagram Visual Information Limited 2005

Reprint 10 9 8 7 6 5 4 3 2 1 0

A catalogue record for this book is available from the British Library

The Unicode™ Standard is reproduced by kind permission of
Unicode, Inc.

ISBN 0 00 716551-X

Printed and bound in Great Britain by Clays Ltd, St Ives plc.

INTRODUCTION

The need to measure

Systems of measurement have been created by people to quantify natural phenomena. Quantifying lengths, weights, temperatures, forces, and so on, helps scientists to describe and understand the natural world. But the first systems of measurement were devised to allow people to deal more effectively with everyday life.

People have measured lengths, weights and time since the earliest civilizations. Accurate measurements of weight were needed, for example, for buying and selling commodities, and of length for building houses, bridges and other structures. But accurate measurements rely on agreed standards and units. At first these were based on familiar measures, such as the length of the arm or the length of a ploughed furrow, but they were neither precise nor standard. During the Middle Ages, people struggled to cope with units that varied from one place to another, a situation that led to many errors, frauds and disputes. As trade between countries increased, so did the confusion. With advances in science and technology, scientists too demanded a more precise way of measuring.

From 1600 onwards, in the Age of Enlightenment and rational thinking, the search began for a logical, uniform system that was easy to use and would form the basis for all forms of measurement. Scholars wanted one basic unit from which all other units would be derived. Having agreed a unit of length, for example, units for area and volume naturally followed, but it could also define a unit of weight, based on the weight of a particular volume of water. Units for length and weight satisfied most commercial needs.

Following the adoption of the decimal system in the early 17th century, people wanted to apply the same simple concept to units of measurements. In April 1790 a French bishop, Charles Maurice de Talleyrand, proposed a new unit of length based on the length of a pendulum that would make one full swing per second. The French Academy of Sciences examined the idea but decided that the swing of a pendulum was not sufficiently standard, it being affected by variations in temperature and gravity at different places on Earth. They recommended instead that the length of the new unit be one ten-millionth of the distance between the North Pole and the Equator, along a meridian. By 1798 the measurement was made and one metre defined. It was used to derive a standard weight – a kilogram, the weight of a cube of water whose side was one tenth of a metre. In 1799 these two standards were lodged in the French National Archives in Paris.

Having created the metric system, the French then abandoned it in 1812 when Emperor Napoleon returned to the old units of measurement. This motivated the British to create invariable standards for the yard and the pound instead, standards which were adopted across the British Empire and were known as imperial units. Imperial units continued to be used in English-speaking countries until the second half of the 20th century and are still largely used in the United States, where they are known as customary units.

The metric system was reintroduced in France and made compulsory there in 1840, from where it gradually spread to other European countries, South America and the rest of the world. An international conference in 1875, attended by delegates from 17 countries, produced the Treaty of the Metre to promote the spread of the metric system, followed in 1889 by the first General Conference of Weights and Measures which approved the prototypes that defined the metre, the kilogram and other metric measures, and so encouraged more countries to adopt the system.

The aim to base all units on a single unit proved unachievable and eventually six basic units were agreed. In 1960 the eleventh General Conference of Weights and Measures extended the metric system to form the International System of Units (SI units), now internationally accepted in science, technology and business. It uses seven basic units – the metre (length), the kilogram (weight), the second (time), the ampere (electrical current), the kelvin (temperature), the mole (mass), and the candela (light intensity).

Units of measurement in the United States

Successive governments in the United States, from that of President Washington onwards, wanted to have a uniform system of measurement throughout the land and in 1866 the metric system was authorized as legal, but not mandatory. Although the United States participated in all the General Conferences of Weights and Measures, it was not until 1968 that Congress ordered a study that recommended that conversion to metrication should be encouraged on a voluntary basis. People being reluctant and slow to change, however, the customary units of inches, yards and miles are still used for everyday purposes. Scientists, however, increasingly use the metric system and the government long ago accepted that the country would eventually come into line with the rest of the world.

About this book

Different standards have been created around the world, and units based on both the imperial and metric systems of measurement are now encountered. As a result, knowledge is needed of how to convert values from one system to another. The simple need to measure has created a complex web of units that now affects every aspect of life.

Likewise, computers now feature in all areas of everyday life. While the digital age has removed the drudgery of repetitive calculation, the proliferation of computer languages and operating systems has also brought the problems of code conversion and a need for standardization. Collins *Measurements and Conversions* addresses this issue with a ready reference to some of the most commonly used character codes in computing and the internet.

The book is divided into 14 sections: how to use this book, length, area, volume, weight, energy, temperature, time, speed, geometry, numbers, astronomy, food, and computers and the internet. Each section provides essential information on the main units of measurement or features of a particular topic. Where relevant, individual sections have conversion formulae, e.g. for metric and imperial conversion equivalents, with conversion tables to provide immediate visual reference. There are sample calculations to illustrate each formula.

Collins *Measurements and Conversions* is an indispensable guide to the international variety of units of measurement and computer coding. It is an essential companion, whether for school, office or home.

CONTENTS

1   How to use this book

12	Unit conversion index	19	International System of Units
14	Glossary of abbreviations	22	Terms and definitions

2   Length

68	Early measurement systems	69	Conversion formulae
68	Measuring small distances	71	Sample calculations
69	Measuring large distances	72	Conversion tables
69	Astronomical measurements		

3   Area

78	Conversion formulae	87	Sample calculations
80	Sample calculations	88	Formulae for geometry of surface area
81	Conversion tables		
85	Countries and continents compared	89	Sample calculations
86	Formulae for geometry of area		

4   Volume

90	Conversion formulae	105	Sample calculations
93	Units of liquid and dry capacity	106	Cooking measures
94	Sample calculations	107	Handy measures
96	Conversion tables	108	Beverage measures
104	Formulae for geometry of volume		

5   Weight

110	Conversion formulae	113	Atomic mass units
112	Sample calculations	114	Conversion tables
113	Atomic mass	118	Scales of hardness

6   Energy

120	Conversion formulae	124	Electromagnetic spectrum
121	Sample calculations	124	Measuring earthquakes
122	Conversion tables	126	Measuring sound
123	Electromagnetic waves		

7 Temperature

128 Systems of measurement   132 Useful temperatures
129 Conversion formulae   133 Wind-chill temperature
129 Conversion tables

8 Time

134 Units of time   138 Time zones of the world
135 Conversion formulae   140 Geological timescale
136 Sample calculations   141 Types of calendar
137 Measuring time   142 Perpetual calendar

9 Speed

158 Conversion formulae   166 Wind speeds
160 Sample calculations   166 Hurricane
161 Conversion tables

10 Geometry

168 Polygons   171 The compass
170 Quadrilaterals   173 Angles
170 Triangles   174 Conversion tables

11 Numbers

176 Standard UK paper sizes 185 Prime numbers
177 Envelope sizes and styles 185 Fibonacci sequence
178 Clothing sizes   186 Fractions, decimals and
180 Body measurements   percentages
181 Gun gauge   188 Square and cube roots
181 Horse measurements   189 Multiplication tables
182 Named numbers   195 Multiplication grid
182 Numerical prefixes   196 Mathematical symbols
183 Prefixes in order of value 197 Arithmetic operations
184 Roman numerals

12 Astromony

198 Planetary features   204 Light years
200 Planetary distances   204 Stellar magnitudes
202 Sidereal period   205 The ten nearest stars
203 The solar system: orbits
     and rotations

Contents

13 Food

206 Cooking measurements
207 Spoonful equivalents for ingredients
208 Kitchen weights

210 Food and energy
211 Food and drink calorie table

14 Computers and the internet

216 Binary numbers
217 Data storage
218 Data transfer rates
219 Computer coding systems: ASCII

221 Computer coding systems: Unicode
226 Common HTML codes
228 Internet addresses
229 Internet country codes

232 Index

1 How to use this book

Measurements and Conversions is divided into 14 sections, each of which is devoted to a particular category of facts and figures. If you know which category you wish to explore, e.g. length, weight, area, just turn to the table of contents to find the relevant page number.

Formulae

Within the measurement sections, you will find a selection of conversion formulae. These are easy-to-use formulae for common conversions: you will need to use a calculator for most of them, although many are simple, approximate conversions. Sample calculations are also provided.

Conversion tables

Each group of units has its conversion tables: pages of quick-reference tables for all imperial and metric measurements from metres to feet, grains to grams. These are particularly handy if you do not have a calculator. It would be impossible to accommodate tables listing every possible conversion, so the material included is not exhaustive.

You can use the following to convert figures larger than those in the table:

(a) separate the total into its parts: e.g., to convert 1536 units of something, first convert the largest part in the table (1000) and then each remaining part (500, 30 and 6). Then add these separate conversions together to find the total conversion; or

(b) move the decimal point in your original figure until it is at the same decimal position as those in the table. Look for the nearest number to this in the table and record the appropriate conversion. Then move the decimal point the same number of places in the opposite direction to give an approximate conversion of your original number.

Note also that, because of lack of space, the figures in the conversion tables are rounded up or down, usually to the third decimal place, and so are not always exact.

Unit conversion index

In this book, there are tables for converting units from the imperial system of measurement to the metric system (and vice versa), and for converting one type of unit to another within the same system. The following unit conversion index enables you to refer quickly to the tables in which a particular unit is converted.

acre 20, 79–81, 83–84
are 20
bit 217
bits per second 218
calorie 120–122
Celsius 128–131
centimetre 20, 70–73, 75
   cubic 20, 91, 94, 97
   square 20, 78, 80, 82–83
   centimetres per
     second 158, 160, 163
centrad 174–75
chain 20, 70–71, 74, 76
   square 20, 78, 80, 82, 84
circular milli-inch *See*
   milli-inch
cubic units *See* individual
   units listed
cup 206
degree (angle) 174–75
dry volume measurements
   See individual units listed
Fahrenheit 128–131
fathom 20, 70–73, 75
feet per minute 158, 160, 162
feet per second 159, 160, 164
fluid volume *See* individual
   units listed
foot 20, 70–73, 75

cubic 21, 91, 95, 98, 100
   square 20, 79, 81–82, 84
furlong 20, 70–71, 74, 76
gallon 21, 90–93, 95, 97–100
   dry (US) 92, 96, 102–03
   fluid (US) 90, 92–97, 99,
     102–03
grade 174–75
grain 21, 110, 112, 114–15
gram 20, 110–12, 114–16
hectare 20, 79–80, 83–84
horsepower 121–22
inch 20, 70–71, 73, 75
   cubic 21, 90–91, 94, 97, 101
   square 20, 78, 80–83
   inches per second 158, 160,
     163
joule 121–22
kelvin 128–31
kilocalorie 121–22
kilogram 20, 111-12, 115-16
kilograms per square cm 111–12,
   115–16
kilojoule 121–22
kilometre 20, 70, 72, 74, 76
   square 20, 79–80, 83–84
   kilometres per hour
     158–62, 164
kilowatt 121–22

knot 159–60, 163
  international 159–64
litre 91–93, 95, 96, 98–103
magnum 108
metre 20, 70–76
  cubic 20, 91–92, 95–96, 98, 100, 102–03
  square 20, 78–82, 84
  metres per minute 158, 160, 162
metres per second 159, 161, 164
micrometre 70–71, 73, 75
  square 78, 80, 82–83
micron *See* micrometre
mile 20, 70, 72, 74, 76
  nautical 70, 72, 74, 76
  square 20, 79–80, 83–84
miles per hour 158–60, 162–64
milli-inch 70–71, 73, 75
  circular 78, 80, 82–83
millilitre 91–95, 99–102
milligram 20
millimetre 20, 70-71, 73, 75
  square 20, 78, 80, 82–83
nautical mile *See* mile
ounce 21, 110–114, 116, 117
  fluid 21, 90–91, 93-94, 97–98, 100–01

fluid (US) 90, 92–95, 97–98, 101–02
  troy 111–14, 116–17
pint 21, 90–91, 93–95, 97–100
  dry (US) 93
  fluid (US) 90, 92-94, 96–98, 101, 103
pound 21, 111-12, 115–16
  pounds per square inch 111–12, 115–16
quart 21, 90–91, 93–95, 97, 99, 100
  dry (US) 92-93
  fluid (US) 90, 92–94, 96–97, 99, 102-03
  square units *See* individual units listed
radian 174–75
stone 21, 111–12, 115–16
spoonful 206
ton
  long (UK) 21, 111–12, 115
  short (US) 111, 113, 115–16
tonne 20, 111–13, 115-17
yard 20, 70–76
  cubic 21, 91, 95, 98, 101
  square 20, 79–82, 84
yards per minute 158, 160, 162

Glossary of abbreviations

'	foot	c	centirad (angular measure)
'	minute (angular measure)	c	centi (10^{-2})
"	inch	cal	calorie
"	second (angular measure)	Cal	kilocalorie
°	degree	cc	cubic centimetre
°C	degree Celsius	cd	candela
°F	degree Fahrenheit	cg	centigrades (angular measure)
°r	degree Réaumur	ch	chain
°R	degree Rankine	ch²	square chain
a	alto (10^{-18})	Ci	curie
a	are	cl	centilitre
A	ampere	cm	centimetre
Å	ångström	cm/s	centimetres per second
ac	acre	cm²	square centimetre
am	attometre	cm³	cubic centimetre
amu	atomic mass unit	cmil	circular milli-inch
as	attosecond	c	coloumb
atm	atmosphere	cu cm	cubic centimetre
AU	astronomical unit	cu ft	cubic foot
B	bel	cu in	cubic inch
bil	billion	cu km	cubic kilometre
Bq	becquerel	cu m	cubic metre
Btu	British thermal unit	cu mm	cubic millimetre
bu	bushel	cu or ³	cubic units
C	coulomb		

cu yd	cubic yard	**fur**	furlong
cwt	hundredweight	**G**	giga (10^9)
d	day	**g**	grade
d	deci (10^{-1})	**g**	gram
da	deca (10^1)	**g/cm²**	grams per square centimetre
dam	dekametre	**g/cm³**	grams per cubic centimetre
dB	decibel		
dl	decilitre	**gal**	gallon
dm	decimetre	**GHz**	gigahertz
dr	dram	**gi**	gill
dry pt	dry pint	**Gm**	gigametre
dry qt	dry quart	**gr**	grain
dwt	pennyweight	**Gs**	gigasecond
E	exa (10^{18})	**h**	hour
eV	electronvolt	**ha**	hectare
F	farad	**H**	henry
f	femto (10^{-15})	**h**	hecto (10^2)
fl dr	fluid dram (drachm)	**hm**	hectometre
fl oz	fluid ounce	**hp**	horsepower
fm	fathom	**hr**	hour
fm	femtometre	**Hz**	hertz
fs	femtosecond	**in**	inch
ft	foot	**in/s**	inches per second
ft/min	feet per minute	**in²**	square inch
ft/s	feet per second	**in³**	cubic inch
ft²	square foot	**J**	joule
ft³	cubic foot	**K**	kelvin

k	kilo (10^3)	**lb/ft³**	pounds per cubic foot
kcal	kilocalorie	**lm**	lumen
kg	kilogram	**lt**	long (UK) ton
kg/cm²	kilograms per square centimetre	**lx**	lux
kg/cm³	kilograms per cubic centimetre	**ly**	light year
		M	mega (10^6)
kg/m²	kilograms per square metre	**m**	milli (10^{-3})
		m	metre
kg/m³	kilograms per cubic metre	**m**	minute
		m/min	metres per minute
kHz	kilohertz	**m/s**	metres per second
kJ	kilojoule	**m²**	square metre
km	kilometre	**m³**	cubic metre
km/h	kilometres per hour	**mg**	milligram
km/s	kilometres per second	**mg**	milligrade (angular measure)
km²	square kilometre	**MHz**	megahertz
km³	cubic kilometre	**mi**	mile
kn	international knot	**mi²**	square mile
ks	kilosecond	**mi³**	cubic mile
kt	kiloton	**mil**	milli-inch
kW	kilowatt	**min**	minim
kWh	kilowatt-hour	**min**	minute
l	litre	**ml**	millilitre
lb	pound	**mm**	millimetre
lb tr	pound troy	**mmHg**	millimetres of mercury
lb/ft²	pounds per square foot		

Mm	Megametre	**q**	quintal
mm²	square millimetre	**qtr**	quarter
mm³	cubic millimetre	**qtr tr**	quarter troy
mol	mole	**qt**	quart
mph	miles per hour	**rad**	radian (angular measure)
mrad	millirad (angular measure)	**R**	röntgen
Ms	megasecond	**S**	conductance
ms	millisecond	**s**	second
Mt	megaton	**sec**	second
N	newton	**sh cwt**	short hundredweight
N	micro (10^{-6})	**sh t**	short (US) ton
n	nano (10^{-9})	**SI**	International System of Units (Système International d'Unités)
n mi	nautical mile		
nm	nanometre		
ns	nanosecond		
oz	ounce	**sq mi**	square mile
oz tr	ounce troy	**sq or ²**	square units
p	pico (10^{-12})	**sr**	steradian
Pa	pascal	**st**	stone
pc	parsec	**st**	stère
P	peta (10^{15})	**T**	tera (10^{12})
pk	peck	**T**	tesla
pm	picometre	**t**	tonne
ps	picosecond	**tbsp**	tablespoon
PSI	pounds per square inch	**Tm**	terametre
pt	pint	**tn**	ton

ton tr	ton troy	**yd**	yard
Ts	terasecond	**yd/min**	yards per minute
tsp	teaspoon	**yd²**	square yard
UK kn	British knot	**yd³**	cubic yard
US dry gal	US dry gallon	**Y**	yotta (10^{24})
US dry pt	US dry pint	**y**	yocto (10^{-24})
US dry qt	US dry quart	**ypm**	yards per minute
US fl gal	US fluid gallon	**Z**	zetta (10^{21})
US fl pt	US fluid pint	**z**	zepto (10^{-24})
US fl qt	US fluid quart	**λ**	lambda
V	volt	**μ**	micron
W	watt	**μm**	micrometre
Wb	weber	**μm²**	square micrometre
W/m²	watts per square metre	**μs**	microsecond
Xu	X-unit	**π**	pi
		Ω	ohm

International System of Units

The International System of Units (or Système International d'Unités – SI) is the current form of the metric system that has been in use since 1960. In the UK, the SI system is used in education, science and, increasingly, in everyday life.

Base units
There are seven base units in SI:

Unit	Symbol	Quantity
metre	m	length/distance
kilogram	kg	mass
ampere	A	electric current
kelvin	K	temperature
candela	cd	luminosity
second	s	time
mole	mol	amount of substance

Supplementary units
There are also two supplementary units:

Unit	Symbol	Quantity
radian	rad	plane angle
steradian	sr	solid angle

Derived units
In addition, the system uses derived units, which are expressed in terms of the seven base units above. For example, velocity is given in metres per second (m/s, m s^{-1}). Other derived units in SI are referred to by special names. For example, the watt (W) is a unit of power; the joule (J) is a unit of energy; and the newton (N) is a unit of force.

Imperial units

Length

1 inch	(in or ")			
1 foot	(ft or ')	12 in		
1 yard	(yd)	36 in	3 ft	
1 fathom	(fm)	72 in	6 ft	2 yd
1 chain	(ch)		66 ft	22 yd
1 furlong	(fur)			220 yd
1 mile	(mi)		5280 ft	1760 yd

Area

square inch	(in²)			
1 square foot	(ft²)	144 in²		
1 square yard	(yd²)		9 ft²	
1 square chain	(ch²)			484 yd²
1 acre				4840 yd²
1 square mile	(mi²)	640 acres		

Metric units

Length

1 micrometre	(μm)	0.001 mm
1 millimetre	(mm)	1 mm
1 centimetre	(cm)	10 mm
1 metre	(m)	1000 mm
1 kilometre	(km)	10^6 mm

Area

1 square millimetre	(mm²)	1 mm²
1 square centimetre	(cm²)	100 mm²
1 square metre	(m²)	10^6 mm²
1 are		10^8 mm²
1 hectare		10^{10} mm²
1 square kilometre	(km²)	10^{12} mm²

Volume

1 cubic millimetre	(mm³, cu mm)	1 mm³
1 cubic centimetre	(cm³, cu cm)	1000 mm³
1 cubic metre	(m³, cu m)	10^9 mm³
1 cubic kilometre	(km³, cu km)	10^{18} mm³

Weight

1 milligram	(mg)	1 mg
1 gram	(g)	1000 mg
1 kilogram	(kg)	10^6 mg
1 tonne	(t)	10^9 mg

Volume	1 cubic inch	(in^3)			
	1 fluid ounce	(fl oz)			
	1 pint	(pt)	20 fl oz		
	1 quart	(qt)	40 fl oz	2 pt	
	1 gallon	(gal)		8 pt	4 qt
	1 cubic foot	(ft^3)	1728 in^3		
	1 cubic yard	(yd^3)	46 656 in^3	27 ft^3	

Weight	1 grain	(gr)			
	1 ounce	(oz)	437.5 gr		
	1 pound	(lb)		16 oz	
	1 stone	(st)			14 lb
	1 ton			35 840 oz	2240 lb

10^{-4} cm	10^{-6} m		
0.1 cm	0.001 m		
1 cm	0.01 m		
100 cm	1 m		
10^5 cm	1000 m		

0.01 cm^2	10^{-6} m^2		
1 cm^2	10^{-4} m^2		
10^4 cm^2	1 m^2		
10^6 cm^2	100 m^2		
10^8 cm^2	10^4 m^2	100 ares	
10^{10} cm^2	10^6 m^2	10^4 ares	100 hectares

10^{-3} cm^3	10^{-9} m^3
1 cm^3	10^{-6} m^3
10^6 cm^3	1 m^3
10^{15} cm^3	10^9 m^3

0.001 g	10^{-6} kg
1 g	0.001 kg
1000 g	1 kg
10^6 g	1000 kg

TERMS AND DEFINITIONS

abampere

Unit of electric current in the centimetre-gram-second (cgs) system of measurement. It is the current, flowing through two infinitely long parallel conductors 1 centimetre apart, that produces a force of 2 dynes per centimetre between them.

1 abampere = 10 amperes.

abcoulomb

Unit of electric charge in the centimetre-gram-second (cgs) system of measurement. It is the charge that each second passes any cross-section of a conductor through which a steady current of 1 ampere is flowing.

1 abcoulomb = 10 coulombs.

abfarad

Unit of electric capacitance in the centimetre-gram-second (cgs) system of measurement. It is the capacitance of a capacitor carrying a charge of 1 abcoulomb and with a potential difference of 1 abvolt between its plates.

1 abfarad = 1000 farads (10^9 farads).

abhenry

Unit of electric inductance in the centimetre-gram-second (cgs) system of measurement. It is the inductance produced when a rate of change of current of 1 abampere per second generates an induced electromotive force (EMF) of 1 abvolt.

1 abhenry = 1 thousand-millionth of a henry (10^{-9} henry).

absolute zero

Temperature at which a substance has no heat at all, and its constituent molecules are stationary. It has the values:

-273.16° Celsius	-459.67° Fahrenheit
0 Kelvin	0° Rankine.

absorptiometer

An instrument for measuring (a) the solubility of a gas, or (b) the absorption of light by a solution (which in certain circumstances is a measure of the concentration of the dissolved substance).

absorption hygrometer

An instrument for measuring the amount of water vapour in air (by determining the increase in weight of a drying agent over which a sample of air is drawn).

abvolt

Unit of potential difference or electromotive force in the centimetre-gram-second (cgs) system of measurement. It is the potential difference that exists between two points when 1 erg of work must be done to transfer 1 abcoulomb of charge from one of the points to the other.

1 abvolt = one tenth-millionth of a volt (10^{-8} volts).

acceleration

Acceleration is the rate of change of velocity or speed. It is measured in units of distance per second per second (distance/second^2), such as metres per second per second (m/sec^2). Negative acceleration (in which velocity decreases over time) is called deceleration, and is measured in exactly the same fashion.

accelerometer

Device for the measurement of acceleration. There are two types: those for linear (straight line) acceleration and those for angular (twisting) acceleration. The first accelerometer was built in 1783 by George Atwood, an English physicist.

acidity

In chemistry and many of its applications, acidity (and alkalinity) are often expressed on the pH scale (acidity is caused by the presence of hydrogen ions, and the pH of a solution is the negative logarithm of its hydrogen ion concentration). A neutral solution, such as pure water, has a pH of 7. A pH of less than 7 indicates an acidic solution; a pH of more than 7 indicates an alkaline solution. The lower the pH, the more acid it is. For any specific acid – such as hydrochloric acid – acidity can also be expressed in terms of the concentration of that acid: for example, in molality (moles per kilogram), normality (gram-equivalents per litre), grams per litre, and so on.

acre

A measure of land: originally the amount of land that a yoke of oxen could plough in a day. Equal to 4840 yd^2.

acute angle

An angle of between 0° and 90°.

aeon, eon

Technically, an aeon/eon is not a specific length of time, simply an extreme one, involving thousands of years. In astronomy and geology, however, it has come to mean a period of precisely 1 US billion (i.e. 1000 million) years.

altazimuth

Astronomical instrument consisting of a telescope that can be rotated against angular scales both vertically and horizontally, for measuring the altitude and azimuth of a celestial object.

altimeter

The decrease in air pressure as altitude increases is the basis for the ordinary altimeter for airplanes. By converting the air pressure to altitude, the instrument indicates height above sea level. Over high terrain the readings would not indicate height above the ground. The solution to this is the use of a radar altimeter. One of the earliest uses was in 1783, when the French physicist Jacques Charles sent a barometer up with a balloon to measure altitude.

altitude

Altitude, or height, is a distance and is therefore measured in standard linear units as appropriate, such as the foot, the metre, the kilometre, and the mile. The altitude of a mountain can be measured in several mathematical ways (such as trigonometry), and through a number of mechanical methods (such as orometry: the use of an aneroid barometer to gauge elevation).

alto-

Prefix meaning a unit valued at 10^{-18} in the metric system.

amagat

Primarily a unit of gas density at 0 °C (273.16 K) and normal pressure (760 millimetres of mercury, mmHg).

1 amagat = 1 mole per 22.4 dm^3 = 0.04464 mole per litre.

Alternatively, a unit of volume: the volume occupied by 1 mole of gas at 0 °C (273.16 K) and normal pressure (760 mmHg). For an ideal gas, this volume corresponds to 22.4 litres. The unit was named after the Dutch physicist E.H. Amagat (1841–1915).

ammeter

Instrument for measuring electric current. It has an electromagnet and a permanent magnet, either one of which is movable, although the moving coil type is more uneven. Ammeters are not as sensitive as galvanometers due to their design, which causes only a small proportion of the current to flow through the coil. Electronic meters (digital meters) are now widely used.

ampere (A)

The unit for measuring electric current in the SI system of measurement. It is the current, flowing in a pair of infinitely long parallel conductors of negligible cross-section located 1 metre apart in a vacuum, that produces a force of 2×10^{-7} newtons per metre between them.

ampere hour

Unit of electric charge equivalent to a current of 1 ampere flowing for 1 hour.

1 ampere hour = 3600 coulombs.

ampere turn

Unit of magnetomotive force in the SI system of measurement, equal to the force produced by a current of 1 ampere flowing round one turn of a conductor.

Ampère, André Marie

French physicist and mathematician (1775–1836) who laid the foundations of the science of electrodynamics (electromagnetism) after the discovery by H. Ch. Ørsted in 1820 of the magnetic effects of electric currents. The basic unit of electric current is named after him.

amu

See atomic mass unit.

anemometer

An instrument for measuring wind speed, usually consisting of a vertical, rotatable shaft with three or four horizontal arms carrying hemispherical cups. The wind blows round the arms and hence the shaft, and the speed of rotation is a measure of wind speed.

aneroid barometer

A type of barometer with an evacuated bellows made of thin corrugated metal. The change in shape of the bellows following changes in atmospheric pressure is made, by means of levers, to move a pointer along a scale calibrated in pressure units. The term aneroid derives from ancient Greek words that together mean 'without being wet', referring to the fact that the device is totally dry, using neither liquid nor fluid metal (mercury).

angles

Angles measure the distance a line turns around a fixed point. Surveyors in particular use angles to measure heights and lengths. The oldest way of measuring angle is the system of degrees, which was devised by the ancient Mesopotamians. A line which describes a full circle turns 360 degrees, so one degree is $\frac{1}{360}$ of a circle. A degree is subdivided into minutes. An alternative system based on the grade, or gon, was developed in 1792, but modern mathematicians prefer to use radians. A radian is the angle at the centre of a circle which cuts off an arc on the circumference that is equal in length to the radius.

ångström (Å)

A unit of length, used mainly to measure the wavelength of light. Named after the Swedish physicist A.J. Ångström (1814–74). Equal to 10^{-10} metres (10^{-8} centimetres).

Ångström, Anders Jonas

Swedish physicist (1814–74) who detected hydrogen in the Sun. In 1855 he deduced that a hot gas emits light at the same wavelengths at which it absorbs light when cooler. He founded the science of spectroscopy.

anomalistic month

The time between two successive passages of the Moon through perigee.

1 anomalistic month = 27.55455 days.

anomalistic year

Equals the time interval between two consecutive passages of the Earth through its perihelion (365 days, 6 hours, 13 minutes, 53 seconds).

apothecaries' system

A system of weights used especially by pharmacists.

are (a)

A unit of measure equal to an area of 100 m² (1 are = 100 m²). *See* also hectare (ha): 100 are = 1 hectares.

area rod

A unit of area equal to 30¼ yd². Also called a square perch or a square pole.

astrolabe

An ancient astronomical instrument that was used to predict the positions of the Sun and stars. The earliest type was probably devised by the Greeks around 100 BCE, and was later developed by the Arabs. It can be set to show the appearance of the sky for any date or time. By the nineteenth century it had been replaced by mechanical clocks.

astronomical distances

Distances in space are so huge, they soon outstrip the metric system. Instead a light-year – the distance that light travels in one year – is used. Nothing travels faster than light: in one second it travels 300,000 kilometres, the equivalent of more than seven times around the Equator; a light-year is about nine and a half million million kilometres. Using light-years is a convenient way of representing very long distances, but it tends to hide the actual magnitude of such distances.

astronomical unit (AU)

A unit of measure based on the distance between the Earth and the Sun. Approximately equal to 1.5×10^8 km.

atmosphere

Unit of pressure.

1 atmosphere = 101 325 pascals = 1.01325×10^5 newtons per square metre = 1.01325 bar (1 bar = 0.9869 atmosphere).

It is equivalent also to 760 millimetres of mercury or 14.72 pounds per square inch.

atomic clock

A timing device whose extreme accuracy is based on the undeviating frequency with which molecules vibrate. It was invented in 1953 by

Charles H. Townes (US) and is closely related to a maser. It makes use of the fact that the nitrogen atom in an ammonia molecule can be made to vibrate continuosly at a constant rate of 24×10^9 times per second, doing so more accurately than any other timing device yet known.

atomic mass unit (amu)

(chemical) A unit of mass equal to ⅟16 of the weighted mass of the three naturally occurring neutral oxygen isotopes.

1 amu chemical = $(1.660 \pm 0.00005) \times 10^{-27}$ kg. Formerly called the atomic weight unit.

(international) A unit of mass equal to half of the mass of a neutral carbon-12 atom.

1 amu international = $(1.660\ 33 \pm 0.00005) \times 10^{-27}$ kg.

(physical) A unit of mass equal to ⅟16 of the mass of an oxygen atom.

1 amu physical = 1.660×10^{-27} kg.

atto-

A prefix which, when it precedes a unit, reduces the unit to 1 UK trillionth/1 US quintillionth (10^{-18}) of its standard size and quantity. For example, 1 attofarad = 0.000000000000000001 farad.

Avogadro, Amedeo

An Italian physicist (1776–1856). Avogadro's law states that equal volumes of gases, at the same temperature and pressure, contain the same number of molecules. He became the first chair of mathematical physics at Turin University. Avogadro introduced the decimal system in Piedmont.

Avogadro's number

The number of molecules (or atoms or ions) in a mole (gram molecular weight) of a substance, equal (for all substances) to 6.02253×10^{23}. It is known alternatively as Avogadro's constant, and was named after the Italian nobleman and physicist Amedeo Avogadro (1776–1856).

avoirdupois system

A system of weights based on the 16-ounce pound and the 16-dram ounce.

baker's dozen

A counting unit equal to 13.

balance

Balance of payments/ balance of trade. The net profit or loss of a country when annual financial totals of exports, imports, investments, grants and tourist expenditures are set against one another. This measurement may alternatively be narrowed down to a comparison between one country and another, and the overall annual profit or loss of one in relation to the other in terms of exports, imports, investments and tourist expenditures.

barleycorn

Basic Anglo-Saxon unit, the length of a corn of barley. The unit survived after 1006, but today is defined as $\frac{1}{3}$ of an inch.

barograph

A device for recording atmospheric pressure. It was not invented until 1681, primarily by the English physicist Robert Hooke, who improved on a device developed in 1683 by the English architect Sir Christopher Wren.

barometer

A device for measuring the varying weight of the atmosphere as the weather changes at a given place. It was devised in 1644 by Evangelista Torricelli, an Italian physicist.

baud

Unit of speed of transmission of telecommunications.
1 baud = 1 pulse or bit per second.
The actual data–signalling rate may not be as fast as the baud rate because of the inclusion also of various control signals. The unit was named after the French telegraph engineer J.M.E. Baudot (1845–1903), who gave his name also to a 5-bit telegraph code of on and off pulses (contrasting with the long and short pulses of the Morse code).

becquerel (Bq)

Unit of radioactivity in the SI system, equal to the number of nuclei in a radioactive element that disintegrate each second. It has replaced the former unit, the curie.
1 becquerel = 2.7×10^{-11} curies.
The unit was named after the French physicist Antoine Henri Becquerel (1852–1908).

Becquerel, Antoine Henri

French physicist (1852–1908). His earliest interest was the plane polarization of light, the phenomenon of phosphorescence and the absorption of light by crystals. He also worked on the subject of terrestrial magnetism. In 1896 he discovered natural radioactivity. In 1903 Becquerel shared the Nobel Prize for Physics with Pierre and Marie Curie.

Beaufort, Sir Francis

Irish-born British rear-admiral and hydrographer (1774–1857). He is best known for introducing the Beaufort scale of wind force. The scale ranges from calm (0) to full hurricane (12). Beaufort joined the navy in 1787, saw active service for more than 20 years, and became official hydrographer to the British Admiralty in 1832.

bel (B)

Unit of sound intensity, used in measuring differences in intensity levels.

1 bel = 10 decibels.

The unit is named after the Scottish-born US physicist and inventor Alexander Bell (1847–1922), inventor of the telephone.

billion (bil)

In the UK, a number equal to 10^{12}; in the US, equal to 10^9. Commonly now also used in the UK to mean 10^9.

binary system

This is a positional notational system with a number base of 2. The only digits used are 0 and 1. Computers use the binary system as their basic operating code ('machine code'). When a computer processes coded signals it does so in a series of electronic pulses. The presence or absence of a pulse can be represented by the digits 1 and 0. When talking about computers, these digits are referred to as 'bits' (an abbreviation for 'binary digits'). A group of eight is called a 'byte'.

bit

Basic unit of information in a digital computing system, corresponding to one or other symbol of the binary system of numeral notation (that is, 1 or 0).

8 bits = 1 byte.

1000 bits = 1 kilobit, 0.125 kilobyte.

bolt

A measure of length, usually for fabric. In the UK, a bolt of cloth equals 42 yards; in the US, a bolt of wallpaper equals 16 yards and a bolt of cloth equals 40 yards.

boutylka

Unit of liquid volume in Russia, closely approximating to the capacity of a standard European wine-bottle (75 centilitres).

British thermal unit (Btu)

Measure of heat needed to raise the temperature of one pound of water by 1°F. Equal to 252 calories.

Bourdon gauge

Type of pressure gauge consisting of a flattened metal tube, closed at one end and bent into a curve. Fluid pressure (gas or liquid) applied to the open end tends to straighten the tube, movement of which makes a pointer move round a scale calibrated in pressures. It was named after the French engineer Eugène Bourdon (1808–84).

bushel (bu)

A measure of dry volume. In the US, 1 bu = 8 gal (64 US pt); in the UK, 1 bu = 8 gal (64 UK pt). The measures are not to be confused:
1.03 US bu = 1 UK bu.

byte

In digital computers, a group of bits processed as 1 unit of data.
1 byte = 8 bits.
1000 bytes = 1 kilobyte.

calibre

A unit of length used to measure the diameter of a tube or the bore of a firearm, in $\frac{1}{100}$ inches or $\frac{1}{1000}$ inches increments.

caliper

A caliper uses two pivoted points to measure small distances. In the past calipers were made of wood, but today they are made of steel. The distance measured by a fixed caliper can be read from a standard ruler, but an adjustable caliper has a calibrated screw which gives the reading directly. When used with a vernier scale a caliper is accurate to 0.025 mm (0.001 in). Pneumatic and electronic calipers are also used.

calorie (cal)

A measure of heat energy representing the amount of heat needed to raise the temperature 1 gram of water by 1 °Celsius. Also called 'small calorie':

1000 cal = 1 kcal or Cal.

See also joule, kilocalorie.

candela

Unit of luminous intensity in the SI system, equal to the intensity of a source of light, frequency 540 x 10^{12} hertz, that gives a radiant intensity of 1⁄683 watts per steradian in a given direction.

carat

A unit of weight equal to 200 mg (3.1 grains). Also used as a measure of gold purity (per 24 parts gold alloy).

Celsius, Anders

Swedish astronomer and mathematician (1701–44) best remembered for the Celsius temperature scale (1742). He proposed 100° as the melting point of ice and 0° as the boiling point of water. He also measured the relative brightness of stars and calculated the distance of the Earth from the Sun.

Celsius scale

Temperature scale on which the two fixed points are the freezing point of pure water (0 °C) and the boiling point of pure water (100 °C). It is the same as the obsolescent centigrade scale.

centi-

Prefix meaning a 100th or 1⁄100 in the metric system; e.g. a centilitre (cl) is a unit of volume equal to 1⁄100 (0.01) litre.

centigrade

A measure of temperature difference representing a single division on a temperature scale. The centigrade scale has 100 equal degrees; the Fahrenheit scale has 212 equal degrees. To convert a centigrade (or celsius) temperature to a Fahrenheit temperature, multiply by 9⁄5 and add 32 to the product. Thus, for example,

100 °Celsius = (100 x 9⁄5) + 32 = 180 + 32 = 212 °Fahrenheit.

centilitre

One-hundredth litre: a small volumetric unit of both liquid and dry capacity in the SI system. It is abbreviated as 'cl'.

    1 centilitre = 0.01 litre, 0.10 decilitre, 10 millilitres
    1 centilitre = 0.0176 UK pint, 0.0211 US pint.

centimetre

One-hundredth metre, a much-used small linear measure in the metric system. It is abbreviated as 'cm'.

    1 centimetre = 0.01 metre, 0.10 decimetre
    1 centimetre = 0.3937008 inch, 0.03281 foot
    100 centimetres = 1 metre

centimetre-gram-second (cgs) system

System of units based on the centimetre (length), gram (mass) and second (time). It was superseded first by the metre-kilogram-second (mks) system, and then by the SI system.

centrad

A measure of a plane angle, especially used to measure the angular deviation of light through a prism. 1 centrad = $\frac{1}{100}$ (0.01) radian.

century

A measure of time equal to 100 years.

chain

A measure of length equal to 22 yd. Also known as Gunter's chain.

chaldron

A measure of volume. In the UK, 1 chaldron = 36 UK bushels (288 gallons); in the US, 1 chaldron = 36 US bushels.

circular inch

A square measure. The cross-sectional measurement of wire used in electrical circuits.

    1 circular inch = 0.785 square inch (a diameter of half an inch).
    (1 square inch = 1.274 circular inch.)

circular mil

A square measure. The cross-sectional measurement of wire used in electrical circuits.

    1 circular mil = one-millionth circular inch (a diameter of 0.001 inch) = 0.000000785 square inch = 0.000050645 square millimetre.

clock

Clocks have been in existence since the earliest times, the first types being called water clocks because they measured time by the amount of water flowing from one container to another. These were made in China as early as 3000 BCE. Not until the 1300s did mechanical clocks, operated by weights or springs, begin to appear. The first clock accurate enough for scientific use was the pendulum clock, invented by the Dutch physicist and astronomer Christian Huygens in 1656, based on experiments made by the Italian astronomer Galileo Galilei in 1581. Electric motors were later used to operate clocks, but the most accurate type yet invented is the atomic clock.

clothes sizes

As clothes became mass-produced, manufacturers needed a standard system of sizing for 'off-the-peg' garments and shoes. Different systems are used in the United States, the United Kingdom and Europe.

conductance

The ability of a material to conduct heat or electricity.

cord

A unit of dry volume, especially used for timber. Equal to 128 ft^3.

coulomb (C)

Unit of electric charge, equal to the quantity of electricity carried by 1 ampere of current in 1 second. It was named after the French physicist Charles Coulomb (1736–1806).

counting stick

A bone or a stick carved into at regular intervals was used in prehistoric times as a means of counting.

crore

An Indian counting unit equal to 10 million.

cubic units (cu or ^{3})

These signify that three quantities measured in the same units have been multiplied together. For example, with a three-dimensional rectangular object, the height, breadth and length may be multiplied togther to give its volume, which is then measured in cubic units.

cubit

The cubit was the basic unit of length used by the Egyptians, Sumerians, Babylonians and Hebrews. The cubit was the distance between the elbow and the tip of the longest finger. The Egyptians had two cubits, a short cubit of 0.45 metres (17.7 inches) and a royal cubit of 0.524 metres (20.6 inches), which was subdivided into hands, palms and digits. The Greeks added a new unit, the foot, which was equal to 16 digits.

cup

A measure of volume (either liquid or solid) used especially in cooking. In the UK, 1 cup = 0.44 UK pt (8.80 UK fluid ounces) ; in the US, 1 cup = 0.53 US pt (8.48 US fluid ounces).

curie (Ci)

Unit of radioactivity equal to 3.7 disintegrations per second (similar to the activity of 1 gram of radium-226). It has been superseded by the becquerel. The unit was named after Marie Curie (1867–1934).

Curie, Marie

French physicist of Polish background (1867–1934). The discovery of radioactivity by Becquerel in 1896 led Marie and her husband Pierre Curie to the isolation of polonium and radium. Marie Curie developed methods for the separation of radium from radioactive residues in sufficient quantities to allow for its characterization and the study of its properties. In 1903 the Curies were awarded half of the Nobel Prize for Physics for their study into the spontaneous radiation discovered by Becquerel, who was awarded the other half of the Prize. In 1911 Marie Curie received a second Nobel Prize, this time in Chemistry, in recognition of her work in radioactivity.

customary units

Many units of length were originally based on agreed familiar lengths, particularly those used in agriculture. In England, for example, 'three barleycorns, round and dry' were used to measure an inch and a furlong was based on the customary length of a furrow ploughed in a field. Gradually the customary measures became standardized. A furlong became an eighth of a mile and was subdivided into chains and rods. An inch was also subdivided – into barleycorns, lines and douzièmes. Furlongs are still used in horse racing – the length of a horse race varying between 5 furlongs and 12 furlongs – and the height of a horse is measured in hands.

customary units now largely obsolete

12 douzièmes = 1 line

4 lines = 1 barleycorn

3 barleycorns = 1 inch

5 1/2 yards = 1 rod

4 rods = 1 chain

10 chains = 1 furlong

8 furlongs = 1 mile

1 mile = 0.33 league

customary units still in use

12 inches (in) = 1 foot (ft)

3 feet = 1 yard (yd)

1760 yards = 1 mile (mi)

cycle

One of a (usually) recurrent series of similar changes, such as a vibration or wave motion. One cycle is the period of motion; the number of cycles per second is the frequency (measured in hertz, which has superseded cycles per second).

day

In normal parlance, 1 day = 24 hours = 1440 minutes = 86 400 seconds.

It begins and ends at midnight, representing one complete revolution of the Earth on its axis, in relation to the Sun. Lunar days (measured in relation to the Moon) and sidereal days (measured in relation to the stars) are not used for scientific purposes although, in accumulation over a year, the differences may be substantial.

The division of the day into twenty-four hours is of comparatively late cultural development, arising initially as a necessity for making trading appointments and deals during daylight.

deca-

Prefix meaning ten in the metric system; e.g. a decametre is a measure of length equal to 10 m.

decade

A measure of time equal to 10 years.

deci-

Prefix meaning $\frac{1}{10}$ in the metric system; e.g. a decilitre (dl) is a measure of liquid volume equal to $\frac{1}{10}$ (0.01) litre.

decibel (dB)

A unit of sound pressure level, equal to ten times the logarithm of the ratio of the square of the r.m.s. value of the sound pressure to the square of the reference pressure (usually the threshold of hearing). By extension, the decibel is used for other power ratios (such as the input and output voltages of an amplifier).

1 decibel = 0.1 (one-tenth) bel.

decimal system

The full name of our everyday counting system is the 'decimal positional notational system'. A decimal system has a number base of 10, i.e. the number on which the decimal system is constructed is 10. In a positional notational system, the exact position of a digit determines its value, e.g. in the number 22 the left-hand digit has 10 times the value of the right-hand digit. Zeros are used to keep the positions and values of the other digits correct, e.g. without the zeros the numbers 20200 and 22 would appear to have the same value.

degree (°)

In geometry, a unit of angle (arc) derived by dividing a complete revolution (circle) into 360 segments; symbol °. Degrees may be subdivided into minutes (symbol ') and seconds (symbol ") of arc.

1 degree = 60 minutes = 3600 seconds.

In thermometry, a unit of difference in temperature on a temperature scale is represented by the symbol °. Common units are degrees Celsius (or centigrade, both written °C) and degrees Fahrenheit (°F). The SI unit of temperature, the kelvin, does not have a degree sign (0 °C = 273 K).

digit

One of ten Arabic symbols representing the numbers 0 to 9. Also used in astronomy as a unit of measure equal to half the diameter of the Sun or Moon. Used in ancient Egypt as a measure of length:

1 digit = 1 finger width.

digitizer

A device for converting analogue quantities to digital form. In 1952 a voltmeter having a digital display was invented by Andrew Kay (US).

dioptre (D)

Unit of lens power, equal to the reciprocal of a lens's focal length in metres. Thus, a positive (converging) lens with a focal length of 50 centimetres (0.5 metre) is + 2 dioptres. Negative (diverging) lenses are ascribed negative dioptre values. The system is most commonly used in specifying the power ('strength') of lenses in spectacles and contact lenses.

douzième

A unit of length equal to $\frac{1}{12}$ line.

dozen

A counting unit equal to 12.

drachm

A unit of weight in the apothecaries' system.
1 drachm = $\frac{1}{8}$ apothecaries' ounce (60 grains).

dram (dr)

A unit of mass equal to $\frac{1}{16}$ oz.
A fluid dram is a unit of liquid volume.
1 dr = $\frac{1}{8}$ fl oz.

dry

Used in the US to distinguish measures of dry (solid) volume as opposed to liquid (fluid) volume. For example, in the UK the pint measures both dry and liquid volume. In the US, 1 fl pt = $\frac{1}{8}$ US gal; 1 dry pt = $\frac{1}{64}$ US bu. 1 US dry pt ≈ 0.969 UK pt ≈ 1.163 US fl pt.

dry quart (dry qt)

A unit of measure for dry (solid) volume in the US.

dynamometer

A device for measuring the power or energy of a machine, such as the horsepower produced by a motor. An absorption type dynamometer absorbs and dissipates the power being measured; the simplest type is the Prony brake, invented by the French engineer Gaspard de Prony in 1821. Other types are the Froude (water) brake, the fan brake, and the electromagnetic brake.

dyne

A unit of force equal to that needed to produce an acceleration of 1 centimetre per second in a mass of 1 gram. Replaced in the international system by the newton (N).
1 dyne = 10^{-5} N.

early units

Early units were based on convenient parts of the body, such as the length of the arm, the width of a finger and the length of a foot and a pace.

EDM (Electronic-distance-measuring equipment)

This instrument measures distances by transmitting an impulse of electromagnetic energy and measuring the time it takes for the impulse to be reflected off an object back to the instrument. The time is converted into a very accurate measure of the distance.

EMU (electromagnetic units)

A system of electrical units based on the unit magnetic pole and a given value of the permittivity of free space (electric constant). Based within the centimetre-gram-second (cgs) system, 1 EMU is in the SI system assigned a value of 8.854×10^{-12} farads per metre.

electronvolt (eV)

A unit of energy representing the energy acquired by an electron in passing through a potential difference of 1 volt.

1 electronvolt (eV) = $(1.6 \pm 0.00007) \times 10^{-19}$ Joules (J).

ESU (electrostatic units)

A system of electrical units defined in terms of the force of attraction or repulsion between two electric charges and a given value of the permittivity of free space (electric constant). Based within the centimetre-gram-second (cgs) system, 1 ESU is in the SI system assigned a value of 8.854×10^{-12} farad per metre.

engineer's chain

A measure of length equal to 100 feet.

erg

A unit of energy equal to the energy produced by a force of 1 dyne acting through a distance of 1 cm. Replaced in the international system by the joule (J).

1 erg = 10^{-7} J.

exa-

Prefix meaning a unit valued at 10^{18} in the metric system.

Fahrenheit, Daniel Gabriel

German physicist (1686–1736) who invented thermometers using alcohol (1709) and mercury, as well as the temperature scale named after him.

farad (F)

Unit of electrical capacitance, equal to the capacitance that carries a charge of 1 coulomb when it is charged by a potential difference of 1 volt. It is a large unit and, in practice, submultiples such as microfarads (10^{-6} farad) or picofarads (10^{-12} farad) are generally used.

1 farad = 10^{-9} electromagnetic unit (EMU) = 9 x 10^{11} electrostatic units (ESU).

faraday

Unit of electric charge, equal to the amount of charge that will liberate 1 mole (1 gram-equivalent weight) of an element during electrolysis. It equals 9.6487 x 10^4 coulombs per mole (gram-equivalent), and is the product of the electric charge and Avogadro's number. The unit is named after Michael Faraday.

Faraday, Michael

English chemist and physicist (1791–1867). He discovered electromagnetic induction, which led to generators, transformers and electromagnets. He also proposed the laws of electrolysis and showed the rotation of polarized light by magnetism.

fathom (fm)

Unit of length, especially used to measure marine depth. Originally based on the span of two outstretched arms.

1 fathom (fm) = 6 feet (ft).

feet per minute

A unit of speed representing the number of feet travelled in 1 minute.

femto-

In the UK, a prefix meaning 1 thousand billionth (10^{-15}); in the US, meaning 1 quadrillionth (10^{-15}).

firkin

A unit of volume, used especially to measure beer or ale. In the UK, 1 firkin = 9 UK gal; in the US, 1 firkin = 9.8 US gal.

fluid

Used to distinguish units of liquid (fluid) volume as opposed to dry (solid) volume.

fluid dram

See dram.

fluid ounce

A unit of liquid volume measurement. In the UK, 1 fl oz = $\frac{1}{20}$ UK pt; in the US, 1 fl oz = $\frac{1}{16}$ US pt.

foot (ft)

A unit of length equal to 12 inches.

force pound

A unit of force equal to 32.174 poundals. Also called pound-force.

furlong (fur)

A unit of length equal to $\frac{1}{8}$ mile (660 ft).

gallon (gal)

A unit of liquid volume equal to 8 pints. The US and UK gallons should not be confused: 1 UK gal = 1.2 US gal.

galvanometer

An instrument for measuring very small electric currents. It has a movable element that is deflected by a flow of current. It contains a permanent magnet and an electromagnet, either one of which could be movable. The first one was invented by the Dutch scientist Hans Christian Øersted. Galvanometers can be converted to ammeters and voltmeters.

gauge

A unit of length used to measure the diameter of a shotgun bore; e.g. six-gauge equals 23.34 mm.

Geiger counter

A device to measure radioactivity that uses ionization of a gas-filled tube when exposed to charged particles. It was invented by the German physicist Hans Geiger in 1908. It is primarily used as a simple way to locate a source of radioactivity. More sophisticated detectors are now available.

geometric degree (°)

A unit of measure of plane angle equal to $\frac{1}{360}$ of the circumference of a circle (1 circle = 360°).

geometric minute (')

A unit of measure for plane angles.

$1' = \frac{1}{60}°$.

giga-

A prefix meaning one billion (10^9). For example, 1 gigametre = 1 billion metres.

gill

A unit of liquid volume. In the UK, 1 gill = $\frac{1}{4}$ UK pt; in US (gi), 1 gi = $\frac{1}{4}$ US fl pt. The two should not be confused: 1 UK gill = $\frac{1}{2}$ US gi.

global positioning system

This instrument bounces radio signals off at least three different satellites to give an exact position.

grade (g)

Primarily another word for degree and, in many European languages, the only word for 'degree'. Despite the potential confusion, however, the term is additionally an alternative for 'grad' or 'gon' (nine-tenths of a degree). In the US, the word 'grade' is also used as a synonym for 'gradient'.

gradient

In geometry, the gradient of a line is its slope (angle with the horizontal), and the gradient of a curve at a particular point is the slope of the tangent at that point. The gradient is generally expressed in degrees. In everyday usage, a gradient is more often expressed as a ratio or a percentage. For example: a road may have an uphill gradient of 1 in 8 (or 1 : 8) which means, strictly, that it rises 1 distance unit for every 8 units on the level. In practice, however, so that gradients can be measured on the ground, 1 in 8 means a rise of 1 unit for every 8 units along the road (that is, up the slope). In percentage terms, this gradient is $12\frac{1}{2}\%$.

gradienter

A device used by surveyors for measuring gradients. It basically comprises a low-powered telescope, a spirit level and a vertical arc calibrated in degrees, mounted on a tripod.

gradiometer

A device that measures the gradient of the Earth's magnetic or gravitational field at a chosen location.

grain (gr)

A unit of mass measurement, used especially in the apothecaries' system.

1 grain = $\frac{1}{7000}$ lb (avoirdupois) = 0.050 gram.

gram (g)

A unit of mass or volume measurement.

1 g = 0.001 kg.

gross

A counting measure equal to 144 (or 12 dozen).

Gunter's chain

In the past surveyors used a chain that measured up to 66 feet (20 metres) and defined the customary unit, the chain. The chain was invented by the English mathematician Edmund Gunter in the early 1600s.

gyrocompass

A compass built around a gyroscope. The gyroscope is mounted so that it has freedom to move about both a horizontal and vertical axis.

gyroscope

A device consisting of a rapidly spinning heavy wheel that maintains its original position when its axis of rotation is moved. This characteristic of being able to resist forces has made it valuable for several purposes. When used for stabilizing ships and aircraft, it is know as a gyrostabilizer. When used as a compass it is known as a gyrocompass.

half life

For a radioactive isotope, the time it takes for half of its nuclei to spontaneously decay, equal to $\log_e 2$ divided by the decay constant. It varies, depending on the isotope, from a few seconds to thousands of years, and can be used as a basis for geological dating.

hand

A unit of length, used especially to measure horses' height.
1 hand = 10.2 cm = 4 in.

hardness

See Mohs' scale of hardness.

hectare (ha)

A measure of area, usually of land, equal to 10 000 m².

hecto-

Prefix meaning 100; e.g. a hectometer (hm) is a unit of length equal to 100 m.

henry (H)

Unit of inductance, equal to the inductance that produces an induced electromotive force (voltage) of 1 volt for a change in current flow of 1 ampere per second. It was named after the American physicist Joseph Henry (1797–1878).

hertz (Hz)

A unit of frequency measurement equal to 1 cycle per second. The unit was named after German physicist Heinrich Rudolf Hertz (1857–94).

Hertz, Heinrich Rudolf

German physicist of Jewish background (1857–94). He confirmed J.C. Maxwell's electromagnetic theory and later studied electromagnetic waves (known also as hertzian waves, or radio waves). He demonstrated that these are long, transverse waves that travel at the speed of light and can be reflected, refracted and polarized like light. Hertz also investigated electric discharge in rarefied gases. The unit of frequency was named after him.

horsepower (hp)

A unit of work representing the power needed to raise 550 pounds (lb) by 1 foot (ft) in 1 second (s).

hour (hr)

A unit of time measurement equal to 60 minutes (3600 seconds).

hundredweight (cwt)

A unit of mass. There are two forms of hundredweight in the avoirdupois system. The traditional hundredweight, used mainly in Britain and English-speaking countries other than in North America, relates to the original form of ton (sometimes called the long, or gross, ton in North America), and is also known as a quintal. The more recent hundredweight, used mainly in North America, really does correspond to 100 lesser units and accordingly relates to a ton consisting of a number of pounds that is much easier to remember (sometimes called the short ton), and is also known as a cental.

1 (long, gross) hundredweight = 112 pounds avdp. = 50.80208 kg
1 short hundredweight = 100 pounds avdp. = 45.35924 kg

hydrometer

An instrument for measuring the density of a liquid, consisting of a glass bulb (containing a weight) at the lower end of a glass stem. It floats in a liquid with the stem upright, and the stem is graduated with a density scale. For solutions of a single substance, density is generally proportional to concentration and, in such cases, the stem may be graduated directly in concentrations.

hygrometer

An instrument for measuring the humidity of a gas, such as air. The type that makes a recording of humidity is called a hygroscope.

inch (in)

A unit of length equal to $\frac{1}{12}$ foot.

inches per second

A unit of speed representing the number of inches travelled in 1 second.

interferometer

An interferometer measures microscopic and astronomical distances very precisely. An optical interferometer uses interference patterns in light waves to measure, for example, the thickness or refractive index of a material or the diameter of a star. In radio astronomy the instrument uses interference in radio waves to measure accurately the position of radio sources. The interferometer was invented by the American physicist Albert Michelson in 1893.

joule (J)

A unit of energy equal to the work done when a force of 1 newton is applied through a distance of 1 metre. Used instead of calorie: 1 J = 0.239 cal. Named after J.P. Joule (1818–89).

Joule, James Prescott

English physicist (1818–1889) who laid foundations for the theory of the conversion of energy. The unit of work or energy is named after him. With Lord Kelvin (William Thomson), he devised an absolute scale of temperature.

keg

A unit of volume, used especially for beer, equal to approximately 30 gallons. Also used as a measure of weight for nails, equal to 100 pounds (lb).

kelvin (K)

A scale of temperature measurement in which each degree is equal to $\frac{1}{273.16}$ of the interval between 0 K (absolute zero) and the triple point of water. K = °C + 273.16. Named after William Thomson, Lord Kelvin (1824–1907).

kilo-

A prefix meaning 1000; e.g. a kilogram (kg) is a unit of mass equal to 1000 grams.

kilocalorie (kcal or Cal)

A unit of energy measurement representing the amount of heat required to raise the temperature of 1 kilogram of water by 1 °C. Also called the 'international calorie'.

1 kcal = 1000 cal.

See also calorie.

kilometre (km)

A unit of length equal to 1000 metres.

kiloparsec

A unit used to measure the distance between galactic bodies.

1 kiloparsec = 3260 light years.

kilowatt (kW)

A unit of power equal to 1000 watts (W).

kilowatt-hour (kWh)

A unit of energy equal to the energy expended when a power of 1 kW is used for 1 hour.

knot (kn)

A nautical unit of speed measurement equal to the velocity at which 1 nautical mile is travelled in 1 hour.

1 kn = 6076 ft per hour.

lakh

An Indian counting unit equal to 100 000.

lambda (λ)

A unit of volume measurement.

1 λ = 1 microlitre (10^{-6} litre).

league

A unit of length equal to 3 miles.

length rod

A unit of length equal to 5½ yards. Also called a perch or a pole.

light year (ly)

A unit of length representing the distance travelled by light through space in one year. 1 light year = 9.4605×10^{12} km (or, in the UK, 9 billion miles; in the US, 9 trillion miles).

litre (l)

A unit of volume measurement equal to the volume of 1 kilogram of water at its maximum density.

1 litre = 1000 cm³.

long distances

On Earth distances between places are given in terms of kilometres. Maps use scales to represent large distances. Progressively smaller scales allow greater and greater areas to be shown, but with decreasing detail.

long (UK) hundredweight (cwt)

A unit of mass equal to 112 lb;

1 hundredweight troy = 100 pounds troy;

1 hundredweight = 4 quarters.

lumen (lm)

> A unit of luminous flux in the SI system, equal to the amount of light given out through a solid angle by a source of 1 candela intensity radiating equally in all directions.

lunar month

> The time between two successive passages of the Moon through conjuction (or opposition). It is also called a synodic month.
> 1 lunar month = 29.53059 days.

lux (lx)

> A unit of illumination in the SI system, equal to 1 lumen per square metre. The unit is alternatively called a metre-candle.

magnum

> A measure of volume, used especially for wine or champagne.
> 1 magnum = $\frac{2}{5}$ gallon.

Mach, Ernst

> Austrian physicist and philosopher (1838–1916). He contributed to the science of projectiles and gave names to the ratio of the speed of flow of a gas to the speed of sound (Mach number) and to the angle of a shock wave to the direction of motion (Mach angle).

manometer

> A device used to measure the pressure of gases. In its simplest form a manometer is a U-shaped glass tube filled with a liquid (usually mercury). The difference of the levels in the two limbs of the tube is proportional to the amount of pressure. The first version was invented in 1661 by the Dutch physicist Christian Huygens.

maser

> A device that generates or amplifies microwaves, mostly for applications in radio astronomy or long-distance radar. The term is an acronym from microwave amplication (by) stimulated emission (of) radiation.

mass quarter

> A unit of mass. In the UK, 1 quarter = $\frac{1}{4}$ UK hundredweight (28 lb); in the US, 1 quarter = $\frac{1}{4}$ US ton (500 lb).

mean solar day

A measure of time representing the interval between consecutive passages of the Sun across the meridian, averaged over 1 year.

1 day = 24 hours (86 400 seconds).

mega-

A prefix meaning 1 million; e.g. a megaton is a unit of weight equal to 1 million tons.

megahertz (MHz)

A unit of frequency equal to 1 million cycles per second.

measuring tapes

A measuring tape is very similar to a ruler. Dress-making tapes measure up to about 180 centimetres and 5 feet. Tapes up to 30 metres, 60 metres and 90 metres (100 feet, 200 feet and 300 feet) are used by people such as surveyors, builders and gardeners. A surveyor's invar tape is made of a mixture of nickel, iron and other metals so that the tape is less subject to variations in temperature and can make extremely precise measurements.

Mercalli, Giuseppe

Italian seismologist (1859–1914) who invented a scale of earthquake intensity based on the degree of damage caused by the ground movement. The scale has been replaced by the Richter scale.

meridian

A line of longitude; a great circle that passes through both poles (the north and south poles of the Earth, or the celestial poles), or a great semicircle that passes from one pole to another.

metre (m)

The metric system, like the decimal system, is based on multiples and fractions of 10. The basic unit, the metre, was originally defined to be one ten-millionth of the distance from the North Pole to the Equator measured along a line of longitude. Rather than measure the whole distance, a shorter distance – that between Dunkirk in France and Barcelona in Spain, both on the same meridian – was measured using triangulation. The full distance was then calculated from astronomical measurements of angle.

Once the length of a metre was agreed, a length of platinum exactly one metre long was constructed in 1799 and kept in the

National Archives in Paris, as the standard by which all other metre
rules were checked. Having created the metric system, the French,
under Napoleon Bonaparte, abandoned it in 1812, but in 1840 it was
re-introduced and made compulsory in France, and thereafter slowly
spread to other countries.

In 1960 the length of a metre was redefined as exactly 1 650 763.73
wavelengths of light given off by isotope 86 of the element krypton.
The advantage of this definition was that it did not rely on
comparison with a standard of reference lodged in Paris. In 1983, the
metre was again redefined, as the distance travelled by light in a
vacuum in 0.0000003 of a second. This last definition is most useful
since it can be reproduced in any laboratory.

When SI units were introduced in 1960, the metre remained the
basic unit of length. Britain began to change to the metric system in
1965 and it is now used in most areas, although distances on road
signs and milestones are still given in miles. In the US, scientists and
other academics increasingly use the metric system, although
customary units are used for everyday measurements.

metres per minute (m/min)

A unit of speed measurement representing the number of metres
travelled in 1 minute.

metric horsepower

A unit of power representing that needed to raise a 75-kg mass
1 metre in 1 second.

metric ounce

A unit of mass equal to 25 grams. Also called a mounce.

metric system

A system of measurement based on the metre.

metric ton

See tonne.

metric units

10 millimetres (mm) = 1 centimetre (cm)
100 centimetres = 1 metre (m)
1000 metres = 1 kilometre (km).

mho

Unit of conductance in the centimetre-gram-second (cgs) system, equal to the reciprocal of an ohm, and therefore also known as a reciprocal ohm. The unit of conductance, of the same size, in the SI system is the siemens.

micro-

A prefix meaning one millionth; e.g. a microlitre is a unit of volume equal to 1 millionth of a litre.

micrometre

This instrument measures solid objects. It has a C-shaped frame and jaws that open and close. The object to be measured is placed between the jaws and the jaws tightened by means of a screw. It was invented by the English scientist William Gascoigne in 1640.

micron (μm)

A unit of length equal to $\frac{1}{1000}$ (0.001) mm. Also called the micrometer.

microscopic lengths

Very small objects, such as blood cells, bacteria and atoms, are measured by enlarging them under a microscope and measuring them against an ordinary scale. The magnification factor is then used to calculate the actual size. The units used are achieved by progressively subdividing a metre by 10.

mile (mi)

Basic longer unit for distance of the imperial system, deriving ultimately from the *mille passus* '1000 (double-) paces' that constituted the old Roman unit and is generally accepted to have measured 1618 yards. Today, a unit of length equal to 1760 yd. Also called the statute mile in the UK.

1 statute mile = 1.609344 kilometres.

miles per hour (mph)

A unit of speed representing the number of miles travelled in 1 hour.

millennium

A period of time equal to 1000 years.

milli-

Prefix meaning 1 thousandth or $\frac{1}{1000}$; e.g. 1 millimetre (mm) is a unit of length equal to $\frac{1}{1000}$ (0.001) of a metre.

Milne, John

English seismologist (1801–80). He invented the modern seismograph, an instrument to record the horizontal movements of the Earth during earthquakes.

minim

A unit of volume, applied to liquids. In the UK, 1 minim = $\frac{1}{480}$ fl oz; in the US, 1 minim = $\frac{1}{480}$ US fl oz. The two should not be confused: 1 UK minim = 0.961 US minim.

minute (m or min)

A unit of time measurement equal to 60 seconds.
60 minutes = 1 hour.

Mohs' scale (of hardness)

Named after Friedrich Mohs the scale is a series of numbers that indicates the hardness of minerals and similar substances, ranging from 1 to 10. The numbers relate to actual minerals, each of which is hard enough to scratch any of those above it on the following list:

Scale number	Mineral
1	talc
2	gypsum
3	calcite
4	fluorite
5	apatite
6	fel(d)spar/orthoclase
7	quartz
8	topaz
9	corundum
10	diamond

Mohs, Friedrich

German mineralogist (1773–1839) who wrote *The Natural History System of Mineralogy* (1821), and *Treatise on Mineralogy* (1825). He classified minerals on the basis of hardnes, and the Mohs' scale of hardness is still in use.

mole (mol)

The amount of a substance that corresponds to its relative molecular mass in grams, or that contains a number of particles (atoms, ions or molecules) equal to Avogadro's constant (6.02253×10^{23}).

Morley, Edward Williams

American scientist (1838–1932). Along with Albert Michelson, he developed a sensitive interferometer, which showed that the speed of light is constant whether measured in the direction of the Earth's movement or perpendicular to that direction.

month

Unit of time based originally on the period between two successive new Moons equal to approximately 27.5 days; also equal to 4 weeks or $\frac{1}{13}$ of a calendar year.

nano-

In the UK, a prefix meaning 1 thousand millionth (10^{-9}); in the US, meaning 1 billionth (10^{-9}). For example, in the UK 1 nanometer = 1 thousand millionth of a metre; in the US 1 nanometre = 1 billionth of a metre.

Napier, John

Scottish mathematician (1550–1617). He invented logarithms and wrote *Mirifici logarithmorum canonis descriptio* (1614), containing the first logarithmic table and the first use of the word logarithm. His *Rabdologiae* (1617) gives various methods for abbreviating arithmetical calculations. One method of multiplication uses a system of numbered rods called Napier's rods, or Napier's bones; this was a major improvement on the ancient system of counters then in use. He introduced the decimal point in writing numbers.

nautical chain

A measure of length equal to 15 feet.

nautical mile (n mi)

A unit of length used in navigation. In the UK, 1 nautical mile = 6080 feet; in the metric system, 1 nautical mile (international) = 1852 metres. Also called the geographical mile.

newton (N)

A unit of force which, when applied, accelerates a mass of 1 kilogram

by 1 metre per second. This unit has replaced the dyne. It was named
after Isaac Newton (1642–1727).

1 newton (N) = 10^5 dynes.

Newton, Isaac

English physicist (1642–1727). His laws of motion and theory of
gravity were published in his most important book, *The Mathematical
Principles of Natural Philosophy* or the *Principia* (1687). He also studied
optics and developed what was to be his greatest contribution to
mathematics: calculus. Newton, a professor of mathematics at
Cambridge by 1669, was always reluctant to publish his findings and
had described his progress to only a few colleagues. This led to a
longstanding feud with German mathematician Leibniz who,
working independently, developed calculus somewhat later.

ohm (Ω)

A unit of electrical resistance. One ohm equals the resistance across
which a potential difference of 1 volt produces a current flow of
1 ampere. Named after G.S. Ohm (1787–1854).

Ohm, Georg Simon

German physicist (1789–1854) whose studies of how the current
flowing in an electric circuit was affected by the applied voltage and
the resistance led to the formulation of the law that has ever since
honoured his name. He is also remembered in the name of the unit
of resistance, the ohm.

orbital second

A unit of time equal to $\frac{1}{31\,557}$ of the tropical year 1900. Also called
Ephemeris second.

ounce (oz)

A unit of mass equal to $\frac{1}{16}$ lb.

ounce troy

A unit of mass in the troy system. Equal to $\frac{1}{12}$ pound troy.

pace

A unit of length/distance equal to about 2½ feet, used in ancient
Rome.

palm

A unit of length used in ancient Egypt, equal to the width of an average palm of the hand (4 digits).

parsec (pc)

A unit of length used for measuring astronomical distances. 1 parsec = 3.26 light years.

pascal (Pa)

A unit of pressure equal to the force of 1 newton acting over an area of 1 square metre.

Pascal, Blaise

French physicist and mathematician (1623–62). In the 1650s he developed the theory of probability (with Pierre de Fermat) and a device – now called Pascal's triangle – for calculating probabilities. He also invented the adding machine, in effect the precursor of today's calculator. In physics, Pascal is remembered for developing what became known as Pascal's law of pressure: pressure applied to a fluid in a vessel is transmitted in all directions equally.

peck (pk)

A unit of dry volume. 1 peck = 2 UK gal; 1 peck = 2 US gal. The two should not be confused: 1 UK peck = 1.032 US peck.

pennyweight (dwt)

A unit of weight in the troy system equal to $\frac{1}{20}$ ounce troy (25 grains).

perch

A unit of length equal to 5½ yards. Also called a pole or a rod.

perigee

The point on a satellite's orbit at which the satellite is nearest the planet it is orbiting.

peta-

In the UK, a prefix meaning 1 thousand billion (10^{15}); in the US, meaning 1 quadrillion (10^{15}).

pi (π)

Symbol and name representing the ratio of a circle's circumference to its diameter. Its value is approximately 3.14.

pica

A unit of length, used by printers, approximately equal to ⅙ in.

pico-

In the UK, a prefix meaning one billionth (10^{-12}). For example, in the UK, 1 picometre = 1 billionth of a metre; in the US, 1 picometre = 1 trillionth of a metre.

pint (pt)

A unit of volume. In the UK, a pint measures either dry or liquid volume: 1 pt = ⅛ UK gal. In the US, two kinds of pint are used: 1 fl pt = ⅛ gal; 1 dry pt = ¼₆₄ bu. The two should not be confused: 1 UK pt ≈ 1.2 US fl pt ≈ 1.03 US dry pt.

pixel

The smallest element of an image that can be individually processed in a video display system.

point

A unit of length, used especially by printers, approximately equal to ¹⁄₇₂ in.

pole

Unit of length equal to 5½ yards. Also called a perch or a rod.

pound (lb)

Unit of mass in the foot-pound-second (FPS) system, now defined as a mass equal to 0.4535923 kilogram (formerly the mass of a cylinder of platinum called the Imperial Standard Pound). It is the basic unit of the avoirdupois (avdp.), troy and apothecaries' weight measurement systems.

1 pound = 16 ounces, 256 drams, 7000 grains = 0.4535924 kilogram.

poundal

A unit of force equal to that needed to give an acceleration of 1 foot per second to a mass of 1 pound.

protractor

A protractor is a circular or semicircular instrument that is graded in degrees to measure angles.

PSI

Pounds per square inch: a unit for measuring pressure. 1 PSI equals the pressure resulting from a force of 1 pound force acting over an area of 1 square inch. *See also* pound.

Pythagoras

Greek mathematician and philosopher (6th century BC). He is associated with mathematical discoveries involving chief musical intervals, relations of numbers, and theorem bearing his name.

quart (qt)

A unit of volume for liquids. In the UK, 1 qt = 2 UK pt; in the US, 1 qt = 2 US fl pt. The two should not be confused: 1 UK qt ≈ 1.2 US qt.

quarter (qr)

An imperial measure of weight originating in the avoirdupois weight system, but traditionally adapted in the US to a slightly diminished though related size.

    1 UK quarter (of a hundredweight) = 2 stones, 28 pounds
        = 12.7006 kilograms
    1 US quarter (of a short hundredweight, or cental) = 25 pounds
        = 11.3398 UK quarters.

quarter troy (qr tr)

A unit of weight equal to 25 troy pounds.

quintal (q)

A unit of mass equal to 100 kg or 100 lb. Called the short hundredweight in the US.

quipu

A mathematical record of statistics which uses knots tied into cords. Used in the Inca Empire of Peru (12th –16th century).

rad

A short form of radian, a unit of measure for plane angles. *See also* centrad.

radar

An acronym (Radio Detection and Ranging). A device/system based on the effect of reflection of radio waves by metallic objects.

Rankine, William John MacQuorn

Scottish engineer (1820–72) who excelled in many areas but is best remembered for the Rankine cycle which describes the changes in pressure and temperature of water in a steam engine. The Rankine cycle is used to rate the performance of steam power plants.

Rankine scale of temperature

A temperature scale on which absolute temperatures are expressed in degrees Fahrenheit. Thus, absolute zero (0 K) is 0 °R, the freezing point of water (0 °C, 32 °F) is 491.67 °R and the boiling point of water (100 °C, 212 °F) is 617.67 °R. To convert Fahrenheit temperatures to Rankine temperatures, add 459.67. The scale was named after the Scottish physicist and engineer William Rankine (1820–72).

ream

A unit of volume, used to measure paper in bulk. One ream equals about 500 sheets.

Réaumur

A unit of temperature named after René Antoine Ferchault de Réaumur, first proposed in 1731. The freezing point of water is 0° Reaumur, the boiling point 80° Reaumur. Hence a degree Reaumur is 1.25 degrees Celsius or kelvin. The Réaumur scale has long been replaced by the Celsius scale.

reputed quart

A unit of volume, used especially for wine, equal to ⅙ of a Winchester wine gallon.

Richter, Charles Francis

American seismologist (1900–85) who, with Beno Gutenberg, devised an absolute scale of earthquake strength, based on the logarithm of the maximum amplitude of earthquake waves on the seismograph, adjusted for distance from the earthquake epicentre. The scale was named after him.

Richter scale

A logarithmic scale for expressing the strength of shocks from an earthquake, corresponding to the varying seismic effects at the ground surface. In part it closely approximates to the Mercalli scale, and may briefly be summarized:

2.0–2.9 perceived only by sensitive seismographic machines
3.0–3.9 slight vibration; hanging objects swing
4.0–4.9 vibration; crockery rattles; small objects displaced
5.0–5.9 furniture moves; masonry cracks and falls; waves on ponds
6.0–6.9 difficult standing; walls and chimneys partly collapse
7.0–7.9 buildings collapse; cracks in ground; landslides
8.0–8.9 damage to underground structures; masses of rock displaced.

r.m.s. value

For an alternating (cyclical) wave form, the root-mean-square value of the varying quantity (such as current or voltage) for a sine wave equal to the peak value divided by the square root of 2.

rod

Unit of length that is the same as a pole (and, in the US, a perch).
1 rod = 16½ feet, 5½ yards = 5.0292 metres.
320 rods = 1 mile.

Roman mile

When the Romans became the dominant power in the Mediterranean, they took over and modified the units of length. They based the foot on the length of one foot and subdivided it into 12 unciae, from which comes our word inch. The Romans also needed a unit to measure longer distances so they used a pace, a double stride, and measured 1000 paces to make a mile, from the Latin *mille* (meaning a thousand). One pace equalled 5 feet, so that the Roman mile of 5000 feet was very close to today's mile at 5280 feet.

röntgen

A unit of radition, equal to the amount of ionizing radiation (for example, X-rays, gamma-rays) that will produce 2.58×10^{-4} coulomb of electric charge in 1 kilogram of dry air. The unit was named after the German physicist Wilhelm Röntgen.

Röntgen, Wilhelm Conrad

German physicist (1854–1923) who discovered X-rays. He demonstrated their medical value, but not their dangers. In 1901 he was awarded the first Nobel Prize for Physics. The unit of radiation was named after him.

rood

A unit of area equal to ¼ acre (1210 yd²).

rulers

A ruler is the most common instrument for measuring millimetres, centimetres and metres; or yards, feet and inches. It is a straight piece of wood, plastic or metal with a scale marked on it. The standard school ruler is 30 centimetres, or 12 inches, long. Carpenters and builders use folding rulers that can measure up to a metre or more. Most instruments include scales for reading off measurements.

score

A counting unit equal to 20.

scruple

A unit of mass in the apothecaries' system equal to 20 grains.

sea mile

A unit of length distinguished from the nautical mile.
1 sea mile = 1000 fathoms (6000 feet).

second

A unit of time equal to ⅟₆₀ minute.

short (US) hundredweight (sh cwt)

US name for the UK quintal or cental. Equal to 100 pounds.

sidereal day

A measure of time approximately equal to 23 hours, 56 minuntes, 4.09 seconds. A sidereal day represents the time needed for one complete rotation of the Earth on its axis.

sidereal month

A measure of time.
1 month = 27.5 days.

sidereal second

A unit of time equal to ⅟₈₆ ₄₀₀ of the interval needed for one complete rotation of the Earth on its axis.

sidereal year

Equals the time that it takes the Earth to revolve around the Sun from one fixed point (usually a star) back to the same point (365 days, 6 hours, 9 minutes, 9 seconds).

siemens (S)

Unit of conductance in the SI system, equal to the conductance of a material of resistance 1 ohm when there is a potential difference (voltage) of 1 volt between its ends. It superseded the mho (reciprocal ohm), which has exactly the same value. It was named after Karl Wilhelm (later William) Siemens (1822–83).

Siemens, William

English electrical engineer of German background (1822–83). Among his inventions were a water metre (1851) and a device for reproducing printing that remained standard until the development of photography. He was also one of the first to apply (1883) electric power to railways. The unit of conductance was named after him.

specialist units

Many industries have created their own standard sizes, but all are based on metres, inches or feet.

square chain

A measure of area equal to 484 yd^2.

square units (sq or ^{2})

These signify that two quantities measured in the same units have been multiplied together. For example, to find the area of a square or rectangle, length and breadth are multiplied together to give the area, which is measured in square units.

steradian

A unit of solid angle in the SI system of units, equal to the angle subtended at the centre of a sphere by an area on its surface equal to the square of its radius. The whole surface subtends an angle of 4π steradians at the centre.

stère

A unit of volume, especially used for measuring timber.
1 stère = 1 m^3.

stone

Measure of weight in Britain and some other countries (although not ordinarily in North America), used particularly in relation to one's own bodyweight (which is referred to then, if not an exact number of stone, as 'n stone m pounds'). Even in Britain, however, this mode of weight measurement is being superseded by units of the metric system (kilograms).

1 stone = 14 pounds = 6.35026 kilograms.

synodic month

See lunar month.

tablespoon (tbsp)

A unit of volume used in cooking and equal to 1.5 centilitres (3 tsp).

16 tbsp = 1 cup.

teaspoon (tsp)

A unit of volume used in cooking and equal to 0.5 centilitre.

3 tsp = 1 tbsp.

tera-

In the UK, a prefix meaning one billion (10^{12}). In the US, meaning 1 trillion (10^{12}). For example, in the UK 1 terametre = 1 billion metres; in the US 1 terametre = 1 trillion metres.

tesla (T)

Unit of magnetic flux density in SI units, equal to 1 weber per square metre, and to the magnetic induction which, on a current of 1 ampere, produces a force of 1 newton. It was named after the American physicist of Serbian background, Nikola Tesla (1856–1943).

Tesla, Nikola

American inventor. A pioneer in the field of high-voltage electricity, he made many discoveries and inventions of great value to the development of radio transmission and to the field of electricity. These include a system of arc lighting, the Tesla induction motor and system of alternating-current transmission, the Tesla coil, generators of high-frequency currents, a transformer to increase oscillating currents to high potentials, a system of wireless communication, and a system of transmitting electric power without wires. He produced the first power system at Niagara Falls. The unit of magnetic flux density was named after him.

theodolite

A theodolite is similar to a transit but is smaller and more accurate.

thermograph

A thermometer, used in meteorology, that makes a continuous recording of temperature.

thermometer

An instrument for measuring temperature. There are many types, the most familiar being the liquid-in-glass thermometer (a graduated capillary tube containing mercury or dyed alcohol which moves along the tube from a bulb reservoir). Almost any physical property that varies with temperature can be employed to indicate changes in temperature. The movement of a coil of dissimilar metals (bimetallic strip), for example, is commonly used in a thermograph. The change of a metal's electrical resistance with temperature is used in a platinum resistance thermometer (for high temperatures), and the generation of an electromotive force (voltage) at a junction between two dissimilar metals is used in a thermocouple-type thermometer.

Thomson, William (1st Baron Kelvin)

Irish-born Scottish physicist and mathematician (1824–1907) who proposed the absolute, or Kelvin, temperature scale (1848) and, at around the same time as Rudolf Celsius, established the second law of thermodynamics. He also invented a tide predictor and a harmonic analyser.

ton

A unit of mass. In the US, 1 ton = 2000 lb. In the UK, 1 ton = 2 240 lb. Called a long ton in the US.

tonne (t)

A unit of mass equal to 1000 kg. Also called a metric ton.

tonne of coal equivalent

A measure of energy production/consumption based on the premise that 1 tonne of coal provides 8000 kilowatt-hours (kWh) of energy.

ton troy (ton tr)

A unit of mass equal to 2000 pounds troy.

Torricelli, Evangelista

Italian physicist and mathematician (1608–47) who was the first to discover the fundamental principles of hydraulics (fluid mechanics). In 1644 he described the barometer, or Torricellian tube. He improved telescopes and microscopes and made several mathematical discoveries. He is said to be the father of hydrodynamics.

total station

An instrument which uses a small telescope and a laser to measure distances and heights. It is set up on a tripod and combines the techniques used in a theodolite and EDM equipment. The total station measures distances and heights that are accurate to the nearest millimetre and displays the result on a liquid-crystal panel.

transit

A transit is an instrument used by surveyors. It consists of a telescope that can rotate vertically and horizontally to measure angles which are read off vertical or horizontal scales. Vernier scales are used to give greater accuracy.

trillion

In the UK, equal to 10^{18}; in the US, equal to 10^{12}.

triple point

For a substance that can exist in three different phases, the temperature and pressure at which they all can coexist. For example, ice, liquid water and water vapour coexist in water's triple point (at a temperature of 273.16 K and pressure of 610 newtons per square metre).

tropical month

The time taken for the Moon to return to the same longitude after making a complete orbit around the Earth (that is, one complete revolution of the Moon on its axis).

1 tropical month = 27.32158 days.

tropical year

Equals the time interval between two consecutive passages of the Sun, in one direction, through the Earth's equatorial plane (or from vernal equinox to vernal equinox; 365 days, 5 hours, 48 minutes, 46 seconds).

troy pound (lb tr)

A unit of mass in the troy system.
1 troy pound = 12 troy ounces.

troy system

A system of mass measurement based on the 20-ounce pound and the 20-pennyweight ounce.

vernier scale

A vernier scale is used alongside other instruments to give more accurate readings. The vernier is slid along the main scale to compare graduations on the two scales. Nine subdivisions on the main scale are matched by ten subdivisions on the vernier scale. The correct reading is given by the subdivision on the vernier which is closest to the subdivision on the main scale.

volt (V)

A unit of electromotive force and potential difference. Equal to the difference in potential between two points of a conducting wire carrying a constant current of 1 ampere (A), when the power released between the points is 1 watt (W). Named after Alessandro Volta.

Volta, Alessandro Giuseppe Anastasi, Conte

Italian physicist (1745–1827) He invented the first electric battery (the voltaic pile) in 1800, whose name is given to the unit of electrical potential difference, the volt. Volta developed a theory of current electricity and made studies of heat and gases.

volt-ampere

Unit that describes the apparent power in an a.c. electric circuit, equal to the product of the root-mean-square (r.m.s.) voltage and the current.

voltmeter

An instrument for measuring voltage that may be one of several types – moving iron, moving coil, electrostatic or digital. The first two types are similar to ammeters. The electrostatic type is more recent, using the principle of mechanical force acting on bodies at different voltages; no current is drawn. The digital-style meter was invented in 1952; it uses solid-state circuits. Around 1970 integrated circuits were introduced, for use when high accuracy is required.

watt (W)

A unit of power equal to that available when 1 J of energy is expended in 1 second.

1 W = 1 volt-ampere; 746 W = 1 horsepower (hp).

Named after the Scottish inventor James Watt.

Watt, James

Scottish inventor (1736–1819). He devised improvements to Thomas Newcomen's steam engine that resulted in a new type of engine with a separate condensing chamber, an air pump to bring steam into the chamber, and parts of the engine insulated. He also perfected a rotary engine. Watt coined the term horsepower. The watt, a unit of power, was named after him.

weber (W)

Unit of magnetic flux, defined as the flux through a surface over which the total normal component of the magnetic induction is 1 tesla per square metre. A magnetic flux change of 1 weber per second in a circuit induces an EMF of 1 volt in it.

1 weber = 1 volt-second = 1 joule per ampere.

Weber, Wilhelm Eduard

German physicist (1804–91). He worked with C.F. Gauss on terrestrial magnetism and devised an electromagnetic telegraph. He introduced the absolute system of electrical units. The coulomb was once known as the weber; now the weber is a magnetic unit.

Winchester quart

A unit of fluid volume equal to 2½ litres.

X-unit (x or XU)

A unit of length used especially for measuring wavelength.

1 x-unit $\approx 10^{-3}$ ångström (10^{-13} m).

yard (yd)

An imperial measure of extremely common usage, although now in Europe largely overtaken by the slightly larger metre of the eponymous metric system.

1 yard = 3 feet, 36 inches = 91.44 centimetres, 0.9144 metre

2 yards = 1 fathom (1.8288 metre)

5.5 yards = 1 rod, pole, or US perch.

yards per minute (ypm)

A unit of speed representing the number of yards travelled in 1 minute.

yardstick

The standard units were not precise, and varied from region to region. In the early nineteenth century a commission was set up in England to produce a precise standard for the yard. A metal yardstick, whose length was related to the length of a pendulum that made one complete swing under certain specified conditions, was lodged in the Houses of Parliament, but was destroyed when the building burned down in 1834. In 1845 a second yardstick was produced and marked 'Mr Bailey's Number 1 Standard Yard' and kept at the National Weights and Measures Laboratory. In 1963 the yard was redefined in relation to the metre, by then the accepted international unit of length.

year

A unit of time measurement determined by the revolution of the Earth around the Sun. The ordinary calendar credits the year with 365 days, plus an extra day (29 February) every fourth year to compensate for accumulated time over.

yocto-

Prefix meaning a unit valued at 10^{-24} in the metric system.

yotta-

Prefix meaning a unit valued at 10^{24} in the metric system.

zepto-

Prefix meaning a unit valued at 10^{-21} in the metric system.

zetta-

Prefix meaning a unit valued at 10^{21} in the metric system.

2 Length

Early measurement systems

Egyptian measurements

1 digit   = one finger width
1 palm   = four digits
1 hand   = five digits
1 cubit   = elbow to finger tip (= 28 digits = 20.6 in)

Roman measurements

1 foot   =   12 unciae (= 12 inches)
1 pace   =   5 feet
Roman mile (*mille passus*)   =   1 000 paces

Agricultural measurements

12 douzièmes	= 1 line		4 rods	= 1 chain
4 lines	= 1 barleycorn		10 chains	= 1 furlong
3 barleycorns	= 1 inch		8 furlongs	= 1 mile
5½ yards	= 1 rod		3 miles	= 1 league

Measuring small distances

Name	Symbol	Value	Metres
Attometre	am	10^{-18} m	0.000 000 000 000 000 001 m
Femtometre	fm	10^{-15} m	0.000 000 000 000 001 m
Picometre	pm	10^{-12} m	0.000 000 000 001 m
Nanometre	nm	10^{-9} m	0.000 000 001 m
Micrometre	µm	10^{-6} m	0.000 001 m
Millimetre	mm	10^{-3} m	0.001 m
Centimetre	cm	10^{-2} m	0.01 m
Decimetre	dm	10^{-1} m	0.1 m
Metre	m		1 m

Measuring large distances

Terametre	Tm	10^{12} m	1 000 000 000 000 m
Gigametre	Gm	10^{9} m	1 000 000 000 m
Megametre	Mm	10^{6} m	1 000 000 m
Myriametre	mym	10^{4} m	10 000 m
Kilometre	km	10^{3} m	1000 m
Hectometre	hm	10^{2} m	100 m
Dekametre	dam	10 m	10 m
Metre	m		1 m

Astronomical measurements

The table below lists standard abbreviations and equivalents for the units used in measuring astronomical distances. These are very large units and are related to the Earth's orbit.

A light year (ly) is the distance light travels – at its speed of 299 792.458 km/s – through space over a tropical year.

An astronomical unit (AU) is the mean distance between the Earth and the Sun.

A parsec (pc) is the distance at which a baseline of 1 AU in length subtends an angle of 1 second.

1 AU	=	149 600 000 km	=	93 000 000 mi
1 ly	=	9 460 500 000 000 km	=	5 878 000 000 000 mi
1 pc	=	30 857 200 000 000 km	=	19 174 000 000 000 mi
1 ly	=	63 240 AU		
1 pc	=	206 265 AU	=	3.262 ly

Conversion formulae

Overleaf are listed the multiplication/division factors for converting units of length from imperial to metric, and vice versa. Note that two kinds of factors are given: quick, for an approximate conversion that can be made without a calculator; and accurate, for an exact conversion.

The bars which appear in the charts are diagrammatic visual representations of the equivalents calculated afterwards.

			Quick	Accurate
Milli-inches (mils) Micrometres (μm)				
	mils ⟶	μm	× 25	× 25.4
	μm ⟶	mils	÷ 25	× 0.0394
Inches (in) Millimetres (mm)				
	in ⟶	mm	× 25	× 25.4
	mm ⟶	in	÷ 25	× 0.0394
Inches (in) Centimetres (cm)				
	in ⟶	cm	× 2.5	× 2.54
	cm ⟶	in	÷ 2.5	× 0.394
Feet (ft) Metres (m)				
	ft ⟶	m	÷ 3.3	× 0.305
	m ⟶	ft	× 3.3	× 3.281
Yards (yd) Metres (m)				
	yd ⟶	m	÷ 1	× 0.914
	m ⟶	yd	× 1	× 1.094
Fathoms (fm) Metres (m)				
	fm ⟶	m	× 2	× 1.829
	m ⟶	fm	÷ 2	× 0.547
Chains (ch) Metres (m)				
	ch ⟶	m	× 20	× 20.1168
	m ⟶	ch	÷ 20	× 0.0497
Furlongs (fur) Metres (m)				
	fur ⟶	m	× 200	× 201.17
	m ⟶	fur	÷ 200	× 0.005
Yards (yd) Kilometres (km)				
	yd ⟶	km	÷ 1000	× 0.00091
	km ⟶	yd	× 1000	× 1093.6
Miles (mi) Kilometres (km)				
	mi ⟶	km	× 1.5	× 1.609
	km ⟶	mi	÷ 1.5	× 0.621
Nautical miles (n mi) Miles (mi)				
	n mi ⟶	mi	× 1.2	× 1.151
	mi ⟶	n mi	÷ 1.2	× 0.869
Nautical miles (n mi) Kilometres (km)				
	n mi ⟶	km	× 2	× 1.852
	km ⟶	n mi	÷ 2	× 0.540

Sample calculations

Milli-inches (mils) to micrometres (μm)
   e.g.   3 mils =
         3 mils x 25.4 = 76.2 μm
         3 mils = 76.2 μm

Micrometres (μm) to milli-inches (mils)
   e.g.   100 μm =
         100 x 0.0394 = 3.94 mils
         100 μm = 3.94 mils

Inches (in) to millimetres (mm)
   e.g.   10 in =
         10 x 25.4 = 254 mm
         10 in = 254 mm

Millimetres (mm) to inches (in)
   e.g.   1000 mm =
         1000 mm x 0.0394 = 39.4 in
         1000 mm = 39.4 in

Inches (in) to centimetres (cm)
   e.g.   50 in =
         50 x 2.54 = 127 cm
         50 in = 127 cm

Centimetres (cm) to inches (in)
   e.g.   100 cm =
         100 x 0.394 = 39.4 in
         100 cm = 39.4 in

Feet (ft) to metres (m)
   e.g.   100 ft =
         100 x 0.305 = 30.5 m
         100 ft = 30.5 m

Metres (m) to feet (ft)
   e.g.   1000 m =
         1000 x 3.281 = 3281 ft
         1000 m = 3281 ft

Yards (yd) to metres (m)
   e.g.   500 yards =
         500 x 0.9144 = 457.2 m
         500 yd = 457.2 m

Metres (m) to yards (yd)
   e.g.   10 metres =
         10 x 1.0936 = 10.936 yd
         10 m = 10.936 yd

Fathoms (fm) to metres (m)
   e.g.   40 fathoms =
         40 x 1.829 = 73.16 m
         40 fm = 73.16 m

Metres (m) to fathoms (fm)
   e.g.   500 metres =
         500 x 0.547 = 273.5 fm
         500 m = 273.5 fm

Chains (ch) to metres (m)
   e.g.   50 chains =
         50 x 20.1168 = 1005.84 m
         50 ch = 1005.84 m

Metres (m) to chains (ch)
   e.g.   1000 metres =
         1000 x 0.0497 = 49.7 ch
         1000 m = 49.7 ch

Furlongs (fur) to metres (m)
   e.g.   50 furlongs =
         50 x 201.168 = 10 058.4 m
         50 fur = 10 058.4 m

Metres (m) to furlongs (fur)
   e.g.   500 metres =
         500 x 0.005 = 2.5 fur
         500 m = 2.5 fur

Yards (yd) to kilometres (km)
    e.g. 550 yards =
            550 x 0.00091 = 0.5005 km
            550 yd = 0.5005 km

Kilometres (km) to yards (yd)
    e.g. 10 kilometres
            10 x 1093.6 = 10 936 yd
            10 km = 10 936 yd

Miles (mi) to kilometres (km)
    e.g. 250 miles
            250 x 1.609 = 402.25 km
            250 mi = 402.25 km

Kilometres (km) to miles (mi)
    e.g. 250 kilometres
            250 x 0.621 = 155.25 mi
            250 km = 155.25 mi

Nautical miles (n mi) to miles (mi)
    e.g. 1500 nautical miles =
            1500 x 1.151 = 1726.5 mi
            1500 n mi = 1726.5 mi

Miles (mi) to nautical miles (n mi)
    e.g. 1500 miles =
            1500 x 0.869 = 1303.5 n mi
            1500 mi = 1303.5 n mi

Nautical miles (n mi) to kilometres (km)
    e.g. 1500 nautical miles =
            1500 x 1.852 = 2778 km
            1500 n mi = 2778 km

Kilometres (km) to nautical miles (n mi)
    e.g. 1500 km =
            1500 x 0.54 = 810 n mi
            1500 km = 810 n mi

Conversion tables

These tables can be used to convert units of length from one measuring system to another. The first group of tables, right, converts imperial to metric; the second, beginning on page 75, converts metric to imperial.

The tables starting with the ones on the right show the conversion of:

- Milli-inches to Micrometres
- Inches to Millimetres
- Inches to Centimetres
- Feet to Metres
- Yards to Metres
- Fathoms to Metres
- Chains to Metres
- Furlongs to Metres
- Yards to Kilometres
- Miles to Kilometres
- Nautical miles to Miles
- Nautical miles to Kilometres.

From page 75 the tables show the conversion of:

- Micrometres to Milli-inches
- Millimetres to Inches
- Centimetres to Inches
- Metres to Feet
- Metres to Yards
- Metres to Fathoms
- Metres to Chains
- Metres to Furlongs
- Kilometres to Yards
- Kilometres to Miles
- Miles to Nautical miles
- Kilometres to Nautical miles.

Milli-inches to Micrometres

mils	µm
1	25.4
2	50.8
3	76.2
4	101.6
5	127.0
6	152.4
7	177.8
8	203.2
9	228.6
10	254.0
20	508.0
30	762.0
40	1016.0
50	1270.0
60	1524.0
70	1778.0
80	2032.0
90	2286.0
100	2540.0

Inches to Millimetres

in	mm
1	25.4
2	50.8
3	76.2
4	101.6
5	127.0
6	152.4
7	177.8
8	203.2
9	228.6
10	254.0
20	508.0
30	762.0
40	1016.0
50	1270.0
60	1524.0
70	1778.0
80	2032.0
90	2286.0
100	2540.0

Inches to Centimetres

in	cm
1	2.54
2	5.08
3	7.62
4	10.16
5	12.70
6	15.24
7	17.78
8	20.32
9	22.86
10	25.40
20	50.80
30	76.20
40	101.60
50	127.00
60	152.40
70	177.80
80	203.20
90	228.60
100	254.00

Feet to Metres

ft	m
1	0.305
2	0.610
3	0.914
4	1.219
5	1.524
6	1.829
7	2.134
8	2.438
9	2.743
10	3.048
20	6.096
30	9.144
40	12.192
50	15.240
60	18.288
70	21.336
80	24.384
90	27.432
100	30.480

Yards to Metres

yd	m
1	0.914
2	1.829
3	2.743
4	3.658
5	4.572
6	5.486
7	6.401
8	7.315
9	8.230
10	9.144
20	18.288
30	27.432
40	36.576
50	45.720
60	54.864
70	64.008
80	73.152
90	82.296
100	91.440

Fathoms to Metres

fm	m
1	1.83
2	3.66
3	5.49
4	7.32
5	9.14
6	10.97
7	12.80
8	14.63
9	16.46
10	18.29
20	36.58
30	54.87
40	73.16
50	91.45
60	109.74
70	128.03
80	146.32
90	164.61
100	182.90

Length

Chains to Metres	
ch	m
1	20.108
2	40.216
3	60.324
4	80.432
5	100.540
6	120.648
7	140.756
8	160.864
9	180.972
10	201.080
20	402.160
30	603.240
40	804.320
50	1005.400
60	1206.480
70	1407.560
80	1608.640
90	1809.720
100	2010.800

Furlongs to Metres	
fur	m
1	201.17
2	402.34
3	603.50
4	804.67
5	1005.84
6	1207.01
7	1408.18
8	1609.34
9	1810.51
10	2011.68
20	4023.36
30	6035.04
40	8046.72
50	10 058.40
60	12 070.08
70	14 081.76
80	16 093.44
90	18 105.12
100	20 116.80

Yards to Kilometres	
yd	km
1	0.091
2	0.183
3	0.274
4	0.366
5	0.457
6	0.549
7	0.640
8	0.731
9	0.823
10	0.914
20	1.829
30	2.743
40	3.658
50	4.572
60	5.486
70	6.401
80	7.315
90	8.230
100	9.144

Miles to Kilometres	
mi	km
1	1.609
2	3.219
3	4.828
4	6.437
5	8.047
6	9.656
7	11.265
8	12.875
9	14.484
10	16.093
20	32.187
30	48.280
40	64.374
50	80.467
60	96.561
70	112.654
80	128.748
90	144.841
100	160.934

Nautical miles to Miles	
n mi	mi
1	1.151
2	2.302
3	3.452
4	4.603
5	5.754
6	6.905
7	8.055
8	9.206
9	10.357
10	11.508
20	23.016
30	34.523
40	46.031
50	57.539
60	69.047
70	80.554
80	92.062
90	103.570
100	115.078

Nautical miles to Kilometres	
n mi	km
1	1.852
2	3.704
3	5.556
4	7.408
5	9.260
6	11.112
7	12.964
8	14.816
9	16.668
10	18.520
20	37.040
30	55.560
40	74.080
50	92.600
60	111.120
70	129.640
80	148.160
90	166.680
100	185.200

Micrometres to Milli-inches	
µm	mils
1	0.039
2	0.079
3	0.118
4	0.157
5	0.197
6	0.236
7	0.276
8	0.315
9	0.354
10	0.394
20	0.787
30	1.181
40	1.575
50	1.969
60	2.362
70	2.756
80	3.150
90	3.543
100	3.937

Millimetres to Inches	
mm	in
1	0.039
2	0.079
3	0.118
4	0.157
5	0.197
6	0.236
7	0.276
8	0.315
9	0.354
10	0.394
20	0.787
30	1.181
40	1.575
50	1.969
60	2.362
70	2.756
80	3.150
90	3.543
100	3.937

Centimetres to Inches	
cm	in
1	0.394
2	0.787
3	1.181
4	1.575
5	1.969
6	2.362
7	2.756
8	3.150
9	3.543
10	3.937
20	7.874
30	11.811
40	15.748
50	19.685
60	23.622
70	27.559
80	31.496
90	35.433
100	39.370

Metres to Feet	
m	ft
1	3.281
2	6.562
3	9.843
4	13.123
5	16.404
6	19.685
7	22.966
8	26.247
9	29.528
10	32.808
20	65.617
30	98.425
40	131.234
50	164.042
60	196.850
70	229.659
80	262.467
90	295.276
100	328.084

Metres to Yards	
m	yd
1	1.094
2	2.187
3	3.281
4	4.374
5	5.468
6	6.562
7	7.655
8	8.749
9	9.843
10	10.936
20	21.872
30	32.808
40	43.745
50	54.681
60	65.617
70	76.553
80	87.489
90	98.425
100	109.361

Metres to Fathoms	
m	fm
1	0.547
2	1.093
3	1.640
4	2.187
5	2.734
6	3.280
7	3.827
8	4.374
9	4.921
10	5.467
20	10.935
30	16.402
40	21.870
50	27.337
60	32.805
70	38.272
80	43.740
90	49.207
100	54.674

Metres to Chains			Metres to Furlongs			Kilometres to Yards	
m	ch		m	fur		km	yd
1	0.0497		1	0.005		1	1093.6
2	0.0994		2	0.010		2	2187.2
3	0.1491		3	0.015		3	3280.8
4	0.1989		4	0.020		4	4374.4
5	0.2487		5	0.025		5	5468.0
6	0.2983		6	0.030		6	6561.6
7	0.3481		7	0.035		7	7655.2
8	0.3979		8	0.040		8	8748.8
9	0.4476		9	0.045		9	9842.4
10	0.4973		10	0.050		10	10 936.0
20	0.9946		20	0.099		20	21 872.0
30	1.4919		30	0.149		30	32 808.0
40	1.9893		40	0.199		40	43 744.0
50	2.4866		50	0.249		50	54 680.0
60	2.9839		60	0.298		60	65 616.0
70	3.4812		70	0.348		70	76 552.0
80	3.9785		80	0.398		80	87 488.0
90	4.4758		90	0.447		90	98 424.0
100	4.9731		100	0.497		100	109 360.0

Kilometres to Miles			Miles to Nautical miles			Kilometres to Nautical miles	
km	mi		in	n mi		km	n mi
1	0.621		1	0.869		1	0.54
2	1.243		2	1.738		2	1.08
3	1.864		3	2.607		3	1.62
4	2.485		4	3.476		4	2.16
5	3.107		5	4.349		5	2.70
6	3.728		6	5.214		6	3.24
7	4.350		7	6.083		7	3.78
8	4.971		8	6.952		8	4.32
9	5.592		9	7.821		9	4.86
10	6.214		10	8.690		10	5.40
20	12.427		20	17.380		20	10.80
30	18.641		30	26.069		30	16.20
40	24.855		40	34.759		40	21.60
50	31.069		50	43.449		50	27.00
60	37.282		60	52.139		60	32.40
70	43.496		70	60.828		70	37.80
80	49.710		80	69.518		80	43.20
90	55.923		90	78.208		90	48.60
100	62.137		100	86.900		100	54.00

3 Area

Conversion formulae

Below are the multiplication/division factors for converting units of area from imperial to metric, and vice versa. Two kinds of factors are given: quick for an approximate conversion, and accurate for an exact conversion.

			Quick	Accurate
Circular mils (cmil)				
Square micrometres (μm²)				
cmil	→	μm²	× 500	× 506.7
μm²	→	cmil	÷ 500	× 0.002
Square inches (in²)				
Square millimetres (mm²)				
in²	→	mm²	× 650	× 645.2
mm²	→	in²	÷ 650	× 0.0016
Square inches (in²)				
Square centimetres (cm²)				
in²	→	cm²	× 6.5	× 6.452
cm²	→	in²	÷ 6.5	× 0.15
Square chains (ch²)				
Square metres (m²)				
ch²	→	m²	× 400	× 404.686
m²	→	ch²	÷ 400	× 0.0025

		Quick	Accurate
Square miles (mi²)			
Square kilometres (km²)			
mi² ⟶ km²		× 2.5	× 2.590
km² ⟶ mi²		÷ 2.5	× 0.386
Square miles (mi²)			
Hectares (ha)			
mi² ⟶ ha		× 250	× 258.999
ha ⟶ mi²		÷ 250	× 0.0039
Hectares (ha)			
Acres			
ha ⟶ acre		× 2.5	× 2.471
acre ⟶ ha		÷ 2.5	× 0.405
Square metres (m²)			
Square yards (yd²)			
m² ⟶ yd²		× 1	× 1.196
yd² ⟶ m²		÷ 1	× 0.836
Square metres (m²)			
Square feet (ft²)			
m² ⟶ ft²		× 11	× 10.764
ft² ⟶ m²		÷ 11	× 0.093

Sample calculations

Circular mils (cmils) to square micrometres (μm^2)

e.g.   2 circular mils =
2 x 506.7 = 1013.4 μm^2
2 cmils = 1013.4 μm^2

Square micrometres (μm^2) to circular mils (cmils)

e.g.   1000 square micrometres =
1000 x 0.002 = 2 cmils
1000 μm^2 = 2 cmils

Square inches (in^2) to square millimetres (mm^2)

e.g.   5 square inches =
5 x 645.16 = 3225.8 mm^2
5 in^2 = 3225.8 mm^2

Square millimetres (mm^2) to square inches (in^2)

e.g.   25 square millimetres =
25 x 0.0016 = 0.0388 in^2
25 mm^2 = 0.0388 in^2

Square inches (in^2) to square centimetres (cm^2)

e.g.   5 square inches =
5 x 6.452 = 32.26 cm^2
5 in^2 = 32.26 cm^2

Square centimetres (cm^2) to square inches (in^2)

e.g.   25 cm^2 =
25 x 0.15 = 3.75 in^2
25 cm^2 = 3.75 in^2

Square chains (ch^2) to square metres (m^2)

e.g.   5 square chains =
5 x 404.686 = 2023.43 m^2
5 ch^2 = 2023.43 m^2

Square metres (m^2) to square chains (ch^2)

e.g.   1500 m^2 =
1500 x 0.0025 = 3.75 ch^2
1500 m^2 = 3.75 ch^2

Square miles (mi^2) to square kilometres (km^2)

e.g.   50 square miles =
50 x 2.590 = 129.5 km^2
50 mi^2 = 129.5 km^2

Square kilometres (km^2) to square miles (mi^2)

e.g.   50 square kilometres =
50 x 0.386 = 19.3 mi^2
50 km^2 = 19.3 mi^2

Square miles (mi^2) to hectares (ha)

e.g.   2 square miles =
2 x 258.999 = 517.998 ha
2 mi^2 = 517.998 ha

Hectares (ha) to square miles (mi^2)

e.g.   1500 hectares =
1500 x 0.0039 = 5.85 mi^2
1500 ha = 5.85 mi^2

Hectares (ha) to acres

e.g.   150 hectares =
150 x 2.471 = 370.65 acres
150 ha = 370.65 acres

Acres to hectares (ha)

e.g.   150 acres =
150 x 0.405 = 60.75 ha
150 acres = 60.75 ha

Square metres (m^2) to square yards (yd^2)

e.g.   15 square metres =
15 x 1.196 = 17.94 yd^2
15 m^2 = 17.94 yd^2

Square yards (yd^2) to square metres (m^2)

e.g.   15 square yards =
15 x 0.836 = 12.54 m^2
15 yd^2 = 12.54 m^2

Square metres (m²) to square feet (ft²)
e.g.   25 square metres =
25 x 10.764 = 269.1 ft²
25 m² = 269.1 ft²

Square feet (ft²) to square metres (m²)
e.g.   25 square feet =
25 x 0.093 = 2.325 m²
25 ft² = 2.325 m²

Square miles (mi²) to acres
How many acres are in 3 square miles?
3 x 640 acres = **1920 acres are in 3 mi²**

Square yards (yd²) to square feet (ft²)
How many square feet in a garden of 24
square yards? 24 x 9 square feet = **216 ft²**

Square inches (in²) to square feet (ft²)
How many square feet are there in 275
square inches?
275 x 0.0069 square feet = **1.8975 ft²**

Acres to square yards (yd²)
How many square yards are there in 1.5
acres?
1.5 x 4840 square yards = **7260 yd²**

Some useful imperial conversions

1 yd²	=	9 ft²	1 mi²	=	640 acres
1 ft²	=	0.111 yd²	1 acre	=	0.0016 mi²
1 acre	=	4840 yd²	1 ft²	=	144 in²
1 yd²	=	0.0002 acres	1 in²	=	0.0069 ft²

Conversion tables

These tables can be used to convert units of length from one
measuring system to another. The tables convert imperial to metric
and metric to imperial.

The tables beginning on page 82 show the conversion of:
- Circular mils to Square micrometres
- Square inches to Square millimetres
- Square inches to Square centimetres
- Square feet to Square metres
- Square yards to Square metres
- Square chains to Square metres
- Acres to Hectares
- Square miles to Hectares
- Square miles to Square kilometres

The tables beginning halfway through page 83 show the
conversion of:
- Square micrometres to Circular mils
- Square centimetres to Square inches
- Square metres to Square feet
- Square metres to Square yards
- Square metres to Square chains
- Hectares to Acres.
- Hectares to Square miles
- Square kilometres to Square miles

Circular mils to Square micrometres	
cmil	µm²
1	506.7
2	1013.4
3	1520.1
4	2026.8
5	2533.5
6	3040.2
7	3546.9
8	4053.6
9	4560.3
10	5067.0
20	10 134.0
30	15 201.0
40	20 268.0
50	25 335.0
60	30 402.0
70	35 469.0
80	40 536.0
90	45 603.0
100	50 670.0

Square inches to Square millimetres	
in²	mm²
1	645.2
2	1290.4
3	1936.6
4	2580.8
5	3226.0
6	3871.2
7	4516.4
8	5161.6
9	5806.8
10	6452.0
20	12 904.0
30	19 356.0
40	25 808.0
50	32 260.0
60	38 712.0
70	45 164.0
80	51 616.0
90	58 068.0
100	64 520.0

Square inches to Square centimetres	
in²	cm²
1	6.452
2	12.903
3	19.355
4	25.806
5	32.258
6	38.710
7	45.161
8	51.613
9	58.064
10	64.516
20	129.032
30	193.548
40	258.064
50	322.580
60	387.096
70	451.612
80	516.128
90	580.644
100	645.160

Square feet to Square metres	
ft²	m²
1	0.093
2	0.186
3	0.279
4	0.372
5	0.465
6	0.557
7	0.650
8	0.743
9	0.836
10	0.929
20	1.858
30	2.787
40	3.716
50	4.645
60	5.574
70	6.503
80	7.432
90	8.361
100	9.290

Square yards to Square metres	
yd²	m²
1	0.836
2	1.672
3	2.508
4	3.345
5	4.181
6	5.017
7	5.853
8	6.689
9	7.525
10	8.361
20	16.723
30	25.084
40	33.445
50	41.806
60	50.168
70	58.529
80	66.890
90	75.251
100	83.613

Square chains to Square metres	
ch²	m²
1	404.686
2	809.372
3	1214.058
4	1618.744
5	2023.430
6	2428.116
7	2832.802
8	3237.488
9	3642.174
10	4046.860
20	8093.720
30	12 140.580
40	16 187.440
50	20 234.300
60	24 281.160
70	28 328.020
80	32 374.880
90	36 421.740
100	40 468.600

Acres to Hectares

acre	ha
1	0.405
2	0.809
3	1.214
4	1.619
5	2.023
6	2.428
7	2.833
8	3.237
9	3.642
10	4.047
20	8.094
30	12.141
40	16.187
50	20.234
60	24.281
70	28.328
80	32.375
90	36.422
100	40.469

Square miles to Hectares

mi²	ha
1	258.999
2	517.998
3	776.997
4	1035.996
5	1294.995
6	1553.994
7	1812.993
8	2071.992
9	2330.991
10	2589.990
20	5179.980
30	7769.970
40	10 359.960
50	12 949.950
60	15 539.940
70	18 129.930
80	20 719.920
90	23 309.910
100	25 899.900

Square miles to Square kilometres

mi²	km²
1	2.590
2	5.180
3	7.770
4	10.360
5	12.950
6	15.540
7	18.130
8	20.720
9	23.310
10	25.900
20	51.800
30	77.700
40	103.600
50	129.499
60	155.399
70	181.299
80	207.199
90	233.099
100	258.999

Square micrometres to Circular mils

µm²	cmil
1	0.002
2	0.004
3	0.006
4	0.008
5	0.010
6	0.012
7	0.014
8	0.016
9	0.018
10	0.020
20	0.040
30	0.060
40	0.080
50	0.100
60	0.120
70	0.140
80	0.160
90	0.180
100	0.200

Square millimetres to Square inches

mm²	in²
1	0.0016
2	0.0031
3	0.0047
4	0.0062
5	0.0078
6	0.0093
7	0.0109
8	0.0124
9	0.0140
10	0.0155
20	0.0310
30	0.0465
40	0.0620
50	0.0775
60	0.0930
70	0.1085
80	0.1240
90	0.1395
100	0.1550

Square centimetres to Square inches

cm²	in²
1	0.155
2	0.310
3	0.465
4	0.620
5	0.775
6	0.930
7	1.085
8	1.240
9	1.395
10	1.550
20	3.100
30	4.650
40	6.200
50	7.750
60	9.300
70	10.850
80	12.400
90	13.950
100	15.500

Square metres to Square feet	
m²	ft²
1	10.764
2	21.528
3	32.292
4	43.056
5	53.820
6	64.583
7	75.347
8	86.111
9	96.875
10	107.639
20	215.278
30	322.917
40	430.556
50	538.196
60	645.835
70	753.474
80	861.113
90	968.752
100	1076.391

Square metres to Square yards	
m²	yd²
1	1.196
2	2.392
3	3.588
4	4.784
5	5.980
6	7.176
7	8.372
8	9.568
9	10.764
10	11.960
20	23.920
30	35.880
40	47.840
50	59.800
60	71.759
70	83.719
80	95.679
90	107.639
100	119.599

Square metres to Square chains	
m²	ch²
1	0.002
2	0.004
3	0.006
4	0.008
5	0.010
6	0.012
7	0.014
8	0.016
9	0.018
10	0.020
20	0.040
30	0.060
40	0.080
50	0.100
60	0.120
70	0.140
80	0.160
90	0.180
100	0.200

Hectares to Acres	
ha	acre
1	2.471
2	4.942
3	7.413
4	9.884
5	12.355
6	14.826
7	17.297
8	19.768
9	22.239
10	24.711
20	49.421
30	74.132
40	98.842
50	123.553
60	148.263
70	172.974
80	197.684
90	222.395
100	247.105

Hectares to Square miles	
ha	mi²
1	0.003 86
2	0.007 72
3	0.011 58
4	0.015 44
5	0.019 31
6	0.023 17
7	0.027 03
8	0.030 89
9	0.034 75
10	0.038 61
20	0.077 22
30	0.115 83
40	0.154 44
50	0.193 05
60	0.231 66
70	0.270 27
80	0.308 88
90	0.347 49
100	0.386 10

Square kilometres to Square miles	
km²	mi²
1	0.386
2	0.772
3	1.158
4	1.544
5	1.931
6	2.317
7	2.703
8	3.089
9	3.475
10	3.861
20	7.722
30	11.583
40	15.444
50	19.305
60	23.166
70	27.027
80	30.888
90	34.749
100	38.610

Countries and continents compared

The comparison of countries

		Square kilometres	Square miles
1	Russian Federation	17 075 000 km²	6 593 000 mi²
2	Canada	9 976 000 km²	3 852 000 mi²
3	China	9 561 000 km²	3 692 000 mi²
4	USA	9 520 000 km²	3 676 000 mi²
5	Brazil	8 512 000 km²	3 286 000 mi²
6	Australia	7 682 000 km²	2 966 000 mi²
7	India	3 288 000 km²	1 269 000 mi²
8	Argentina	2 777 000 km²	1 072 000 mi²

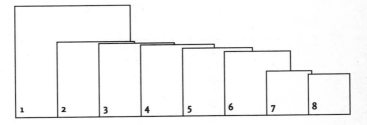

The comparison of continents

		Square kilometres	Square miles
A	Asia	44 250 000 km²	17 085 000 mi²
B	Africa	30 264 000 km²	11 685 000 mi²
C	North America	24 398 000 km²	9 420 000 mi²
D	South America	17 793 000 km²	6 870 000 mi²
E	Antarctica	13 209 000 km²	5 100 000 mi²
F	Europe	9 907 000 km²	3 825 000 mi²
G	Australasia	8 534 000 km²	3 295 000 mi²

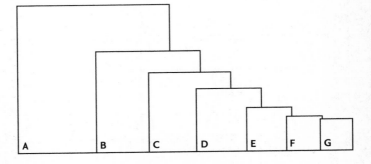

Formulae for geometry of area

$$\pi = 3.1416$$

Abbreviations

a = length of top
b = length of base
h = perpendicular height
r = length of radius

Circle

$$\pi \times r^2$$

Rectangle

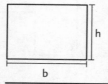

$$b \times h$$

Parallelogram

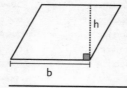

$$b \times h$$

Triangle

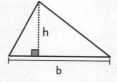

$$\tfrac{1}{2} \times b \times h$$

Trapezium

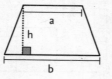

$$\frac{(a + b)\,h}{2}$$

Sample calculations

If r = 10 cm, r² = 100 cm,
then the area of this circle is:

3.1416 x 100 = 314.16 cm²

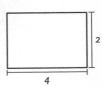

If the sides are 4 cm and 2 cm,
then the area of this rectangle is:

4 x 2 = 8 cm²

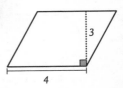

If b = 4 cm and h = 3 cm, then the
area of this parallelogram is:

4 x 3 = 12 cm²

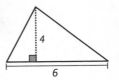

If b = 6 cm and h = 4 cm, then the
area of this triangle is:

½ x 6 x 4 = 3 x 4 = 12 cm²

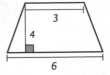

If a = 3 cm, b = 6 cm and h = 4 cm,
then the area of this trapezium is:

(3 + 6) x 4 x ½ = 18 cm²

Formulae for geometry of surface area

$$\pi = 3.1416$$

Abbreviations

b	=	breadth of base
h	=	perpendicular height
l	=	length of base
r	=	length of radius

Cube

$$h \times b \times 6$$

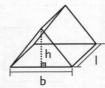

Prism

$$(b \times h) + (3 \times l \times b)$$

Cylinder

$$(2 \times \pi \times r \times l) + (2 \times \pi \times r^2)$$

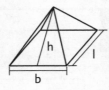

Pyramid

$$(2 \times b \times h) + (b^2)$$

Sphere

$$4 \times \pi \times r^2$$

Sample calculations

If h = 4 cm and b = 4 cm,

then the surface area of this cube is:

4 x 4 x 6 = 16 x 6 = 96 cm²

If b = 3 cm; h = 2 cm and l = 4 cm,

then the surface area of this prism is:

(3 x 2) + (3 x 4 x 3) = 6 + (12 x 3) =
6 + 36 = 42 cm²

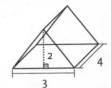

If r = 10 cm; r² = 100 cm and l = 5 cm,

the surface area of this cylinder is:

(2 x 3.1416 x 10 x 5) + (2 x 3.1416 x 100) =
314.16 + 628.32 = 942.48 cm²

If b = 5 cm; h = 8 cm and l = 5 cm,

the surface area of this pyramid is:

(2 x 5 x 8) + 5²
80 + 25 = 105 cm²

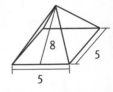

If r² = 100 cm, then the area of this
sphere is:

4 x 3.1416 x 100 = 1256.64 cm²

4 Volume

Conversion formulae

Below are the multiplication/division factors for converting units of volume from one measuring system to another. Note that two kinds of factors are given: quick, for an approximate conversion that can be made without a calculator; and accurate, for an exact conversion.

1

1

UK gallons (gal)
US fluid gallons (fl gal)

		Quick	Accurate
UK gal ⟶ US fl gal		× 1	× 1.201
US fl gal ⟶ UK gal		÷ 1	× 0.833

1

1

UK quarts (qt)
US fluid quarts (fl qt)

UK qt ⟶ US fl qt		× 1	× 1.201
US fl qt ⟶ UK qt		÷ 1	× 0.833

1

1

UK pints (pt)
US fluid pints (fl pt)

UK pt ⟶ US fl pt		× 1	× 1.201
US fl pt ⟶ UK pt		÷ 1	× 0.833

1

1

UK fluid ounces (fl oz)
US fluid ounces (fl oz)

UK fl oz ⟶ US fl oz		× 1	× 0.961
US fl oz ⟶ UK fl oz		÷ 1	× 1.041

1

2

UK fluid ounces (fl oz)
Cubic inches (in³)

UK fl oz ⟶ in³		× 2	× 1.734
in³ ⟶ UK fl oz		÷ 2	× 0.577

		Quick	Accurate
1 16	Cubic inches (in³) Cubic centimetres (cm³)		
	in³ ⟶ cm³	× 16	× 16.387
	cm³ ⟶ in³	÷ 16	× 0.061
1 28	UK fluid ounces (fl oz) Millilitres (ml)		
	UK fl oz ⟶ ml	× 28	× 28.413
	ml ⟶ UK fl oz	÷ 28	× 0.035
1 1	UK quarts (qt) Litres (l)		
	UK qt ⟶ l	× 1	× 1.137
	l ⟶ UK qt	÷ 1	× 0.880
1 4·5	UK gallons (gal) Litres (l)		
	UK gal ⟶ l	× 4.5	× 4.546
	l ⟶ UK gal	÷ 4.5	× 0.220
1 2	Litres (l) UK pints (pt)		
	l ⟶ UK pt	× 2	× 1.760
	UK pt ⟶ l	÷ 2	× 0.568
1 35	Cubic metres (m³) Cubic feet (ft³)		
	m³ ⟶ ft³	× 35	× 35.315
	ft³ ⟶ m³	÷ 35	× 0.028
1 1	Cubic metres (m³) Cubic yards (yd³)		
	m³ ⟶ yd³	× 1	× 1.308
	yd³ ⟶ m³	÷ 1	× 0.765

			Quick	Accurate
1	*Cubic metres (m³)* *UK gallons (gal)*			
220	m³ ⟶ UK gal		× 220	× 219.970
	UK gal ⟶ m³		÷ 220	× 0.005

			Quick	Accurate
1	*US fluid ounces (fl oz)* *Millilitres (ml)*			
30	US fl oz ⟶ ml		× 30	× 29.572
	ml ⟶ US fl oz		÷ 30	× 0.034

			Quick	Accurate
1	*US fluid gallons (fl gal)* *Litres (l)*			
4	US fl gal ⟶ l		× 4	× 3.785
	l ⟶ US fl gal		÷ 4	× 0.264

			Quick	Accurate
1	*Litres (l)* *US fluid pints (fl pt)*			
2	l ⟶ US fl pt		× 2	× 2.113
	US fl pt ⟶ l		÷ 2	× 0.473

			Quick	Accurate
1	*Litres (l)* *US fluid quarts (fl qt)*			
1	l ⟶ US fl qt		× 1	× 1.056
	US fl qt ⟶ l		÷ 1	× 0.947

			Quick	Accurate
1	*Cubic metres (m³)* *US fluid gallons (fl gal)*			
264	m³ ⟶ US fl gal		× 264	× 264.173
	US fl gal ⟶ m³		÷ 264	× 0.004

			Quick	Accurate
1	*Cubic metres (m³)* *US dry gallons (dry gal)*			
227	m³ ⟶ dry gal		× 227	× 227.020
	dry gal ⟶ m³		÷ 227	× 0.004

Units of liquid and dry capacity

US units of liquid capacity

60 minims (min)	=	1 fluid dram (fl dr)	=	0.2256 in^3
8 fluid drams	=	1 fluid ounce (fl oz)	=	1.8047 in^3
4 fluid ounces	=	1 gill (gi)	=	7.2187 in^3
4 gills	=	1 pint (pt)	=	28.875 in^3
2 pints	=	1 quart (qt)	=	57.750 in^3
4 quarts	=	1 gallon (gal)	=	231.00 in^3

US units of dry capacity

1 dry pint (dry pt)	=	½ dry quart (dry qt)	=	33.600 in^3
2 dry pints	=	1 dry quart	=	67.201 in^3
8 dry quarts	=	1 peck (pk)	=	537.60 in^3
4 pecks	=	1 bushel (bu)	=	2150.4 in^3

UK/imperial units of liquid and dry capacity

60 minims (min)	=	1 fluid drachm (fl dr)	=	0.2167 in^3
8 fluid drachms	=	1 fluid ounce (fl oz)	=	1.7339 in^3
5 fluid ounces	=	1 gill (gi)	=	8.6690 in^3
4 gills	=	1 pint (pt)	=	34.677 in^3
2 pints	=	1 quart (qt)	=	69.355 in^3
4 quarts	=	1 gallon (gal)	=	277.42 in^3
2 gallons	=	1 peck (pk)	=	554.84 in^3
4 pecks	=	1 bushel (bu)	=	2219.4 in^3
36 bushels	=	1 chaldron	=	7 979 898 in^3

Metric units at capacity

1000 microlitres/lambdas (λ) =		1 mil (ml)	=	0.000001 m^3
10 millilitres/mils	=	1 centilitre (cl)	=	0.00001 m^3
10 centilitres	=	1 decilitre (dl)	=	0.0001 m^3
10 decilitres	=	1 litre (l)	=	0.001 m^3
1000 litres	=	1 stère (st)	=	1 m^3

Volume

Sample calculations

US gallons (US gal) to US fluid gallons (US fl gal)
e.g. 10 US gallons =
10 x 1.201 = 12.01 US fl gal
10 US gal = 12.01 US fl gal

US fluid gallons (US fl gal) to US gallons (US gal)
e.g. 10 US fluid gallons =
10 x 0.833 = 8.33 US gal
10 US fl gal = 8.33 US gal

UK quarts (UK qt) to US fluid quarts (US fl qt)
e.g. 5 UK quarts =
5 x 1.201 = 6.005 US fl qt
5 UK qt = 6.005 US fl qt

US fluid quarts (US fl qt) to UK quarts (UK qt)
e.g. 5 US fluid quarts =
5 x 0.833 = 4.165 UK qt
5 US fl qt = 4.165 UK qt

UK pints (UK pt) to US fluid pints (US fl pt)
e.g. 5 UK pints =
5 x 1.201 = 6.005 US fl pt
5 UK pt = 6.005 US fl pt

US fluid pints (US fl pt) to UK pints (UK pt)
e.g. 5 US fluid pints =
5 x 0.833 = 4.165 UK pt
5 US fl pt = 4.165 UK pt

UK fluid ounces (UK fl oz) to US fluid ounces (US fl oz)
e.g. 8 UK fluid ounces =
8 x 0.961 = 7.688 US fl oz
8 UK fl oz = 7.688 US fl oz

US fluid ounces (US fl oz) to UK fluid ounces (UK fl oz)
e.g. 8 US fluid ounces =
8 x 1.041 = 8.328 UK fl oz
8 US fl oz = 8.328 UK fl oz

UK fluid ounces (fl oz) to cubic inches (in^3)
e.g. 25 fluid ounces =
25 x 1.734 = 43.35 in^3
25 fl oz = 43.35 in^3

Cubic inches (in^3) to UK fluid ounces (fl oz)
e.g. 50 cubic inches =
50 x 0.577 = 28.85 UK fl oz
50 in^3 = 28.85 UK fl oz

Cubic inches (in^3) to cubic centimetres (cm^3)
e.g. 50 cubic inches =
50 x 16.387 = 819.35 cm^3
50 in^3 = 819.35 cm^3

Cubic centimetres (cm^3) to cubic inches (in^3)
e.g. 50 cubic centimetres
50 x 0.061 = 3.05 in^3
50 cm^3 = 3.05 in^3

UK fluid (fl oz) ounces to millilitres (ml)
e.g. 8 fluid ounces
8 x 28.413 = 227.304 ml
8 fl oz = 227.304 ml

Millilitres (ml) to UK fluid ounces (fl oz)
e.g. 250 millilitres =
250 x 0.035 = 8.75 UK fl oz
250 ml = 8.75 UK fl oz

UK quarts (UK qt) to litres (l)
 e.g. 8 UK quarts =
   8 x 1.137 = 9.096 l
   8 UK qt = 9.096 l

Litres (l) to UK quarts (UK qt)
 e.g. 25 l =
   25 x 0.0880 = 2.2 UK qt
   25 l = 2.2 UK qt

UK gallons (UK gal) to litres (l)
 e.g. 8 UK gallons =
   8 x 4.456 = 6.368 l
   8 UK gal = 6.368 l

Litres (l) to UK gallons (UK gal)
 e.g. 25 litres =
   25 x 0.220 = 5.5 UK gal
   25 l = 5.5 UK gal

UK pints (UK pt) to litres (l)
 e.g. 8 UK pints =
   8 x 0.568 = 4.544 l
   8 UK pt = 4.544 l

Litres (l) to UK pints (UK pt)
 e.g. 25 litres =
   25 x 1.760 = 44 UK pt
   25 l = 44 UK pt

Cubic feet (ft^3) to cubic metres (m^3)
 e.g. 50 cubic feet =
   50 x 0.028 = 1.40 m^3
   50 ft^3 = 1.40 m^3

Cubic metres (m^3) to cubic feet (ft^3)
 e.g. 5 cubic metres =
   5 x 35.315 = 176.575 ft^3
   5 m^3 = 176.575 ft^3

Cubic yards (yd^3) to cubic metres (m^3)
 e.g. 25 cubic yards =
   25 x 0.765 = 19.125 m^3
   25 yd^3 = 32.7 m^3

Cubic metres (m^3) to cubic yards (yd^3)
 e.g. 25 cubic metres =
   25 x 1.308 = 32.7 yd^3
   25 m^3 = 32.7 yd^3

UK gallons (UK gal) to cubic metres (m^3)
 e.g. 25 UK gallons =
   25 x 10.005 = 250.125 m^3
   25 UK gal = 250.125 m^3

Cubic metres (m^3) to UK gallons (UK gal)
 e.g. 25 cubic metres =
   25 x 219.969 = 5499.25 UK gal
   25 m^3 = 5499.25 UK gal

US fluid ounces (US fl oz) to millilitres (ml)
 e.g. 8 US fluid ounces =
   8 x 29.574 = 236.592 ml
   8 US fl oz = 236.576 ml

Millilitres (ml) to US fluid ounces (US fl oz)
 e.g. 250 ml =
   250 x 0.034 = 8.5 US fl oz
   250 ml = 8.5 US fl oz

US fluid gallons (US fl gal) to litres (l)
 e.g. 5 US fluid gallons =
   5 x 3.785 = 18.925 l
   5 US fl gal = 18.925 l

Litres (l) to US fluid gallons (US fl gal)
 e.g. 5 litres =
   5 x 0.264 = 1.32 US fl gal
   5 l = 1.32 US fl gal

US fluid pints (US fl pt) to litres (l)
    e.g. 5 US fluid pints =
          5 x 0.473 = 2.365 l
          5 US fl pt = 2.365 l

Litres (l) to US fluid pints (US fl pt)
    e.g. 5 litres =
          5 x 2.133 = 10.665 US fl pt
          5 l = 10.665 US fl pt

US fluid quarts (US fl qt) to litres (l)
    e.g. 2 US fluid quarts =
          2 x 0.946 = 1.893 l
          2 US fl qt = 1.893 l

Litres (l) to US fluid quarts (US fl qt)
    e.g. 5 litres =
          5 x 1.056 = 5.28 US fl qt
          5 l = 5.28 US fl qt

US fluid gallons (US fl gal) to cubic metres (m³)
    e.g. 2 US fluid gallons =
          2 x 0.004 = 0.008 m^3
          2 US fl gal = 0.008 m^3

Cubic metres (m³) to US fluid gallons (US fl gal)
    e.g. 5 cubic metres =
          5 x 264.173 = 1 320.865 US fl gal
          5 m^3 = 1 320.865 US fl gal

US dry gallons (US dry gal) to cubic metres (m³)
    e.g. 1 US dry gallon =
          1 x 0.004 = 0.004 m^3
          1 US dry gal = 0.004 m^3

Cubic metres (m³) to US dry gallons (US dry gal)
    e.g. 10 cubic metres =
          10 x 227.020 = 2270.2
          US dry gal
          10 m^3 = 2270.2 US dry gal

Conversion tables

The conversion tables are used to convert units of volume from one measuring system to another. The tables beginning on page 97 are used to convert:

- UK gallons to US fluid gallons
- UK quarts to US fluid quarts
- US fluid pints to UK pints
- US fluid ounces to UK fluid ounces
- UK fluid ounces to Cubic inches
- Cubic inches to Cubic centimetres
- Cubic feet to Cubic metres
- Cubic yards to Cubic metres
- UK gallons to Cubic metres
- UK gallons to Litres
- UK pints to US fluid pints
- UK fluid ounces to US fluid ounces
- US fluid gallons to UK gallons
- US fluid quarts to UK quarts
- UK quarts to Litres
- UK pints to Litres
- UK fluid ounces to Millilitres

UK gallons to US fluid gallons	
UK gal	US fl gal
1	1.201
2	2.402
3	3.603
4	4.804
5	6.005
6	7.206
7	8.407
8	9.608
9	10.809
10	12.010
20	24.020
30	36.030
40	48.040
50	60.050
60	72.060
70	84.070
80	96.080
90	108.090
100	120.100

UK quarts to US fluid quarts	
UK qt	US fl qt
1	1.201
2	2.402
3	3.603
4	4.804
5	6.005
6	7.206
7	8.407
8	9.608
9	10.809
10	12.010
20	24.020
30	36.030
40	48.040
50	60.050
60	72.060
70	84.070
80	96.080
90	108.090
100	120.100

US fluid pints to UK pints	
UK fl pt	UK pt
1	0.833
2	1.665
3	2.498
4	3.331
5	4.164
6	4.996
7	5.829
8	6.662
9	7.494
10	8.327
20	16.654
30	24.981
40	33.308
50	41.635
60	49.962
70	58.289
80	66.616
90	74.943
100	83.270

US fluid ounces to UK fluid ounces	
US fl oz	UK fl oz
1	1.041
2	2.082
3	3.122
4	4.163
5	5.204
6	6.245
7	7.286
8	8.327
9	9.367
10	10.408
20	20.816
30	31.224
40	41.632
50	52.040
60	62.448
70	72.856
80	83.264
90	93.672
100	104.080

UK fluid ounces to Cubic inches	
UK fl oz	in^3
1	1.734
2	3.468
3	5.202
4	6.935
5	8.669
6	10.403
7	12.137
8	13.871
9	15.605
10	17.339
20	34.677
30	52.016
40	69.355
50	86.694
60	104.032
70	121.371
80	138.710
90	156.048
100	173.387

Cubic inches to Cubic centimetres	
in^3	cm^3
1	16.387
2	32.774
3	49.161
4	65.548
5	81.935
6	98.322
7	114.709
8	131.096
9	147.484
10	163.871
20	327.741
30	491.612
40	655.482
50	819.353
60	983.224
70	1147.094
80	1310.965
90	1474.835
100	1638.706

Cubic feet to Cubic metres		Cubic yards to Cubic metres		UK gallons to Cubic metres	
ft^3	m^3	yd^3	m^3	UK gal	m^3
1	0.028	1	0.765	1	0.005
2	0.057	2	1.529	2	0.009
3	0.085	3	2.294	3	0.014
4	0.113	4	3.058	4	0.018
5	0.142	5	3.823	5	0.023
6	0.170	6	4.587	6	0.027
7	0.198	7	5.352	7	0.032
8	0.227	8	6.116	8	0.036
9	0.255	9	6.881	9	0.041
10	0.283	10	7.646	10	0.045
20	0.566	20	15.291	20	0.091
30	0.850	30	22.937	30	0.136
40	1.133	40	30.582	40	0.182
50	1.416	50	38.228	50	0.227
60	1.699	60	45.873	60	0.273
70	1.982	70	53.519	70	0.318
80	2.266	80	61.164	80	0.364
90	2.549	90	68.810	90	0.409
100	2.832	100	76.455	100	0.455

UK gallons to Litres		UK pints to US fluid pints		UK fluid ounces to US fluid ounces	
UK gal	l	UK pt	US fl pt	UK pt	US fl oz
1	4.546	1	1.201	1	0.961
2	9.092	2	2.402	2	1.922
3	13.638	3	3.603	3	2.882
4	18.184	4	4.804	4	3.843
5	22.730	5	6.005	5	4.804
6	27.277	6	7.206	6	5.765
7	31.823	7	8.407	7	6.726
8	36.369	8	9.608	8	7.686
9	40.915	9	10.809	9	8.647
10	45.461	10	12.010	10	9.608
20	90.922	20	24.020	20	19.216
30	136.383	30	36.030	30	28.824
40	181.844	40	48.040	40	38.432
50	227.305	50	60.050	50	48.040
60	272.765	60	72.060	60	57.648
70	318.226	70	84.070	70	67.256
80	363.687	80	96.080	80	76.864
90	409.148	90	108.090	90	86.472
100	454.609	100	120.100	100	96.080

US fluid gallons to UK gallons

US fl gal	UK gal
1	0.833
2	1.665
3	2.498
4	3.331
5	4.164
6	4.998
7	5.829
8	6.662
9	7.494
10	8.327
20	16.654
30	24.981
40	33.308
50	41.635
60	49.962
70	58.289
80	66.616
90	74.943
100	83.270

US fluid quarts to UK quarts

US fl qt	UK qt
1	0.833
2	1.665
3	2.498
4	3.331
5	4.164
6	4.996
7	5.829
8	6.662
9	7.494
10	8.327
20	16.654
30	24.981
40	33.308
50	41.635
60	49.962
70	58.289
80	66.616
90	74.943
100	83.270

UK quarts to Litres

UK qt	l
1	1.137
2	2.273
3	3.410
4	4.546
5	5.683
6	6.819
7	7.956
8	9.092
9	10.229
10	11.365
20	22.730
30	34.096
40	45.461
50	56.826
60	68.191
70	79.556
80	90.922
90	102.287
100	113.652

UK pints to Litres

UK pt	l
1	0.568
2	1.137
3	1.705
4	2.273
5	2.841
6	3.410
7	3.978
8	4.546
9	5.114
10	5.683
20	11.365
30	17.048
40	22.730
50	28.413
60	34.096
70	39.778
80	45.461
90	51.143
100	56.826

UK fluid ounces to Millilitres

UK fl oz	ml
1	28.413
2	56.826
3	85.239
4	113.652
5	142.065
6	170.478
7	198.891
8	227.305
9	255.718
10	284.131
20	568.261
30	852.392
40	1136.523
50	1420.654
60	1704.784
70	1988.915
80	2273.046
90	2557.177
100	2841.307

Metric to UK imperial conversions

The tables that follow convert metric units to UK imperial units.

Volume

Millilitres to UK fluid ounces		Litres to UK pints		Litres to UK quarts	
ml	UK fl oz	l	UK pt	l	UK qt
1	0.035	1	1.760	1	0.880
2	0.070	2	3.520	2	1.760
3	0.106	3	5.279	3	2.640
4	0.141	4	7.039	4	3.520
5	0.176	5	8.799	5	4.399
6	0.211	6	10.559	6	5.279
7	0.246	7	12.318	7	6.159
8	0.282	8	14.078	8	7.039
9	0.317	9	15.838	9	7.919
10	0.352	10	17.598	10	8.799
20	0.704	20	35.195	20	17.598
30	1.056	30	52.793	30	26.396
40	1.408	40	70.390	40	35.195
50	1.760	50	87.988	50	43.994
60	2.112	60	105.585	60	52.793
70	2.464	70	123.183	70	61.591
80	2.816	80	140.780	80	70.390
90	3.168	90	158.378	90	79.189
100	3.520	100	175.975	100	87.988

Litres to UK gallons		Cubic metres to UK gallons		Cubic metres to Cubic feet	
l	UK gal	m³	UK gal	m³	ft³
1	0.220	1	219.969	1	35.315
2	0.440	2	439.938	2	70.629
3	0.660	3	659.907	3	105.944
4	0.880	4	879.877	4	141.259
5	1.100	5	1099.846	5	176.573
6	1.320	6	1319.815	6	211.888
7	1.540	7	1539.785	7	247.203
8	1.760	8	1759.754	8	282.517
9	1.980	9	1979.723	9	317.832
10	2.200	10	2199.692	10	353.147
20	4.399	20	4399.385	20	706.293
30	6.599	30	6599.077	30	1059.440
40	8.799	40	8798.769	40	1412.587
50	10.999	50	10 998.462	50	1765.734
60	13.198	60	13 198.154	60	2118.880
70	15.398	70	15 397.846	70	2472.027
80	17.598	80	17 597.539	80	2825.174
90	19.797	90	19 797.231	90	3178.320
100	21.997	100	21 996.923	100	3531.467

Cubic metres to Cubic yards

m^3	yd^3
1	1.308
2	2.616
3	3.924
4	5.232
5	6.540
6	7.848
7	9.156
8	10.464
9	11.772
10	13.080
20	26.159
30	39.239
40	52.318
50	65.398
60	78.477
70	91.557
80	104.636
90	117.716
100	130.795

Cubic centimetres to Cubic inches

cm^3	in^3
1	0.061
2	0.122
3	0.183
4	0.244
5	0.305
6	0.366
7	0.427
8	0.488
9	0.549
10	0.610
20	1.220
30	1.831
40	2.441
50	3.051
60	3.661
70	4.271
80	4.882
90	5.492
100	6.102

Cubic inches to UK fluid ounces

in^3	UK fl oz
1	0.577
2	1.153
3	1.730
4	2.307
5	2.884
6	3.460
7	4.037
8	4.614
9	5.191
10	5.767
20	11.535
30	17.302
40	23.069
50	28.837
60	34.604
70	40.371
80	46.138
90	51.906
100	57.673

US imperial to metric conversions
The conversion tables to the right are used to convert US imperial units of volume to metric units.

US fluid ounces to Millilitres

US fl oz	ml
1	29.572
2	59.145
3	88.717
4	118.289
5	147.862
6	177.434
7	207.006
8	236.579
9	266.152
10	295.724
20	591.447
30	887.171
40	1182.894
50	1478.618
60	1774.341
70	2070.065
80	2365.788
90	2661.512
100	2957.235

US fluid pints to Litres

US fl pt	l
1	0.473
2	0.946
3	1.420
4	1.893
5	2.366
6	2.839
7	3.312
8	3.785
9	4.259
10	4.732
20	9.464
30	14.195
40	18.927
50	23.659
60	28.391
70	33.123
80	37.854
90	42.586
100	47.318

US fluid quarts to Litres

US fl qt	l
1	0.947
2	1.894
3	2.840
4	3.787
5	4.734
6	5.681
7	6.628
8	7.575
9	8.521
10	9.468
20	18.937
30	28.405
40	37.873
50	47.341
60	56.810
70	66.278
80	75.746
90	85.215
100	94.683

US fluid gallons to Litres

US fl gal	l
1	3.785
2	7.571
3	11.356
4	15.141
5	18.927
6	22.712
7	26.497
8	30.282
9	34.068
10	37.853
20	75.706
30	113.559
40	151.412
50	189.265
60	227.118
70	264.971
80	302.824
90	340.677
100	378.530

US fluid gallons to Cubic metres

US fl gal	m^3
1	0.004
2	0.008
3	0.011
4	0.015
5	0.019
6	0.023
7	0.026
8	0.030
9	0.034
10	0.038
20	0.076
30	0.114
40	0.151
50	0.189
60	0.227
70	0.265
80	0.303
90	0.341
100	0.379

US dry gallons to Cubic metres

US dry gal	m^3
1	0.004
2	0.009
3	0.013
4	0.018
5	0.022
6	0.026
7	0.031
8	0.035
9	0.040
10	0.044
20	0.088
30	0.132
40	0.176
50	0.220
60	0.264
70	0.308
80	0.352
90	0.396
100	0.440

Metric to US imperial conversions
The tables to the right convert metric units to US imperial units.

Millilitres to US fluid ounces

ml	US fl oz
1	0.034
2	0.068
3	0.101
4	0.135
5	0.169
6	0.203
7	0.237
8	0.271
9	0.304
10	0.338
20	0.676
30	1.014
40	1.353
50	1.691
60	2.029
70	2.367
80	2.705
90	3.043
100	3.382

Litres to
US fluid pints

l	US fl pt
1	2.113
2	4.227
3	6.340
4	8.454
5	10.567
6	12.680
7	14.794
8	16.907
9	19.020
10	21.134
20	42.268
30	63.401
40	84.535
50	105.669
60	126.803
70	147.937
80	169.070
90	190.204
100	211.338

Litres to
US fluid quarts

l	US fl qt
1	1.056
2	2.112
3	3.168
4	4.225
5	5.281
6	6.337
7	7.393
8	8.449
9	9.505
10	10.562
20	21.123
30	31.685
40	42.246
50	52.808
60	63.369
70	73.931
80	84.493
90	95.054
100	105.616

Litres to
US fluid gallons

l	US fl gal
1	3.785
2	7.571
3	11.356
4	15.141
5	18.927
6	22.712
7	26.497
8	30.282
9	34.068
10	37.853
20	75.706
30	113.559
40	151.412
50	189.265
60	227.118
70	264.971
80	302.824
90	340.677
100	378.530

Cubic metres to
US fluid gallons

m^3	US fl gal
1	0.004
2	0.008
3	0.011
4	0.015
5	0.019
6	0.023
7	0.026
8	0.030
9	0.034
10	0.038
20	0.076
30	0.114
40	0.151
50	0.189
60	0.227
70	0.265
80	0.303
90	0.341
100	0.379

Cubic metres to
US dry gallons

m^3	US dry gal
1	1.056
2	2.112
3	3.168
4	4.225
5	5.281
6	6.337
7	7.393
8	8.449
9	9.505
10	10.562
20	21.123
30	31.685
40	42.246
50	52.808
60	63.369
70	73.931
80	84.493
90	95.054
100	105.616

Formulae for geometry of volume

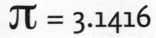

Abbreviations

a	=	length of top
b	=	length of base
h	=	perpendicular height
r	=	length of radius

$$\pi = 3.1416$$

Cube or cuboid

$$b \times h \times l$$

Prism

$$\frac{b \times h \times l}{2}$$

Pyramid

$$\frac{b \times h \times l}{3}$$

Cylinder

$$\pi \times r^2 \times l$$

Sphere

$$\frac{4 \times \pi \times r^3}{3}$$

Cone

$$\frac{\pi \times r^2 \times h}{3}$$

Sample calculations

The volume of this cube is

$5 \times 5 \times 5 = 125 \text{ cm}^3$

The volume of this prism is

$\dfrac{6 \times 8 \times 5}{2} = 120 \text{ cm}^3$

The volume of this pyramid is

$\dfrac{7 \times 8 \times 9}{3} = 168 \text{ m}^3$

The volume of this cylinder is

$\pi \times 40^2 \times 110 = 552\ 921.6 \text{ mm}^3$

The volume of this sphere is

$\dfrac{4 \times \pi \times 50^3}{3} = 523\ 600 \text{ m}^3$

The volume of this cone is

$\dfrac{\pi \times 8^2 \times 10}{3} = 670.208 \text{ cm}^3$

Cooking measures

Although the names of the units are often the same, US measures are slightly different from UK imperial measures – for example, the US pint is 16 ounces, and the UK imperial pint is 20 ounces. US cooks use different measures for liquids and solids; in the imperial system used in the UK, a fluid ounce is equal to a dry ounce. On average, US units are roughly ⅘ the size of UK units. *See also* Cooking measurements on page 206.

UK liquid and dry measures

60 minims	=	1 dram	4 quarts	=	1 gallon
8 drams	=	1 fl oz	1 gallon	=	10 lb (weight in water)
5 fl oz	=	1 gill			
1 gill	=	¼ pint	2 gallons	=	1 peck
1 pint	=	20 fl oz	4 pecks	=	1 bushel
2 pints	=	1 quart	36 bushels	=	1 chaldron

US liquid measures

60 minims	=	1 fl dram
8 fl drams	=	1 fl oz
4 fl oz	=	1 gill
4 gills	=	1 pint
2 pints	=	1 quart
4 quarts	=	1 gallon

US dry measures

1 dry pint	=	½ dry quart
2 dry pints	=	1 dry quart
8 dry quarts	=	1 peck
4 pecks	=	1 bushel

Water weights

1 fl oz water	=	1 oz	1 quart water	=	2½ lb
1 pint water	=	1¼ lb	1 gallon water	=	10 lb

Handy measures

Object	Imperial		Metric
1 thimbleful	30 drops		2.5 ml
60 drops	1 teaspoon		5 ml
1 teaspoon	1 dram		5 ml
1 dessertspoon	2 drams		10 ml
1 tablespoon	4 drams		15 ml
2 tablespoons	1 fl oz		30 ml
1 wine glass	2 fl oz		60 ml
1 tea cup	5 fl oz (1 gill)		140 ml
1 mug	10 fl oz (½ pint)		280 ml

Beverage measures

Beer measures

1 nip	=	¼ pint
1 small	=	½ pint
1 large	=	1 pint
1 flagon	=	1 quart
1 firkin	=	9 gallons
1 anker	=	10 gallons
1 kilderkin	=	2 firkins
1 barrel	=	2 kilderkins
1 hogshead	=	1½ barrels
1 butt	=	2 hogsheads
1 tun	=	2 butts
		216 gallons

Handy measures

small jigger	=	1 fl oz
small wine glass	=	2 fl oz
cocktail glass	=	¼ pint
sherry glass	=	¼ pint
large wine glass	=	¼ pint
tumbler	=	½ pint

Wine measures

10 gallons	=	1 anker
1 hogshead	=	63 gallons
2 hogsheads	=	1 pipe
2 pipes	=	1 tun
1 puncheon	=	84 gallons
1 butt (sherry)	=	110 gallons

US spirits measures

1 pony	=	½ jigger
1 jigger	=	1½ shot
1 shot	=	1 fl oz
1 pint	=	16 shots
1 fifth	=	25⅗ shots
		1⅗ pints
		⅘ quart
		0.758 litre
1 quart	=	32 shots
		1¼ fifths
1 magnum of wine	=	2 quarts
		2½ bottles

Champagne bottle sizes

a Bottle = 75 ml or 26.5 fl oz
b Magnum = 2 bottles
c Jeroboam = 4 bottles
d Rehoboam = 6 bottles
e Methuselah = 8 bottles
f Salamanazar = 12 bottles ·
g Balthazar = 16 bottles
h Nebuchadnezzar = 20 bottles

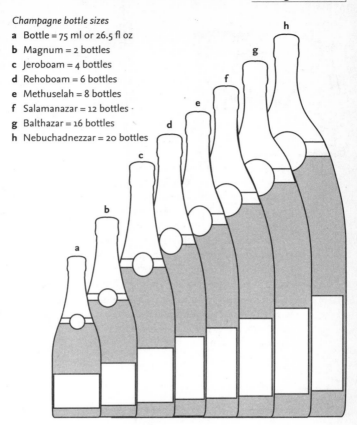

5 Weight

Conversion formulae

Below are listed the multiplication/division factors for converting units of weight from imperial to metric, and vice versa, and from one unit to another in the same system. Note that two kinds of factors are given: quick, for an approximate conversion that can be made without a calculator; and accurate, for an exact conversion.

The term 'weight' differs in everyday use from its scientific use. In everyday terms, we use weight to describe how much substance an object has. In science, the term 'mass' is used to describe this quantity of matter. Weight is used to describe the gravitational force on an object and is equal to its mass multiplied by the gravitational field strength. In scientific terms, mass remains constant but weight varies according to the strength of gravity. All units that follow are strictly units of mass rather than weight, apart from the pressure units kg/cm^2 and PSI.

			Quick	Accurate
Grams (g) *Grains (gr)*				
g	→	gr	× 15	× 15.432
gr	→	g	÷ 15	× 0.065
Ounces (oz) *Grams (g)*				
oz	→	g	× 28	× 28.349
g	→	oz	÷ 28	× 0.035

	Quick	Accurate
Ounces troy (oz tr)		
Grams (g)		
oz tr ⟶ g	× 31	× 31.103
g ⟶ oz tr	÷ 31	× 0.032
Stones (st)		
Kilograms (kg)		
st ⟶ kg	× 6	× 6.350
kg ⟶ st	÷ 6	× 0.157
Long (UK) tons (l t)		
Tonnes (t)		
lt ⟶ t	× 1	× 1.016
t ⟶ lt	÷ 1	× 0.984
Kilograms (kg)		
Pounds (lb)		
kg ⟶ lb	× 2	× 2.205
lb ⟶ kg	÷ 2	× 0.454
Kilograms per square centimetre (kg/cm²)		
Pounds per square inch (PSI)		
kg/cm² ⟶ PSI	× 14	× 14.223
PSI ⟶ kg/cm²	÷ 14	× 0.070
Tonnes (t)		
Short (US) tons (sh t)		
t ⟶ sh t	× 1	× 1.102
sh t ⟶ t	÷ 1	× 0.907
Ounces troy (oz tr)		
Ounces (oz)		
oz tr ⟶ oz	× 1	× 1.097
oz ⟶ oz tr	÷ 1	× 0.911

Weight

Sample calculations

Grains (gr) to grams (g)
 e.g. 100 grains =
   100 x 0.065 = 6.5 g
   100 gr = 6.5 g

Grams (g) to grains (gr)
 e.g. 100 grams =
   100 x 15.432 = 1543.2 gr
   100 g = 1 543.2 gr

Ounces (oz) to grams (g)
 e.g. 4 ounces =
   4 x 28.349 = 113.396 g
   4 oz = 113.396 g

Grams (g) to ounces (oz)
 e.g. 100 grams =
   100 x 0.035 = 3.5 oz
   100 g = 3.5 oz

Ounces troy (oz tr) to grams (g)
 e.g. 12 ounces troy =
   12 x 31.103 = 373.236 g
   12 oz tr = 373.236 g

Grams (g) to ounces troy (oz tr)
 e.g. 250 grams =
   250 x 0.032 = 8 oz tr
   250 g = 8 oz tr

Stones (st) to kilograms (kg)
 e.g. 10 stones =
   10 x 6.350 = 63.5 kg
   10 st = 63.5 kg

Kilograms (kg) to stones (st)
 e.g. 70 kilograms =
   70 x 0.157 = 10.99 st
   70 kg = 10.99 st

Long (UK) tons (l t) to tonnes (t)
 e.g. 40 long (UK) tons =
   40 x 1.016 = 40.64 t
   40 l t = 40.64 t

Tonnes (t) to long (UK) tons (l t)
 e.g. 100 tonnes =
   100 x 0.984 = 98.4 l t
   100 t = 98.4 l t

Pounds (lb) to kilograms (kg)
 e.g. 60 pounds =
   60 x 0.454 = 27.24 kg
   60 lb = 27.24 kg

Kilograms (kg) to pounds (lb)
 e.g. 5 kilograms =
   5 x 2.205 = 11.025 lb
   5 kg = 11.025 lb

Pounds per square inch (PSI) to kilograms per square centimetre (kg/cm^2)
 e.g. 30 pounds per square inch =
   30 x 0.070 = 2.1 kg/cm^2
   30 PSI = 2.1 kg/cm^2

Kilograms per square centimetre (kg/cm^2) to pounds per square inch (PSI)
 e.g. 1 kilogram per square centimetre =
   1 x 14.223 = 14.223 PSI
   1 kg/cm^2 = 14.223 PSI

Short (US) tons (sh t) to tonnes (t)
e.g. 40 short (US) tons =
40 x 0.907 = 36.28 t
40 sh t = 36.28 t

Tonnes (t) to short (US) tons (sh t)
e.g. 5 tonnes =
5 x 1.102 = 5.51 sh t
5 t = 5.51 sh t

Ounces troy (oz tr) to ounces (oz)
e.g. 3 ounces troy =
3 x 1.097 = 3.291 oz
3 oz tr = 3.291 oz

Ounces (oz) to ounces troy (oz tr)
e.g. 4 ounces =
4 x 0.911 = 3.644 oz tr
4 oz = 3.644 oz tr

Atomic mass

An atom's mass is measured in multiples of an atomic mass unit (amu). This table shows the three types of amu. Note that the amu differs from the 'atomic unit of mass' which is the electron's rest mass = 9.1084×10^{-31} kg.

Atomic mass units

Atomic mass units (amu)	Derivation	Equivalent in kg
1 amu (international) =	One-twelfth the mass of carbon-12, the principle isotope of carbon	1.66033×10^{-27} kg
1 amu (physical) =	One-sixteenth the mass of oxygen-16 (99.8% of all oxygen found on Earth)	1.65981×10^{-27} kg
1 amu (chemical) =	One-sixteenth of the average mass of a mixture of the three oxygen isotopes	1.66026×10^{-27} kg

Conversion tables

The conversion tables can be used to convert units of weight from one measuring system to another. The tables below are used to convert:

- Grains to Grams
- Ounces to Grams
- Ounces troy to Grams
- Pounds to Kilograms
- Pounds per square inch to Kilograms per square centimetre
- Stones to Kilograms
- Short (US) tons to Tonnes
- Long (UK) tons to Tonnes
- Grams to Grains

- Grams to Ounces
- Grams to Ounces troy
- Kilograms to Pounds
- Pounds per square inch to Kilograms per square centimetre
- Kilograms to Stones
- Tonnes to Short (US) tons
- Tonnes to Long (UK) tons
- Ounces to Ounces troy
- Ounces troy to Ounces

Grains to Grams		Ounces to Grams		Ounces troy to Grams	
gr	g	oz	g	oz tr	g
1	0.065	1	28.349	1	31.103
2	0.130	2	56.699	2	62.207
3	0.194	3	85.048	3	93.310
4	0.259	4	113.398	4	124.414
5	0.324	5	141.747	5	155.517
6	0.389	6	170.097	6	186.621
7	0.454	7	198.446	7	217.724
8	0.518	8	226.796	8	248.829
9	0.583	9	255.145	9	279.931
10	0.648	10	283.495	10	311.035
20	1.296	20	566.990	20	622.070
30	1.944	30	850.485	30	933.104
40	2.592	40	1133.980	40	1244.139
50	3.240	50	1417.475	50	1555.174
60	3.888	60	1700.970	60	1866.209
70	4.536	70	1984.465	70	2177.243
80	5.184	80	2267.960	80	2488.278
90	5.832	90	2551.455	90	2799.313
100	6.480	100	2834.900	100	3110.348

Pounds to Kilograms

lb	kg
1	0.454
2	0.907
3	1.361
4	1.814
5	2.268
6	2.722
7	3.175
8	3.629
9	4.082
10	4.536
20	9.072
30	13.608
40	18.144
50	22.680
60	27.216
70	31.751
80	36.287
90	40.823
100	45.359

Pounds per square inch to Kilograms per square centimetre

PSI	kg/cm²
10	0.703
15	1.055
20	1.406
22	1.547
24	1.687
26	1.828
28	1.986
30	2.109
32	2.250
34	2.390
36	2.531
38	2.671
40	2.812
45	3.164
50	3.515
55	3.867
60	4.218

Stones to Kilograms

st	kg
1	6.350
2	12.700
3	19.050
4	25.401
5	31.751
6	38.101
7	44.452
8	50.802
9	57.152
10	63.502
20	127.006
30	190.509
40	254.012
50	317.515
60	381.018
70	444.521
80	508.023
90	571.526
100	635.029

Short (US) tons to Tonnes

sh t	t
1	0.907
2	1.814
3	2.721
4	3.628
5	4.535
6	5.443
7	6.350
8	7.257
9	8.164
10	9.071
20	18.143
30	27.215
40	36.287
50	45.359
60	54.431
70	63.502
80	72.574
90	81.646
100	90.718

Long (UK) tons to Tonnes

l t	t
1	1.016
2	2.032
3	3.048
4	4.064
5	5.080
6	6.096
7	7.112
8	8.128
9	9.144
10	10.160
20	20.320
30	30.481
40	40.641
50	50.802
60	60.962
70	71.123
80	81.283
90	91.444
100	101.604

Grams to Grains

g	gr
1	15.432
2	30.865
3	46.297
4	61.729
5	77.162
6	92.594
7	108.027
8	123.459
9	138.891
10	154.324
20	308.647
30	462.971
40	617.294
50	771.618
60	925.942
70	1080.265
80	1234.589
90	1388.912
100	1543.236

Weight

Grams to Ounces	
g	oz
1	0.035
2	0.071
3	0.106
4	0.141
5	0.176
6	0.212
7	0.247
8	0.282
9	0.317
10	0.353
20	0.705
30	1.058
40	1.411
50	1.764
60	2.116
70	2.469
80	2.822
90	3.175
100	3.527

Grams to Ounces troy	
g	oz tr
1	0.032
2	0.064
3	0.096
4	0.129
5	0.161
6	0.193
7	0.225
8	0.257
9	0.289
10	0.322
20	0.643
30	0.965
40	1.286
50	1.608
60	1.929
70	2.251
80	2.572
90	2.894
100	3.215

Kilograms to Pounds	
kg	lb
1	2.205
2	4.409
3	6.614
4	8.818
5	11.023
6	13.228
7	15.432
8	17.637
9	19.842
10	22.046
20	44.092
30	66.139
40	88.185
50	110.231
60	132.277
70	154.324
80	176.370
90	198.416
100	220.462

Kilograms per square centimetre to Pounds per square inch	
kg/cm^2	PSI
0.6	8.534
0.8	11.378
1.0	14.223
1.2	17.068
1.4	19.912
1.6	22.757
1.8	25.601
2.0	28.446
2.2	31.291
2.4	34.135
2.6	36.980
2.8	39.824
3.0	42.669
3.2	45.514
3.5	49.781
4.0	56.892
4.5	64.004

Kilograms to Stones	
kg	st
1	0.157
2	0.315
3	0.472
4	0.630
5	0.787
6	0.945
7	1.102
8	1.260
9	1.417
10	1.574
20	3.149
30	4.724
40	6.299
50	7.874
60	9.448
70	11.023
80	12.598
90	14.173
100	15.747

Tonnes to Short (US) tons	
t	sh t
1	1.102
2	2.205
3	3.307
4	4.409
5	5.512
6	6.614
7	7.716
8	8.818
9	9.921
10	11.023
20	22.046
30	33.069
40	44.092
50	55.116
60	66.139
70	77.162
80	88.185
90	99.208
100	110.231

Tonnes to Long (UK) tons			Ounces to Ounces troy			Ounces troy to Ounces	
t	l t		oz	oz tr		oz tr	oz
1	0.984		1	0.911		1	1.097
2	1.968		2	1.823		2	2.194
3	2.953		3	2.734		3	3.291
4	3.937		4	3.646		4	4.389
5	4.921		5	4.557		5	5.486
6	5.905		6	5.468		6	6.583
7	6.889		7	6.380		7	7.680
8	7.874		8	7.291		8	8.777
9	8.858		9	8.203		9	9.874
10	9.842		10	9.114		10	10.971
20	19.684		20	18.229		20	21.943
30	29.526		30	27.344		30	32.914
40	39.368		40	36.458		40	43.886
50	49.211		50	45.573		50	54.857
60	59.052		60	54.687		60	65.828
70	68.894		70	63.802		70	76.800
80	78.737		80	72.917		80	87.771
90	88.579		90	82.031		90	98.743
100	98.421		100	91.146		100	109.714

Scales of hardness

Solids vary in their degree of hardness, which indicates their resistance to being scratched or cut.

A Mohs' scale

Mohs' scale is used to measure the relative hardness of minerals. The framework uses the 10 minerals – talc to diamond – shown in the scale. Each of these minerals is assigned a numerical value from 1 to 10: the higher the number, the harder the mineral.

Order is determined by the ability of a mineral to scratch all those that have a lower number and to be scratched by those with a higher number. Once this is established, it is possible to place all other minerals on the scale by means of the same scratching procedure.

B Knoop scale

Another system of measuring the hardness of minerals is the Knoop scale. The Knoop scale gives absolute rather than relative measurements. Readings on this scale are made by measuring the size of the indentation made by a diamond-shaped device dropped on the material.

Again, the higher the number the harder the substance, but the intervals between minerals and levels of hardness differ greatly from scale to scale. Minerals with values between 1 and 7 on Mohs' scale fall below 1000 on the Knoop scale, and between 8 and 9 fall below 2000, but diamond falls at 7000.

C Common-object scale

A simple way of measuring hardness uses common objects, whose hardness on the Mohs' scale is known:

a) fingernail (2–2.5 Mohs')   b) penny (4)
c) knife blade (5–6)   d) knife sharpener (8–9)

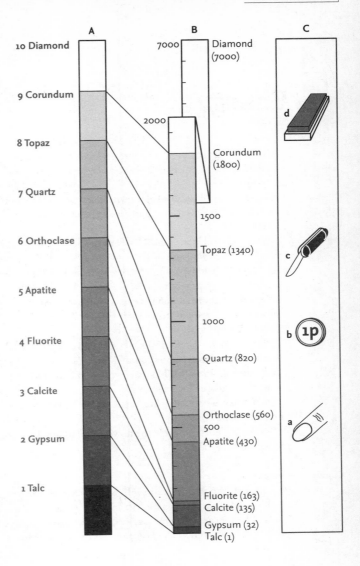

A

10 Diamond

9 Corundum

8 Topaz

7 Quartz

6 Orthoclase

5 Apatite

4 Fluorite

3 Calcite

2 Gypsum

1 Talc

B

7000

Diamond (7000)

2000

Corundum (1800)

1500

Topaz (1340)

1000

Quartz (820)

Orthoclase (560)
500
Apatite (430)

Fluorite (163)
Calcite (135)
Gypsum (32)
Talc (1)

C

d

c

b   1p

a

6 Energy

The joule (J) is the amount of energy needed to move a mass of one kilogram through one metre with an acceleration of one metre per second per second.

The erg is the amount of energy needed to move one gram through one centimetre with an acceleration of one centimetre per second per second.

The calorie (cal) is the amount of energy needed to raise the temperature of one gram of water by one degree Celsius from 14.5 °C to 15.5 °C (58.1 °F to 59.9 °F). 1000 cal = 1 kcal. 1 cal = 4.2 J. *See also* Food and energy, page 210.

The British thermal unit (Btu) is the energy needed to raise the temperature of one pound of water from 60 °F to 61 °F (15.5 °C to 16.1 °C).

The watt (W) is the power provided when one joule is used for one second. 1000 watts are known as a kilowatt (kW).

The kilowatt hour (kWh) is the energy expended when one kilowatt is available for one hour.

The British horsepower (hp) is the power needed to raise 550 lb one foot in one second.

The metric horsepower is the power needed to raise 75 kg one metre in one second.

Conversion formulae

Page 121 lists the multiplication/division factors for converting units of energy from imperial to metric, and vice versa. Note that two kinds of factors are given: quick, for an approximate conversion that can be made without a calculator; and accurate, for an exact conversion.

	Quick	Accurate
Kilowatts (kW) Horsepower (hp)		
kW ⟶ hp	× 1.5	× 1.341
hp ⟶ kW	÷ 1.5	× 0.746
Calories (cal) Joules (J)		
cal ⟶ J	× 4	× 4.187
J ⟶ cal	÷ 4	× 0.239
Kilocalories (kcal) Kilojoules (kJ)		
kcal ⟶ kJ	× 4	× 4.187
kJ ⟶ kcal	÷ 4	× 0.239

Sample calculations

Kilowatts (kW) to horsepower (hp)
    e.g. 10 kilowatts =
        10 x 1.341 = 13.41 hp
        10 kW = 13.41 hp

Horsepower (hp) to kilowatts (kW)
    e.g. 500 horsepower =
        500 x 0.746 = 373 kW
        500 hp = 373 kW

Calories (cal) to Joules (J)
    e.g. 350 calories =
        350 x 4.187 = 1465.45 J
        350 cal = 1465.45 J

Joules (J) to calories (cal)
    e.g. 150 Joules
        150 x 0.239 = 35.85 cal
        150 J = 35.85 cal

Kilocalories (kcal) to kilojoules (kJ)
    e.g. 50 kilocalories =
        50 x 4.187 = 209.35 kJ
        50 kcal = 209.35 kJ

Kilojoules (kJ) to kilocalories (kcal)
    e.g. 150 kilojoules =
        150 x 0.239 = 35.85 kcal
        150 kJ = 35.85 kcal

Conversion tables

The tables can be used to convert units of energy from metric to imperial systems, and vice versa.

Horsepower to Kilowatts

hp	kW
1	0.746
2	1.491
3	2.237
4	2.983
5	3.729
6	4.474
7	5.220
8	5.966
9	6.711
10	7.457
20	14.914
30	22.371
40	29.828
50	37.285
60	44.742
70	52.199
80	59.656
90	67.113
100	74.570

Kilowatts to Horsepower

kW	hp
1	1.341
2	2.682
3	4.023
4	5.364
5	6.705
6	8.046
7	9.387
8	10.728
9	12.069
10	13.410
20	26.820
30	40.231
40	53.641
50	67.051
60	80.461
70	93.871
80	107.280
90	120.690
100	134.100

Joules to Calories

J	cal
1	0.239
2	0.478
3	0.716
4	0.955
5	1.194
6	1.433
7	1.672
8	1.911
9	2.150
10	2.388
20	4.777
30	7.165
40	9.554
50	11.942
60	14.330
70	16.719
80	19.108
90	21.496
100	23.885

Kilojoules to Kilocalories

kJ	kcal
1	0.239
2	0.478
3	0.716
4	0.955
5	1.194
6	1.433
7	1.672
8	1.911
9	2.150
10	2.388
20	4.777
30	7.165
40	9.554
50	11.942
60	14.330
70	16.719
80	19.108
90	21.496
100	23.885

Calories to Joules

cal	J
1	4.187
2	8.374
3	12.560
4	16.747
5	20.934
6	25.121
7	29.308
8	33.494
9	37.681
10	41.868
20	83.736
30	125.604
40	167.472
50	209.340
60	251.208
70	293.076
80	334.944
90	376.812
100	418.680

Kilocalories to Kilojoules

kcal	kJ
1	4.187
2	8.374
3	12.560
4	16.747
5	20.934
6	25.121
7	29.308
8	33.494
9	37.681
10	41.868
20	83.736
30	125.604
40	167.472
50	209.340
60	251.208
70	293.076
80	334.944
90	376.812
100	418.680

Electromagnetic waves

Light and radio waves, X-rays and other forms of energy are transmitted through space as electromagnetic waves. These waves have alternating high and low points – crests (**a**) and troughs (**b**) – like actual waves. The distance between wave crests or troughs is called the wavelength (**c**); this is measured in metres. The amplitude of the wave (**d**) is the distance between the crest or trough and the midpoint of the wave pattern. Frequency refers to the number of waves per second passing through a certain point; this is measured in hertz (Hz).

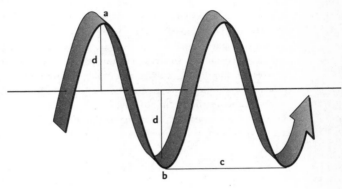

Units of frequency
1000 hertz (Hz) = 1 kilohertz (kHz)
1000 kilohertz = 1 megahertz (MHz)
1000 megahertz = 1 gigahertz (GHz)

Units of wavelength
1000 X-units (Xu) = 1 ångström (Å) = 10^{-10} m
10 000 ångströms = 1 micron (μ) = 10^{-6} m
1000 microns = 1 millimetre = 10^{-3} m

Electromagnetic spectrum

Below is the electromagnetic spectrum, showing the different forms of energy in order of frequency and wavelength. The top part of the diagram shows the frequency in hertz; the lower part measures the wavelength in metres.

1 Radio waves These waves transmit television and radio signals. This section of the spectrum is divided into bands, from VLF (very low frequency) – used for time signals, to SHF (super-high frequency) – used for space and satellite communication.

2 Radar and microwaves Radar bounces waves off objects, allowing unseen objects to be seen; microwaves can cook food quickly.

3 Infrared waves These waves are emitted by all hot objects.

4 Visible light The band of visible light from red to violet.

5 Ultraviolet light In small amounts, these waves produce vitamin D and cause skin to tan; in larger amounts they can damage living cells.

6 X-rays Used to photograph the internal structures of the body.

7 Gamma rays Emitted during the decay of some radioisotopes, these waves can be very damaging to the body.

8 Cosmic rays Caused by nuclear explosions and reactions in space, nearly all of these waves are absorbed by the Earth's atmosphere.

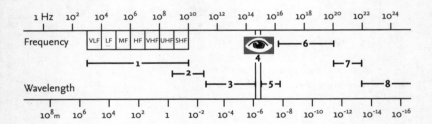

Measuring earthquakes

Earthquake magnitude is measured in units on the Richter scale, which measures the amount of energy released. Each year there are more than 300 000 earth tremors with Richter magnitudes of 2 to 2.9. An earthquake of 8.5 or higher occurs about every 5 to 10 years.

Intensity

The intensity of an earthquake is measured on the Mercalli scale; the numbers refer to an earthquake's effect at a specific place on the Earth's surface.

Below are listed numbers on the Mercalli scale and the characteristics of each.

No	Characteristic
I	instrumental (detected only by seismograph)
II	feeble (noticed only by people at rest)
III	slight (similar to vibrations from a passing truck)
IV	moderate (felt indoors, parked cars rock)
V	rather strong (felt generally, wakes sleepers)
VI	strong (trees sway, some damage)
VII	very strong (general alarm, walls crack)
VIII	destructive (walls collapse)
IX	ruinous (some houses collapse, ground cracks)
X	disastrous (buildings destroyed, rails bend)
XI	very disastrous (landslides, few buildings survive)
XII	catastrophic (total destruction)

Listed below are the Mercalli and Richter scales, with equivalents in joules, and a table comparing the Richter scale with joules.

Mercalli	Richter	Joules	Richter	Joules
I	3.5	$<1.6 \times 10^7$ J	0	6.3×10^{-2} J
II	3.5	1.6×10^7 J	1	1.6×10 J
III	4.2	7.5×10^8 J	2	4.0×10^3 J
IV	4.5	4.0×10^9 J	3	1.0×10^6 J
V	4.8	2.1×10^{10} J	4	2.5×10^8 J
VI	5.4	5.7×10^{11} J	5	6.3×10^{10} J
VII	6.1	2.8×10^{13} J	6	1.6×10^{13} J
VIII	6.5	2.5×10^{14} J	7	4.0×10^{15} J
IX	6.9	2.3×10^{15} J	8	1.0×10^{18} J
X	7.3	2.1×10^{16} J	9	2.5×10^{20} J
XI	8.1	1.7×10^{18} J	10	6.3×10^{22} J
XII	>8.1	$>1.7 \times 10^{18}$ J		

Measuring sound

The loudness of a sound is measured by the size of its vibrations; this is measured in decibels (dB).

Decibel scale

The dB scale is relative and increases exponentially, beginning with the smallest sound change that can be heard by humans (0–1 dB). A 20 dB sound is 10 times louder than a 10 dB sound; a 30 dB sound is 100 times as loud as a 10dB sound. Noises at the level of 120–130 dB can cause pain in humans; higher levels can cause permanent ear damage.

Wave amplitude

Amplitude (a) is the distance between a wave peak or trough and an intermediate line of equilibrium. The greater the amount of energy transmitted in a sound wave, the greater is the wave's amplitude and the louder the sound heard.

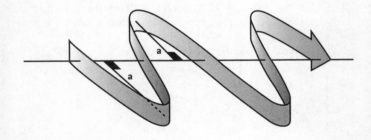

Decibel ratings of some common noises

A	0 dB	human minimum audibility
B	30 dB	soft whisper at 5 m
C	50 dB	inside urban home
D	55 dB	light traffic at 15 m
E	60 dB	conversation at 1 m
F	85 dB	pneumatic drill at 15 m
G	90 dB	heavy traffic at 15 m
H	100 dB	loud shout at 15 m
I	105 dB	aeroplane take-off at 600 m
J	117 dB	inside full-volume disco
K	120 dB	aeroplane take-off at 60 m
L	130 dB	pain threshold for humans
M	140 dB	aeroplane take-off at 30 m

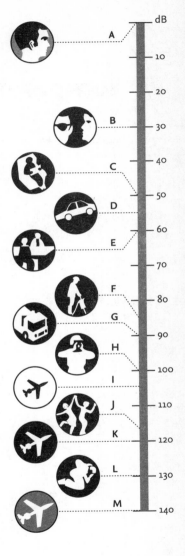

7 Temperature

Systems of measurement

Below, the different systems of temperature measurement are compared: Fahrenheit (°F), Celsius (°C), Réaumur (°r), Kelvin (K) and Rankine (°R).

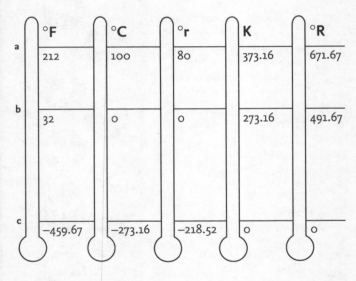

	°F	°C	°r	K	°R
a	212	100	80	373.16	671.67
b	32	0	0	273.16	491.67
c	−459.67	−273.16	−218.52	0	0

a boiling point of water   b freezing point of water
c absolute zero

Conversion formulae

Fahrenheit to others

Fahrenheit to Celsius
°F ➡ °C
(°F − 32) ÷ 1.8

Fahrenheit to Kelvin
°F ➡ K
(°F + 459.67) ÷ 1.8

Fahrenheit to Réaumur
°F ➡ °r
(°F + 459.67) ÷ 1.8 − 273.16 ÷ 1.25

Fahrenheit to Rankine
F ➡ °R
°F + 459.67

Celsius to others

Celsius to Fahrenheit
°C ➡ °F
(°C x 1.8) + 32

Celsius to Kelvin
°C ➡ K
°C + 273.16

Celsius to Réaumur
°C ➡ °r
°C ÷ 1.25

Celsius to Rankine
°C ➡ °R
(°C + 273.16) x 1.8

Kelvin to others

Kelvin to Fahrenheit
K ➡ °F
(K x 1.8) − 459.67

Kelvin to Celsius
K ➡ °C
K − 273.16

Conversion tables

The following tables can be used to convert units of temperature from one measuring system to another. The tables starting on page 130 show the conversion of Fahrenheit to Celsius to Kelvin.

Fahrenheit to Celsius to Kelvin

°F	°C	K
−40.0	−40	233
−38.2	−39	234
−36.4	−38	235
−34.6	−37	236
−32.8	−36	237
−31.0	−35	238
−29.2	−34	239
−27.4	−33	240
−25.6	−32	241
−23.8	−31	242
−22.0	−30	243
−20.2	−29	244
−18.4	−28	245
−16.6	−27	246
−14.8	−26	247
−13.0	−25	248
−11.2	−24	249
−9.4	−23	250
−7.6	−22	251
−5.8	−21	252

Fahrenheit to Celsius to Kelvin

°F	°C	K
−4.0	−20	253
−2.2	−19	254
−0.4	−18	255
1.4	−17	256
3.2	−16	257
5.0	−15	258
6.8	−14	259
8.6	−13	260
10.4	−12	261
12.2	−11	262
14.0	−10	263
15.8	−9	264
17.6	−8	265
19.4	−7	266
21.2	−6	267
23.0	−5	268
24.8	−4	269
26.6	−3	270
28.4	−2	271
30.2	−1	272

Fahrenheit to Celsius to Kelvin

°F	°C	K
32.0	0	273
33.8	1	274
35.6	2	275
37.4	3	276
39.2	4	277
41.0	5	278
42.8	6	279
44.6	7	280
46.4	8	281
48.2	9	282
50.0	10	283
51.8	11	284
53.6	12	285
55.4	13	286
57.2	14	287
59.0	15	288
60.8	16	289
62.6	17	290
64.4	18	291
66.2	19	292

Fahrenheit to Celsius to Kelvin

°F	°C	K
68.0	20	293
69.8	21	294
71.6	22	295
73.4	23	296
75.2	24	297
77.0	25	298
78.8	26	299
80.6	27	300
82.4	28	301
84.2	29	302
86.0	30	303
87.8	31	304
89.6	32	305
91.4	33	306
93.2	34	307
95.0	35	308
96.8	36	309
98.6	37	310
100.4	38	311
102.2	39	312

Fahrenheit to Celsius to Kelvin

°F	°C	K
104.0	40	313
105.8	41	314
107.6	42	315
109.4	43	316
111.2	44	317
113.0	45	318
114.8	46	319
116.6	47	320
118.4	48	321
120.2	49	322
122.0	50	323
123.8	51	324
125.6	52	325
127.4	53	326
129.2	54	327
131.0	55	328
132.8	56	329
134.6	57	330
136.4	58	331
138.2	59	332

Fahrenheit to Celsius to Kelvin

°F	°C	K
140.0	60	333
141.8	61	334
143.6	62	335
145.4	63	336
147.2	64	337
149.0	65	338
150.8	66	339
152.6	67	340
154.4	68	341
156.2	69	342
158.0	70	343
159.8	71	344
161.6	72	345
163.4	73	346
165.2	74	347
167.0	75	348
168.8	76	349
170.6	77	350
172.4	78	351
174.2	79	352

Fahrenheit to Celsius to Kelvin		
°F	°C	K
176.0	80	353
177.8	81	354
179.6	82	355
181.4	83	356
183.2	84	357
185.0	85	358
186.8	86	359
188.6	87	360
190.4	88	361
192.2	89	362
194.0	90	363
195.8	91	364
197.6	92	365
199.4	93	366
201.2	94	367
203.0	95	368
204.8	96	369
206.6	97	370
208.4	98	371
210.2	99	372

Fahrenheit to Celsius to Kelvin		
°F	°C	K
212.0	100	373
213.8	101	374
215.6	102	375
217.4	103	376
219.2	104	377
221.0	105	378
222.8	106	379
224.6	107	380
226.4	108	381
228.2	109	382
230.0	110	383
231.8	111	384
233.6	112	385
235.4	113	386
237.2	114	387
239.0	115	388
240.8	116	389
242.6	117	390
244.4	118	391
246.2	119	392

Useful temperatures

Condition	°C	°F
Water freezes	0	32
Mild winter day	10	50
Warm spring day	20	68
Hot summer day	30	86
Body temperature	37	98.6
Heat wave	40	104
Water boils	100	212

Below is a table of Fahrenheit/Celsius conversions for common oven temperatures.

°F	°C	Oven
225	110	very cool
250	130	
275	140	cool
300	150	
325	170	moderate
350	180	
375	190	moderately hot
400	200	
425	220	hot
450	230	
475	240	very hot

For other conversions, use the following formulae:

°F to °C	Subtract 32, then divide by 1.8.
°C to °F	Multiply by 1.8, then add 32.

Wind-chill temperature

Wind chill is the combined effect of low temperature and wind speed. At any given temperature, the stronger the wind blows, the colder it feels.

A wind-chill temperature of between 15 °F and 0 °F (−9 °C to −18 °C) feels very cold. At wind-chill temperatures below −20 °F (−29 °C) there is a serious risk of frostbite, and at wind-chill temperatures below −60 °F (−50 °C) exposed flesh will freeze in about 30 seconds.

Equivalent wind-chill temperatures

Air temperature (°F)

Wind speed (mph)	50	40	30	20	10	0	−10	−20	−30	−40	−50	−60
40	26	10	−6	−21	−37	−53	−69	−85	−100	−116	−132	−148
35	27	11	−4	−20	−35	−49	−67	−82	−98	−113	−129	−145
30	28	13	−2	−18	−33	−48	−63	−79	−94	−109	−125	−140
25	30	16	0	−15	−29	−44	−59	−74	−88	−104	−118	−133
20	32	18	4	−10	−25	−39	−53	−67	−82	−96	−110	−124
15	36	22	9	−5	−18	−36	−45	−58	−72	−85	−99	−112
10	40	28	16	4	−9	−21	−33	−46	−58	−70	−83	−95
0	48	37	27	16	6	−5	−15	−26	−36	−47	−57	−68

Wind speeds greater than 40 mph have little additional effect on air temperature.

# Time

Listed below are the names of time periods that are artificially derived, as opposed to astronomical periods.

Name	Period	Name	Period
bicentennial	200 years	olympiad	4 years
biennial	2 years	quadrennial	4 years
century	100 years	quadricentennial	400 years
day	24 hours	quincentennial	500 years
decade	10 years	quindecennial	15 years
centennial	100 years	quinquennial	5 years
decennial	10 years	semicentennial	50 years
duodecennial	12 years	septennial	7 years
half-century	50 years	sesquicentennial	150 years
half-decade	5 years	sexennial	6 years
half-millennium	500 years	tricennial	30 years
hour	60 minutes	triennial	3 years
leap year	366 days	undecennial	11 years
millennium	1000 years	vicennial	20 years
minute	60 seconds	week	7 days
month	28–31 days	year	365 days
novennial	9 years	year	12 months
octennial	8 years	year	52 weeks

Days, hours, minutes

Below are listed the basic subdivisions of a day and their equivalents.

1 day	=	24 hours	=	1440 minutes	=	86 400 seconds
1 hour	=	$\frac{1}{24}$ day	=	60 minutes	=	3600 seconds
1 minute	=	$\frac{1}{1440}$ day	=	$\frac{1}{60}$ hour	=	60 seconds
1 second	=	$\frac{1}{86\,400}$ day	=	$\frac{1}{3600}$ hour	=	$\frac{1}{60}$ minute

Time intervals

Names for recurring time intervals

annual	yearly
biannual	twice a year (at unequally spaced intervals)
bimonthly	every two months: twice a month
biweekly	every two weeks: twice a week
diurnal	daily: of a day
perennial	occurring year after year
semiannual	every six months (at equally spaced intervals)
semidiurnal	twice a day
semiweekly	twice a week
trimonthly	every three months
triweekly	every three weeks: three times a week
thrice weekly	three times a week

Conversion formulae

Seconds (s) to minutes (min) ÷ 60	*Minutes (min) to seconds (s)* x 60
Seconds (s) to hours (hr) ÷ 3600	*Hours (hr) to seconds* x 3600
Minutes (min) to hours (hr) ÷ 60	*Hours (hr) to minutes* x 60
Hours (hr) to days ÷ 24	*Days to hours (hr)* x 24
Days to weeks ÷ 7	*Weeks to days* x 7
Weeks to months ÷ 4	*Months to weeks* x 4
Months to years ÷ 12	*Years to months* x 12

Sample calculations

Seconds to minutes
e.g. 10 000 seconds =
10 000 ÷ 60 = 166.66 minutes
10 000 seconds = 166.66 minutes

Minutes to seconds
e.g. 50 minutes =
50 x 60 = 3000 seconds
50 minutes = 3000 seconds

Minutes to hours
e.g. 500 minutes =
500 ÷ 60 = 8.33 hours
500 minutes = 8.33 hours

Hours to minutes
e.g. 5 hours =
5 x 60 = 300 minutes
5 hours = 300 minutes

Hours to seconds
e.g. 2 hours =
2 x 3600 = 7200 seconds
2 hours = 7200 seconds

Seconds to hours
e.g. 100 000 seconds =
100 000 ÷ 3600 = 27.77 hours
100 000 seconds = 27.77 hours

Hours to day
e.g. 96 hours =
96 ÷ 24 = 4 days
96 hours = 4 days

Days to hours
e.g. 3 days =
3 x 24 = 72 hours
3 days = 72 hours

Days to weeks
e.g. 70 days =
70 ÷ 7 = 10 weeks
70 days = 10 weeks

Weeks to days
e.g. 15 weeks =
15 x 7 = 105 days
15 weeks = 105 days

Weeks to months
e.g. 20 weeks =
20 ÷ 4 = 5 months
20 weeks = 5 months

Months to weeks
e.g. 15 months =
15 x 4 = 60 weeks
15 months = 60 weeks

Months to years
e.g. 192 months =
192 ÷ 12 = 16 years
192 months = 16 years

Years to months
e.g. 20 years =
20 x 12 = 240 months
20 years = 240 months

Measuring time

Measuring time in seconds
Standard metric prefixes are added to the second to give a range of
units of different sizes based on the second.

1 terasecond (Ts)	10^{12} s	31 689 years
1 gigasecond (Gs)	10^{9} s	31.7 years
1 megasecond (Ms)	10^{6} s	11.6 days
1 kilosecond (ks)	10^{3} s	16.67 minutes
1 second		
1 millisecond (ms)	10^{-3} s	0.001 seconds
1 microsecond (µs)	10^{-6} s	0.000 001 seconds
1 nanosecond (ns)	10^{-9} s	0.000 000 001 seconds
1 picosecond (ps)	10^{-12} s	0.000 000 000 001 seconds
1 femtosecond (fs)	10^{-15} s	0.000 000 000 000 001 seconds
1 attosecond (as)	10^{-18} s	0.000 000 000 000 000 001 seconds

Astronomical time
Time can be measured by motion; in fact, the motion of the Earth,
Sun, Moon and stars provided humans with the first means of
measuring time.

Years, months, days
Sidereal times are calculated by the Earth's position according to
fixed stars. The anomalistic year is measured according to the
Earth's orbit in relation to the perihelion (Earth's minimum distance
to the Sun). Tropical times refer to the apparent passage of the Sun
and the actual passage of the Moon across the Earth's equatorial
plane. The synodic month is based on the phases of the Moon. Solar
time (as in a mean solar day) refers to periods of darkness and light
averaged over a year.

Time	Days	Hours	Minutes	Seconds
sidereal year	365	6	9	10
anomalistic year	365	6	13	53
tropical year	365	5	48	45
sidereal month	27	7	43	11
tropical month	27	7	43	5
synodic month	29	12	44	3
mean solar day	0	24	0	0
sidereal day	0	23	56	4

Time zones of the world

Some countries, including the UK, adopt Daylight Saving Time (DST) in order to receive more daylight in summer. Clocks are put forward 1 hour in spring and back 1 hour in autumn. The maps below do not reflect DST adjustments.

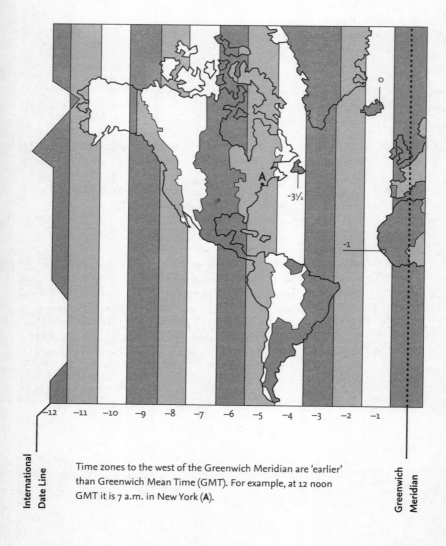

Time zones to the west of the Greenwich Meridian are 'earlier' than Greenwich Mean Time (GMT). For example, at 12 noon GMT it is 7 a.m. in New York (**A**).

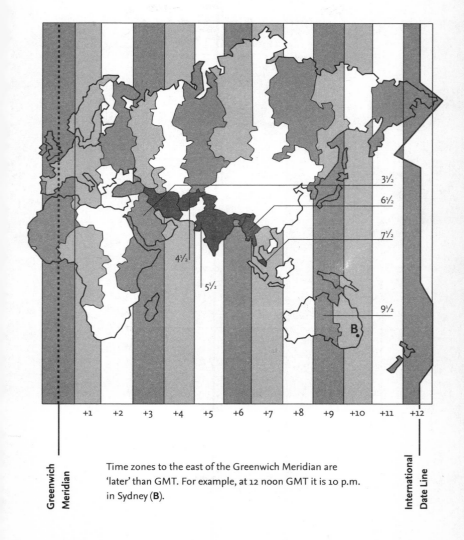

Time zones to the east of the Greenwich Meridian are
'later' than GMT. For example, at 12 noon GMT it is 10 p.m.
in Sydney (**B**).

Geological timescale

Note: Dates are in
millions of years
before the present.

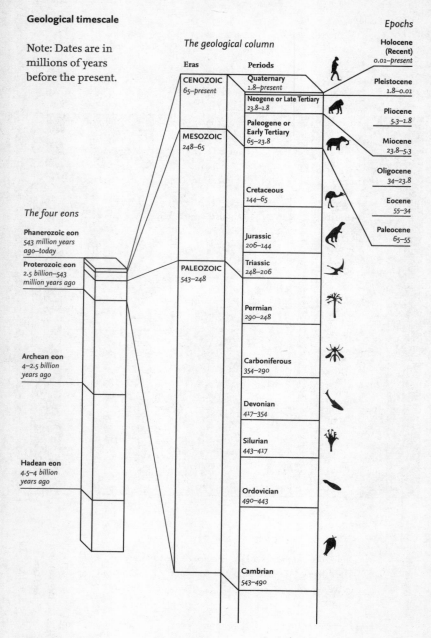

The geological column

Epochs

Holocene (Recent)	0.01–present
Pleistocene	1.8–0.01
Pliocene	5.3–1.8
Miocene	23.8–5.3
Oligocene	34–23.8
Eocene	55–34
Paleocene	65–55

Eras

CENOZOIC	65–present
MESOZOIC	248–65
PALEOZOIC	543–248

Periods

Quaternary	1.8–present
Neogene or Late Tertiary	23.8–1.8
Paleogene or Early Tertiary	65–23.8
Cretaceous	144–65
Jurassic	206–144
Triassic	248–206
Permian	290–248
Carboniferous	354–290
Devonian	417–354
Silurian	443–417
Ordovician	490–443
Cambrian	543–490

The four eons

Phanerozoic eon
*543 million years
ago–today*

Proterozoic eon
*2.5 billion–543
million years ago*

Archean eon
*4–2.5 billion
years ago*

Hadean eon
*4.5–4 billion
years ago*

Types of calendar

The number of days in a year varies among cultures and from year to year.

Gregorian

The Gregorian calendar is a 16th-century adaptation of the Julian calendar devised in the 1st century BCE. The year in this calendar is based on the solar year, which lasts about 365¼ days. In this system, years whose number is not divisible by 4 have 365 days, as do centennial years unless the figures before the noughts are divisible by 4. All other years have 366 days; these are leap years. Below are the names of the months and number of days for a non-leap year.

January	31	July	31
February	28*	August	31
March	31	September	30
April	30	October	31
May	31	November	30
June	30	December	31

* 29 in leap years.

Jewish

A year in the Jewish calendar has 13 months if its number, when divided by 9, leaves 0, 3, 6, 8, 11, 14 or 17; otherwise, it has 12 months. The year is based on the lunar year, but its number of months varies to keep broadly in line with the solar cycle. Its precise number of days is fixed with reference to particular festivals that must not fall on certain days of the week.

Below are the names of the months and number of days in each for the year 5766, a 12-month year (2006 AD in Gregorian).

Tishri	30	Nisan	30
Cheshvan	30*	Iyar	29
Kislev	30*	Sivan	30
Tevet	29	Tammuz	29
Shevat	30	Av	30
Adar	30	Elul	29
Veadar†	29		

* 29 in some years. † In 13-month years, the month Veadar, with 29 days, falls between Adar and Nisan.

Muslim

A year in the Muslim calendar has 355 days if its number, when divided by 30, leaves 2, 5, 7, 10, 13, 16, 18, 21, 24, 26 or 29; otherwise it has 354 days. As in the Jewish calendar, years are based on the lunar cycle.

Below are the names of the months and number of days in each for the Muslim year 1427 (2006 AD in Gregorian).

Muharram	30	Rajab	30
Safar	29	Sha'ban	29
Rabi I	30	Ramadan	30
Rabi II	29	Shawwal	29
Jumada I	30	Dhu l-Qa'da	30
Jumada II	30	Dhu l-hijjah	29

Perpetual calendar

To discover on which day of the week any date between the years 1780 and 2046 falls, look up the year in the key and the letter shown to the right will indicate which of the calendars A–N you should consult.

1780	N	1803	G	1826	A	1849	B
1781	B	1804	H	1827	B	1850	C
1782	C	1805	C	1828	J	1851	D
1783	D	1806	D	1829	E	1852	L
1784	L	1807	E	1830	F	1853	G
1785	G	1808	M	1831	G	1854	A
1786	A	1809	A	1832	H	1855	B
1787	B	1810	B	1833	C	1856	J
1788	J	1811	C	1834	D	1857	E
1789	E	1812	K	1835	E	1858	F
1790	F	1813	F	1836	M	1859	G
1791	G	1814	G	1837	A	1860	H
1792	H	1815	A	1838	B	1861	C
1793	C	1816	I	1839	C	1862	D
1794	D	1817	D	1840	K	1863	E
1795	E	1818	E	1841	F	1864	M
1796	M	1819	F	1842	G	1865	A
1797	A	1820	N	1843	A	1866	B
1798	B	1821	B	1844	I	1867	C
1799	C	1822	C	1845	D	1868	K
1800	D	1823	D	1846	E	1869	F
1801	E	1824	L	1847	F	1870	G
1802	F	1825	G	1848	N	1871	A

1872	I	1916	N	1960	M	2004	L
1873	D	1917	B	1961	A	2005	G
1874	E	1918	C	1962	B	2006	A
1875	F	1919	D	1963	C	2007	B
1876	N	1920	L	1964	K	2008	J
1877	B	1921	G	1965	F	2009	E
1878	C	1922	A	1966	G	2010	F
1879	D	1923	B	1967	A	2011	G
1880	L	1924	J	1968	I	2012	H
1881	G	1925	E	1969	D	2013	C
1882	A	1926	F	1970	E	2014	D
1883	B	1927	G	1971	F	2015	E
1884	J	1928	H	1972	N	2016	M
1885	E	1929	C	1973	B	2017	A
1886	F	1930	D	1974	C	2018	B
1887	G	1931	E	1975	D	2019	C
1888	H	1932	M	1976	L	2020	K
1889	C	1933	A	1977	G	2021	F
1890	D	1934	B	1978	A	2022	G
1891	E	1935	C	1979	B	2023	A
1892	M	1936	K	1980	J	2024	I
1893	A	1937	F	1981	E	2025	D
1894	B	1938	G	1982	F	2026	E
1895	C	1939	A	1983	G	2027	F
1896	K	1940	I	1984	H	2028	N
1897	F	1941	D	1985	C	2029	B
1898	G	1942	E	1986	D	2030	C
1899	A	1943	F	1987	E	2031	D
1900	B	1944	N	1988	M	2032	L
1901	C	1945	B	1989	A	2033	G
1902	D	1946	C	1990	B	2034	A
1903	E	1947	D	1991	C	2035	B
1904	M	1948	L	1992	K	2036	J
1905	A	1949	G	1993	F	2037	E
1906	B	1950	A	1994	G	2038	F
1907	C	1951	B	1995	A	2039	G
1908	K	1952	J	1996	I	2040	H
1909	F	1953	E	1997	D	2041	C
1910	G	1954	F	1998	E	2042	D
1911	A	1955	G	1999	F	2043	E
1912	I	1956	H	2000	N	2044	M
1913	D	1957	C	2001	B	2045	A
1914	E	1958	D	2002	C	2046	B
1915	F	1959	E	2003	D		

A

1786
1797
1809
1815
1826
1837
1843
1854
1865
1871
1882
1893
1899
1905
1911
1922
1933
1939
1950
1961
1967
1978
1989
1995
2006
2017
2023
2034
2045

JANUARY
S	M	T	W	T	F	S
1	2	3	4	5	6	7
8	9	10	11	12	13	14
15	16	17	18	19	20	21
22	23	24	25	26	27	28
29	30	31				

FEBRUARY
S	M	T	W	T	F	S
			1	2	3	4
5	6	7	8	9	10	11
12	13	14	15	16	17	18
19	20	21	22	23	24	25
26	27	28				

MARCH
S	M	T	W	T	F	S
			1	2	3	4
5	6	7	8	9	10	11
12	13	14	15	16	17	18
19	20	21	22	23	24	25
26	27	28	29	30	31	

APRIL
S	M	T	W	T	F	S
30						1
2	3	4	5	6	7	8
9	10	11	12	13	14	15
16	17	18	19	20	21	22
23	24	25	26	27	28	29

MAY
S	M	T	W	T	F	S
	1	2	3	4	5	6
7	8	9	10	11	12	13
14	15	16	17	18	19	20
21	22	23	24	25	26	27
28	29	30	31			

JUNE
S	M	T	W	T	F	S
				1	2	3
4	5	6	7	8	9	10
11	12	13	14	15	16	17
18	19	20	21	22	23	24
25	26	27	28	29	30	

JULY
S	M	T	W	T	F	S
30	31					1
2	3	4	5	6	7	8
9	10	11	12	13	14	15
16	17	18	19	20	21	22
23	24	25	26	27	28	29

AUGUST
S	M	T	W	T	F	S
		1	2	3	4	5
6	7	8	9	10	11	12
13	14	15	16	17	18	19
20	21	22	23	24	25	26
27	28	29	30	31		

SEPTEMBER
S	M	T	W	T	F	S
					1	2
3	4	5	6	7	8	9
10	11	12	13	14	15	16
17	18	19	20	21	22	23
24	25	26	27	28	29	30

OCTOBER
S	M	T	W	T	F	S
1	2	3	4	5	6	7
8	9	10	11	12	13	14
15	16	17	18	19	20	21
22	23	24	25	26	27	28
29	30	31				

NOVEMBER
S	M	T	W	T	F	S
			1	2	3	4
5	6	7	8	9	10	11
12	13	14	15	16	17	18
19	20	21	22	23	24	25
26	27	28	29	30		

DECEMBER
S	M	T	W	T	F	S
31					1	2
3	4	5	6	7	8	9
10	11	12	13	14	15	16
17	18	19	20	21	22	23
24	25	26	27	28	29	30

B

1781
1787
1798
1810
1821
1827
1838
1849
1855
1866
1877
1883
1894
1900
1917
1923
1934
1945
1951
1962
1973
1979
1990
2001
2007
2018
2029
2035
2046

JANUARY

S	M	T	W	T	F	S
		1	2	3	4	5	6
7	8	9	10	11	12	13
14	15	16	17	18	19	20
21	22	23	24	25	26	27
28	29	30	31			

FEBRUARY

S	M	T	W	T	F	S
				1	2	3
4	5	6	7	8	9	10
11	12	13	14	15	16	17
18	19	20	21	22	23	24
25	26	27	28			

MARCH

S	M	T	W	T	F	S
				1	2	3
4	5	6	7	8	9	10
11	12	13	14	15	16	17
18	19	20	21	22	23	24
25	26	27	28	29	30	31

APRIL

S	M	T	W	T	F	S
1	2	3	4	5	6	7
8	9	10	11	12	13	14
15	16	17	18	19	20	21
22	23	24	25	26	27	28
29	30					

MAY

S	M	T	W	T	F	S
		1	2	3	4	5
6	7	8	9	10	11	12
13	14	15	16	17	18	19
20	21	22	23	24	25	26
27	28	29	30	31		

JUNE

S	M	T	W	T	F	S
					1	2
3	4	5	6	7	8	9
10	11	12	13	14	15	16
17	18	19	20	21	22	23
24	25	26	27	28	29	30

JULY

S	M	T	W	T	F	S
1	2	3	4	5	6	7
8	9	10	11	12	13	14
15	16	17	18	19	20	21
22	23	24	25	26	27	28
29	30	31				

AUGUST

S	M	T	W	T	F	S
			1	2	3	4
5	6	7	8	9	10	11
12	13	14	15	16	17	18
19	20	21	22	23	24	25
26	27	28	29	30	31	

SEPTEMBER

S	M	T	W	T	F	S
30						1
2	3	4	5	6	7	8
9	10	11	12	13	14	15
16	17	18	19	20	21	22
23	24	25	26	27	28	29

OCTOBER

S	M	T	W	T	F	S
	1	2	3	4	5	6
7	8	9	10	11	12	13
14	15	16	17	18	19	20
21	22	23	24	25	26	27
28	29	30	31			

NOVEMBER

S	M	T	W	T	F	S
				1	2	3
4	5	6	7	8	9	10
11	12	13	14	15	16	17
18	19	20	21	22	23	24
25	26	27	28	29	30	

DECEMBER

S	M	T	W	T	F	S
30	31					1
2	3	4	5	6	7	8
9	10	11	12	13	14	15
16	17	18	19	20	21	22
23	24	25	26	27	28	29

C

1782
1793
1799
1805
1811
1822
1833
1839
1850
1861
1867
1878
1889
1895
1901
1907
1918
1929
1935
1946
1957
1963
1974
1985
1991
2002
2013
2019
2030
2041

JANUARY

S	M	T	W	T	F	S
		1	2	3	4	5
6	7	8	9	10	11	12
13	14	15	16	17	18	19
20	21	22	23	24	25	26
27	28	29	30	31		

FEBRUARY

S	M	T	W	T	F	S
					1	2
3	4	5	6	7	8	9
10	11	12	13	14	15	16
17	18	19	20	21	22	23
24	25	26	27	28		

MARCH

S	M	T	W	T	F	S
31					1	2
3	4	5	6	7	8	9
10	11	12	13	14	15	16
17	18	19	20	21	22	23
24	25	26	27	28	29	30

APRIL

S	M	T	W	T	F	S
	1	2	3	4	5	6
7	8	9	10	11	12	13
14	15	16	17	18	19	20
21	22	23	24	25	26	27
28	29	30				

MAY

S	M	T	W	T	F	S
			1	2	3	4
5	6	7	8	9	10	11
12	13	14	15	16	17	18
19	20	21	22	23	24	25
26	27	28	29	30	31	

JUNE

S	M	T	W	T	F	S
30						1
2	3	4	5	6	7	8
9	10	11	12	13	14	15
16	17	18	19	20	21	22
23	24	25	26	27	28	29

JULY

S	M	T	W	T	F
	1	2	3	4	5	6
7	8	9	10	11	12	13
14	15	16	17	18	19	20
21	22	23	24	25	26	27
28	29	30	31			

AUGUST

S	M	T	W	T	F	S
				1	2	3
4	5	6	7	8	9	10
11	12	13	14	15	16	17
18	19	20	21	22	23	24
25	26	27	28	29	30	31

SEPTEMBER

S	M	T	W	T	F	S
1	2	3	4	5	6	7
8	9	10	11	12	13	14
15	16	17	18	19	20	21
22	23	24	25	26	27	28
29	30					

OCTOBER

S	M	T	W	T	F	S
		1	2	3	4	5
6	7	8	9	10	11	12
13	14	15	16	17	18	19
20	21	22	23	24	25	26
27	28	29	30	31		

NOVEMBER

S	M	T	W	T	F	S
					1	2
3	4	5	6	7	8	9
10	11	12	13	14	15	16
17	18	19	20	21	22	23
24	25	26	27	28	29	30

DECEMBER

S	M	T	W	T	F	S
1	2	3	4	5	6	7
8	9	10	11	12	13	14
15	16	17	18	19	20	21
22	23	24	25	26	27	28
29	30	31				

D

1783
1794
1800
1806
1817
1823
1834
1845
1851
1862
1882
1873
1879
1890
1902
1913
1919
1930
1941
1947
1958
1969
1975
1986
1997
2003
2014
2025
2031
2042

JANUARY

S	M	T	W	T	F	S
			1	2	3	4
5	6	7	8	9	10	11
12	13	14	15	16	17	18
19	20	21	22	23	24	25
26	27	28	29	30	31	

FEBRUARY

S	M	T	W	T	F	S
						1
2	3	4	5	6	7	8
9	10	11	12	13	14	15
16	17	18	19	20	21	22
23	24	25	26	27	28	

MARCH

S	M	T	W	T	F	S
30	31					1
2	3	4	5	6	7	8
9	10	11	12	13	14	15
16	17	18	19	20	21	22
23	24	25	26	27	28	29

APRIL

S	M	T	W	T	F	S
		1	2	3	4	5
6	7	8	9	10	11	12
13	14	15	16	17	18	19
20	21	22	23	24	25	26
27	28	29	30			

MAY

S	M	T	W	T	F	S
				1	2	3
4	5	6	7	8	9	10
11	12	13	14	15	16	17
18	19	20	21	22	23	24
25	26	27	28	29	30	31

JUNE

S	M	T	W	T	F	S
1	2	3	4	5	6	7
8	9	10	11	12	13	14
15	16	17	18	19	20	21
22	23	24	25	26	27	28
29	30					

JULY

S	M	T	W	T	F	S
		1	2	3	4	5
6	7	8	9	10	11	12
13	14	15	16	17	18	19
20	21	22	23	24	25	26
27	28	29	30	31		

AUGUST

S	M	T	W	T	F	S
31					1	2
3	4	5	6	7	8	9
10	11	12	13	14	15	16
17	18	19	20	21	22	23
24	25	26	27	28	29	30

SEPTEMBER

S	M	T	W	T	F	S
	1	2	3	4	5	6
7	8	9	10	11	12	13
14	15	16	17	18	19	20
21	22	23	24	25	26	27
28	29	30				

OCTOBER

S	M	T	W	T	F	S
			1	2	3	4
5	6	7	8	9	10	11
12	13	14	15	16	17	18
19	20	21	22	23	24	25
26	27	28	29	30	31	

NOVEMBER

S	M	T	W	T	F	S
30						1
2	3	4	5	6	7	8
9	10	11	12	13	14	15
16	17	18	19	20	21	22
23	24	25	26	27	28	29

DECEMBER

S	M	T	W	T	F	S
	1	2	3	4	5	6
7	8	9	10	11	12	13
14	15	16	17	18	19	20
21	22	23	24	25	26	27
28	29	30	31			

E

1789
1795
1801
1807
1818
1829
1835
1846
1857
1863
1874
1885
1891
1903
1914
1925
1931
1942
1953
1959
1970
1981
1981
1987
1998
2009
2015
2026
2037
2043

JANUARY

S	M	T	W	T	F	S
				1	2	3
4	5	6	7	8	9	10
11	12	13	14	15	16	17
18	19	20	21	22	23	24
25	26	27	28	29	30	31

FEBRUARY

S	M	T	W	T	F	S
1	2	3	4	5	6	7
8	9	10	11	12	13	14
15	16	17	18	19	20	21
22	23	24	25	26	27	28

MARCH

S	M	T	W	T	F	S
1	2	3	4	5	6	7
8	9	10	11	12	13	14
15	16	17	18	19	20	21
22	23	24	25	26	27	28
29	30	31				

APRIL

S	M	T	W	T	F	S
			1	2	3	4
5	6	7	8	9	10	11
12	13	14	15	16	17	18
19	20	21	22	23	24	25
26	27	28	29	30		

MAY

S	M	T	W	T	F	S
31					1	2
3	4	5	6	7	8	9
10	11	12	13	14	15	16
17	18	19	20	21	22	23
24	25	26	27	28	29	30

JUNE

S	M	T	W	T	F	S
	1	2	3	4	5	6
7	8	9	10	11	12	13
14	15	16	17	18	19	20
21	22	23	24	25	26	27
28	29	30				

JULY

S	M	T	W	T	F	S
			1	2	3	4
5	6	7	8	9	10	11
12	13	14	15	16	17	18
19	20	21	22	23	24	25
26	27	28	29	30	31	

AUGUST

S	M	T	W	T	F	S
30	31					1
2	3	4	5	6	7	8
9	10	11	12	13	14	15
16	17	18	19	20	21	22
23	24	25	26	27	28	29

SEPTEMBER

S	M	T	W	T	F	S
		1	2	3	4	5
6	7	8	9	10	11	12
13	14	15	16	17	18	19
20	21	22	23	24	25	26
27	28	29	30			

OCTOBER

S	M	T	W	T	F	S
				1	2	3
4	5	6	7	8	9	10
11	12	13	14	15	16	17
18	19	20	21	22	23	24
25	26	27	28	29	30	31

NOVEMBER

S	M	T	W	T	F	S
1	2	3	4	5	6	7
8	9	10	11	12	13	14
15	16	17	18	19	20	21
22	23	24	25	26	27	28
29	30					

DECEMBER

S	M	T	W	T	F	S
		1	2	3	4	5
6	7	8	9	10	11	12
13	14	15	16	17	18	19
20	21	22	23	24	25	26
27	28	29	30	31		

F

1790
1802
1813
1819
1830
1841
1847
1858
1869
1875
1886
1897
1909
1915
1926
1937
1943
1954
1965
1971
1982
1993
1999
2010
2021
2027
2038

JANUARY
S	M	T	W	T	F	S
31					1	2
3	4	5	6	7	8	9
10	11	12	13	14	15	16
17	18	19	20	21	22	23
24	25	26	27	28	29	30

FEBRUARY
S	M	T	W	T	F	S
	1	2	3	4	5	6
7	8	9	10	11	12	13
14	15	16	17	18	19	20
21	22	23	24	25	26	27
28						

MARCH
S	M	T	W	T	F	S
	1	2	3	4	5	6
7	8	9	10	11	12	13
14	15	16	17	18	19	20
21	22	23	24	25	26	27
28	29	30	31			

APRIL
S	M	T	W	T	F	S
				1	2	3
4	5	6	7	8	9	10
11	12	13	14	15	16	17
18	19	20	21	22	23	24
25	26	27	28	29	30	

MAY
S	M	T	W	T	F	S
30	31					1
2	3	4	5	6	7	8
9	10	11	12	13	14	15
16	17	18	19	20	21	22
23	24	25	26	27	28	29

JUNE
S	M	T	W	T	F	S
		1	2	3	4	5
6	7	8	9	10	11	12
13	14	15	16	17	18	19
20	21	22	23	24	25	26
27	28	29	30			

JULY
S	M	T	W	T	F	S
				1	2	3
4	5	6	7	8	9	10
11	12	13	14	15	16	17
18	19	20	21	22	23	24
25	26	27	28	29	30	31

AUGUST
S	M	T	W	T	F	S
1	2	3	4	5	6	7
8	9	10	11	12	13	14
15	16	17	18	19	20	21
22	23	24	25	26	27	28
29	30	31				

SEPTEMBER
S	M	T	W	T	F	S
			1	2	3	4
5	6	7	8	9	10	11
12	13	14	15	16	17	18
19	20	21	22	23	24	25
26	27	28	29	30		

OCTOBER
S	M	T	W	T	F	S
31					1	2
3	4	5	6	7	8	9
10	11	12	13	14	15	16
17	18	19	20	21	22	23
24	25	26	27	28	29	30

NOVEMBER
S	M	T	W	T	F	S
	1	2	3	4	5	6
7	8	9	10	11	12	13
14	15	16	17	18	19	20
21	22	23	24	25	26	27
28	29	30				

DECEMBER
S	M	T	W	T	F	S
			1	2	3	4
5	6	7	8	9	10	11
12	13	14	15	16	17	18
19	20	21	22	23	24	25
26	27	28	29	30	31	

G

1785
1791
1803
1814
1825
1831
1842
1853
1859
1870
1881
1887
1898
1910
1921
1927
1938
1949
1955
1966
1977
1983
1994
2005
2011
1011
1033
2039

JANUARY
S	M	T	W	T	F	S
30	31					1
2	3	4	5	6	7	8
9	10	11	12	13	14	15
16	17	18	19	20	21	22
23	24	25	26	27	28	29

FEBRUARY
S	M	T	W	T	F	S
		1	2	3	4	5
6	7	8	9	10	11	12
13	14	15	16	17	18	19
20	21	22	23	24	25	26
27	28					

MARCH
S	M	T	W	T	F	S
		1	2	3	4	5
6	7	8	9	10	11	12
13	14	15	16	17	18	19
20	21	22	23	24	25	26
27	28	29	30	31		

APRIL
S	M	T	W	T	F	S
					1	2
3	4	5	6	7	8	9
10	11	12	13	14	15	16
17	18	19	20	21	22	23
24	25	26	27	28	29	30

MAY
S	M	T	W	T	F	S
1	2	3	4	5	6	7
8	9	10	11	12	13	14
15	16	17	18	19	20	21
22	23	24	25	26	27	28
29	30	31				

JUNE
S	M	T	W	T	F	S
			1	2	3	4
5	6	7	8	9	10	11
12	13	14	15	16	17	18
19	20	21	22	23	24	25
26	27	28	29	30		

JULY
S	M	T	W	T	F	S
31					1	2
3	4	5	6	7	8	9
10	11	12	13	14	15	16
17	18	19	20	21	22	23
24	25	26	27	28	29	30

AUGUST
S	M	T	W	T	F	S
	1	2	3	4	5	6
7	8	9	10	11	12	13
14	15	16	17	18	19	20
21	22	23	24	25	26	27
28	29	30	31			

SEPTEMBER
S	M	T	W	T	F	S
				1	2	3
4	5	6	7	8	9	10
11	12	13	14	15	16	17
18	19	20	21	22	23	24
25	26	27	28	29	30	

OCTOBER
S	M	T	W	T	F	S
30	31					1
2	3	4	5	6	7	8
9	10	11	12	13	14	15
16	17	18	19	20	21	22
23	24	25	26	27	28	29

NOVEMBER
S	M	T	W	T	F	S
		1	2	3	4	5
6	7	8	9	10	11	12
13	14	15	16	17	18	19
20	21	22	23	24	25	26
27	28	29	30			

DECEMBER
S	M	T	W	T	F	S
				1	2	3
4	5	6	7	8	9	10
11	12	13	14	15	16	17
18	19	20	21	22	23	24
25	26	27	28	29	30	31

H

1792
1804
1832
1860
1888
1928
1956
1984
2012
2040

JANUARY

S	M	T	W	T	F	S
1	2	3	4	5	6	7
8	9	10	11	12	13	14
15	16	17	18	19	20	21
22	23	24	25	26	27	28
29	30	31				

FEBRUARY

S	M	T	W	T	F	S
			1	2	3	4
5	6	7	8	9	10	11
12	13	14	15	16	17	18
19	20	21	22	23	24	25
26	27	28	29			

MARCH

S	M	T	W	T	F	S
				1	2	3
4	5	6	7	8	9	10
11	12	13	14	15	16	17
18	19	20	21	22	23	24
25	26	27	28	29	30	31

APRIL

S	M	T	W	T	F	S
1	2	3	4	5	6	7
8	9	10	11	12	13	14
15	16	17	18	19	20	21
22	23	24	25	26	27	28
29	30					

MAY

S	M	T	W	T	F	S
		1	2	3	4	5
6	7	8	9	10	11	12
13	14	15	16	17	18	19
20	21	22	23	24	25	26
27	28	29	30	31		

JUNE

S	M	T	W	T	F	S
					1	2
3	4	5	6	7	8	9
10	11	12	13	14	15	16
17	18	19	20	21	22	23
24	25	26	27	28	29	30

JULY

S	M	T	W	T	F	S
1	2	3	4	5	6	7
8	9	10	11	12	13	14
15	16	17	18	19	20	21
22	23	24	25	26	27	28
29	30	31				

AUGUST

S	M	T	W	T	F	S
			1	2	3	4
5	6	7	8	9	10	11
12	13	14	15	16	17	18
19	20	21	22	23	24	25
26	27	28	29	30	31	

SEPTEMBER

S	M	T	W	T	F	S
30						1
2	3	4	5	6	7	8
9	10	11	12	13	14	15
16	17	18	19	20	21	22
23	24	25	26	27	28	29

OCTOBER

S	M	T	W	T	F	S
	1	2	3	4	5	6
7	8	9	10	11	12	13
14	15	16	17	18	19	20
21	22	23	24	25	26	27
28	29	30	31			

NOVEMBER

S	M	T	W	T	F	S
				1	2	3
4	5	6	7	8	9	10
11	12	13	14	15	16	17
18	19	20	21	22	23	24
25	26	27	28	29	30	

DECEMBER

S	M	T	W	T	F	S
30	31					1
2	3	4	5	6	7	8
9	10	11	12	13	14	15
16	17	18	19	20	21	22
23	24	25	26	27	28	29

1816
1844
1872
1912
1940
1968
1996
2024

JANUARY

S	M	T	W	T	F	S
	1	2	3	4	5	6
7	8	9	10	11	12	13
14	15	16	17	18	19	20
21	22	23	24	25	26	27
28	29	30	31			

FEBRUARY

S	M	T	W	T	F	S
				1	2	3
4	5	6	7	8	9	10
11	12	13	14	15	16	17
18	19	20	21	22	23	24
25	26	27	28	29		

MARCH

S	M	T	W	T	F	S
31					1	2
3	4	5	6	7	8	9
10	11	12	13	14	15	16
17	18	19	20	21	22	23
24	25	26	27	28	29	30

APRIL

S	M	T	W	T	F	S
	1	2	3	4	5	6
7	8	9	10	11	12	13
14	15	16	17	18	19	20
21	22	23	24	25	26	27
28	29	30				

MAY

S	M	T	W	T	F	S
			1	2	3	4
5	6	7	8	9	10	11
12	13	14	15	16	17	18
19	20	21	22	23	24	25
26	27	28	29	30	31	

JUNE

S	M	T	W	T	F	S
30						1
2	3	4	5	6	7	8
9	10	11	12	13	14	15
16	17	18	19	20	21	22
23	24	25	26	27	28	29

JULY

S	M	T	W	T	F	S
	1	2	3	4	5	6
7	8	9	10	11	12	13
14	15	16	17	18	19	20
21	22	23	24	25	26	27
28	29	30	31			

AUGUST

S	M	T	W	T	F	S
				1	2	3
4	5	6	7	8	9	10
11	12	13	14	15	16	17
18	19	20	21	22	23	24
25	26	27	28	29	30	31

SEPTEMBER

S	M	T	W	T	F	S
1	2	3	4	5	6	7
8	9	10	11	12	13	14
15	16	17	18	19	20	21
22	23	24	25	26	27	28
29	30					

OCTOBER

S	M	T	W	T	F	S
		1	2	3	4	5
6	7	8	9	10	11	12
13	14	15	16	17	18	19
20	21	22	23	24	25	26
27	28	29	30	31		

NOVEMBER

S	M	T	W	T	F	S
					1	2
3	4	5	6	7	8	9
10	11	12	13	14	15	16
17	18	19	20	21	22	23
24	25	26	27	28	29	30

DECEMBER

S	M	T	W	T	F	S
1	2	3	4	5	6	7
8	9	10	11	12	13	14
15	16	17	18	19	20	21
22	23	24	25	26	27	28
29	30	31				

J

1788
1828
1856
1884
1924
1952
1980
2008
2036

JANUARY

S	M	T	W	T	F	S
			1	2	3	4	5
6	7	8	9	10	11	12
13	14	15	16	17	18	19
20	21	22	23	24	25	26
27	28	29	30	31		

FEBRUARY

S	M	T	W	T	F	S
					1	2
3	4	5	6	7	8	9
10	11	12	13	14	15	16
17	18	19	20	21	22	23
24	25	26	27	28	29	

MARCH

S	M	T	W	T	F	S
30	31					1
2	3	4	5	6	7	8
9	10	11	12	13	14	15
16	17	18	19	20	21	22
23	24	25	26	27	28	29

APRIL

S	M	T	W	T	F	S
		1	2	3	4	5
6	7	8	9	10	11	12
13	14	15	16	17	18	19
20	21	22	23	24	25	26
27	28	29	30			

MAY

S	M	T	W	T	F	S
				1	2	3
4	5	6	7	8	9	10
11	12	13	14	15	16	17
18	19	20	21	22	23	24
25	26	27	28	29	30	31

JUNE

S	M	T	W	T	F	S
1	2	3	4	5	6	7
8	9	10	11	12	13	14
15	16	17	18	19	20	21
22	23	24	25	26	27	28
29	30					

JULY

S	M	T	W	T	F	S
		1	2	3	4	5
6	7	8	9	10	11	12
13	14	15	16	17	18	19
20	21	22	23	24	25	26
27	28	29	30	31		

AUGUST

S	M	T	W	T	F	S
31					1	2
3	4	5	6	7	8	9
10	11	12	13	14	15	16
17	18	19	20	21	22	23
24	25	26	27	28	29	30

SEPTEMBER

S	M	T	W	T	F	S
	1	2	3	4	5	6
7	8	9	10	11	12	13
14	15	16	17	18	19	20
21	22	23	24	25	26	27
28	29	30				

OCTOBER

S	M	T	W	T	F	S
			1	2	3	4
5	6	7	8	9	10	11
12	13	14	15	16	17	18
19	20	21	22	23	24	25
26	27	28	29	30	31	

NOVEMBER

S	M	T	W	T	F	S
30						1
2	3	4	5	6	7	8
9	10	11	12	13	14	15
16	17	18	19	20	21	22
23	24	25	26	27	28	29

DECEMBER

S	M	T	W	T	F	S
	1	2	3	4	5	6
7	8	9	10	11	12	13
14	15	16	17	18	19	20
21	22	23	24	25	26	27
28	29	30	31			

K

1812
1840
1868
1896
1908
1936
1964
1992
2020

JANUARY
S	M	T	W	T	F	S
			1	2	3	4
5	6	7	8	9	10	11
12	13	14	15	16	17	18
19	20	21	22	23	24	25
26	27	28	29	30	31	

FEBRUARY
S	M	T	W	T	F	S
						1
2	3	4	5	6	7	8
9	10	11	12	13	14	15
16	17	18	19	20	21	22
23	24	25	26	27	28	29

MARCH
S	M	T	W	T	F	S
1	2	3	4	5	6	7
8	9	10	11	12	13	14
15	16	17	18	19	20	21
22	23	24	25	26	27	28
29	30	31				

APRIL
S	M	T	W	T	F	S
			1	2	3	4
5	6	7	8	9	10	11
12	13	14	15	16	17	18
19	20	21	22	23	24	25
26	27	28	29	30		

MAY
S	M	T	W	T	F	S
31					1	2
3	4	5	6	7	8	9
10	11	12	13	14	15	16
17	18	19	20	21	22	23
24	25	26	27	28	29	30

JUNE
S	M	T	W	T	F	S
	1	2	3	4	5	6
7	8	9	10	11	12	13
14	15	16	17	18	19	20
21	22	23	24	25	26	27
28	29	30				

JULY
S	M	T	W	T	F	S
			1	2	3	4
5	6	7	8	9	10	11
12	13	14	15	16	17	18
19	20	21	22	23	24	25
26	27	28	29	30	31	

AUGUST
S	M	T	W	T	F	S
30	31					1
2	3	4	5	6	7	8
9	10	11	12	13	14	15
16	17	18	19	20	21	22
23	24	25	26	27	28	29

SEPTEMBER
S	M	T	W	T	F	S
		1	2	3	4	5
6	7	8	9	10	11	12
13	14	15	16	17	18	19
20	21	22	23	24	25	26
27	28	29	30			

OCTOBER
S	M	T	W	T	F	S
				1	2	3
4	5	6	7	8	9	10
11	12	13	14	15	16	17
18	19	20	21	22	23	24
25	26	27	28	29	30	31

NOVEMBER
S	M	T	W	T	F	S
1	2	3	4	5	6	7
8	9	10	11	12	13	14
15	16	17	18	19	20	21
22	23	24	25	26	27	28
29	30					

DECEMBER
S	M	T	W	T	F	S
		1	2	3	4	5
6	7	8	9	10	11	12
13	14	15	16	17	18	19
20	21	22	23	24	25	26
27	28	29	30	31		

L

1784
1824
1852
1880
1920
1948
1976
2004
2032

JANUARY

S	M	T	W	T	F	S
				1	2	3
4	5	6	7	8	9	10
11	12	13	14	15	16	17
18	19	20	21	22	23	24
25	26	27	28	29	30	31

FEBRUARY

S	M	T	W	T	F	S
1	2	3	4	5	6	7
8	9	10	11	12	13	14
15	16	17	18	19	20	21
22	23	24	25	26	27	28
29						

MARCH

S	M	T	W	T	F	S
	1	2	3	4	5	6
7	8	9	10	11	12	13
14	15	16	17	18	19	20
21	22	23	24	25	26	27
28	29	30	31			

APRIL

S	M	T	W	T	F	S
				1	2	3
4	5	6	7	8	9	10
11	12	13	14	15	16	17
18	19	20	21	22	23	24
25	26	27	28	29	30	

MAY

S	M	T	W	T	F	S
30	31					1
2	3	4	5	6	7	8
9	10	11	12	13	14	15
16	17	18	19	20	21	22
23	24	25	26	27	28	29

JUNE

S	M	T	W	T	F	S
		1	2	3	4	5
6	7	8	9	10	11	12
13	14	15	16	17	18	19
20	21	22	23	24	25	26
27	28	29	30			

JULY

S	M	T	W	T	F	S
				1	2	3
4	5	6	7	8	9	10
11	12	13	14	15	16	17
18	19	20	21	22	23	24
25	26	27	28	29	30	31

AUGUST

S	M	T	W	T	F	S
1	2	3	4	5	6	7
8	9	10	11	12	13	14
15	16	17	18	19	20	21
22	23	24	25	26	27	28
29	30	31				

SEPTEMBER

S	M	T	W	T	F	S
			1	2	3	4
5	6	7	8	9	10	11
12	13	14	15	16	17	18
19	20	21	22	23	24	25
26	27	28	29	30		

OCTOBER

S	M	T	W	T	F	S
31					1	2
3	4	5	6	7	8	9
10	11	12	13	14	15	16
17	18	19	20	21	22	23
24	25	26	27	28	29	30

NOVEMBER

S	M	T	W	T	F	S
	1	2	3	4	5	6
7	8	9	10	11	12	13
14	15	16	17	18	19	20
21	22	23	24	25	26	27
28	29	30				

DECEMBER

S	M	T	W	T	F	S
			1	2	3	4
5	6	7	8	9	10	11
12	13	14	15	16	17	18
19	20	21	22	23	24	25
26	27	28	29	30	31	

M

1796
1808
1836
1864
1892
1904
1932
1960
1988
2016
2044

JANUARY

S	M	T	W	T	F	S
31					1	2
3	4	5	6	7	8	9
10	11	12	13	14	15	16
17	18	19	20	21	22	23
24	25	26	27	28	29	30

FEBRUARY

S	M	T	W	T	F	S
	1	2	3	4	5	6
7	8	9	10	11	12	13
14	15	16	17	18	19	20
21	22	23	24	25	26	27
28	29					

MARCH

S	M	T	W	T	F	S
		1	2	3	4	5
6	7	8	9	10	11	12
13	14	15	16	17	18	19
20	21	22	23	24	25	26
27	28	29	30	31		

APRIL

S	M	T	W	T	F	S
					1	2
3	4	5	6	7	8	9
10	11	12	13	14	15	16
17	18	19	20	21	22	23
24	25	26	27	28	29	30

MAY

S	M	T	W	T	F	S
1	2	3	4	5	6	7
8	9	10	11	12	13	14
15	16	17	18	19	20	21
22	23	24	25	26	27	28
29	30	31				

JUNE

S	M	T	W	T	F	
			1	2	3	4
5	6	7	8	9	10	11
12	13	14	15	16	17	18
19	20	21	22	23	24	25
26	27	28	29	30		

JULY

S	M	T	W	T	F	S
31					1	2
3	4	5	6	7	8	9
10	11	12	13	14	15	16
17	18	19	20	21	22	23
24	25	26	27	28	29	30

AUGUST

S	M	T	W	T	F	S
	1	2	3	4	5	6
7	8	9	10	11	12	13
14	15	16	17	18	19	20
21	22	23	24	25	26	27
28	29	30	31			

SEPTEMBER

S	M	T	W	T	F	S
				1	2	3
4	5	6	7	8	9	10
11	12	13	14	15	16	17
18	19	20	21	22	23	24
25	26	27	28	29	30	

OCTOBER

S	M	T	W	T	F	S
30	31					1
2	3	4	5	6	7	8
9	10	11	12	13	14	15
16	17	18	19	20	21	22
23	24	25	26	27	28	29

NOVEMBER

S	M	T	W	T	F	S
		1	2	3	4	5
6	7	8	9	10	11	12
13	14	15	16	17	18	19
20	21	22	23	24	25	26
27	28	29	30			

DECEMBER

S	M	T	W	T	F	S
				1	2	3
4	5	6	7	8	9	10
11	12	13	14	15	16	17
18	19	20	21	22	23	24
25	26	27	28	29	30	31

N

1780
1820
1848
1876
1916
1944
1972
2000
2028

JANUARY
S	M	T	W	T	F	S
30	31					1
2	3	4	5	6	7	8
9	10	11	12	13	14	15
16	17	18	19	20	21	22
23	24	25	26	27	28	29

FEBRUARY
S	M	T	W	T	F	S
		1	2	3	4	5
6	7	8	9	10	11	12
13	14	15	16	17	18	19
20	21	22	23	24	25	26
27	28	29				

MARCH
S	M	T	W	T	F	S
			1	2	3	4
5	6	7	8	9	10	11
12	13	14	15	16	17	18
19	20	21	22	23	24	25
26	27	28	29	30	31	

APRIL
S	M	T	W	T	F	S
30						1
2	3	4	5	6	7	8
9	10	11	12	13	14	15
16	17	18	19	20	21	22
23	24	25	26	27	28	29

MAY
S	M	T	W	T	F	S
	1	2	3	4	5	6
7	8	9	10	11	12	13
14	15	16	17	18	19	20
21	22	23	24	25	26	27
28	29	30	31			

JUNE
S	M	T	W	T	F	S
				1	2	3
4	5	6	7	8	9	10
11	12	13	14	15	16	17
18	19	20	21	22	23	24
25	26	27	28	29	30	

JULY
S	M	T	W	T	F	S
30	31					1
2	3	4	5	6	7	8
9	10	11	12	13	14	15
16	17	18	19	20	21	22
23	24	25	26	27	28	29

AUGUST
S	M	T	W	T	F	S
		1	2	3	4	5
6	7	8	9	10	11	12
13	14	15	16	17	18	19
20	21	22	23	24	25	26
27	28	29	30	31		

SEPTEMBER
S	M	T	W	T	F	S
					1	2
3	4	5	6	7	8	9
10	11	12	13	14	15	16
17	18	19	20	21	22	23
24	25	26	27	28	29	30

OCTOBER
S	M	T	W	T	F	S
1	2	3	4	5	6	7
8	9	10	11	12	13	14
15	16	17	18	19	20	21
22	23	24	25	26	27	28
29	30	31				

NOVEMBER
S	M	T	W	T	F	S
			1	2	3	4
5	6	7	8	9	10	11
12	13	14	15	16	17	18
19	20	21	22	23	24	25
26	27	28	29	30		

DECEMBER
S	M	T	W	T	F	S
31					1	2
3	4	5	6	7	8	9
10	11	12	13	14	15	16
17	18	19	20	21	22	23
24	25	26	27	28	29	30

$\mathcal{9}$ Speed

Conversion formulae

Below are listed the multiplication/division factors for converting units of speed from imperial to metric, and vice versa; and, also, for converting from one unit to another within the same system. Two kinds of factors are given: quick, for a conversion that can be made without a calculator; and accurate, for an exact conversion.

			Quick	Accurate
Miles per hour (mph)				
Kilometres per hour (km/h)				
mph	⟶	km/h	× 1.5	× 1.609
km/h	⟶	mph	÷ 1.5	× 0.621
Yards per minute (ypm)				
Metres per minute (m/min)				
ypm	⟶	m/min	× 1	× 1.094
m/min	⟶	ypm	÷ 1	× 0.914
Feet per minute (ft/min)				
Metres per minute (m/min)				
ft/min	⟶	m/min	× 3	× 0.305
m/min	⟶	ft/min	÷ 3	× 3.281
Inches per second (in/s)				
Centimetres per second (cm/s)				
in/s	⟶	cm/s	× 2.5	× 2.54
cm/s	⟶	in/s	÷ 2.5	× 0.394

		Quick	Accurate
International knots (kn)			
Miles per hour (mph)			
kn ⟶ mph		× 1	× 1.151
mph ⟶ kn		÷ 1	× 0.869
British knots (UK kn)			
International knots (kn)			
UK kn ⟶ kn		× 1	× 1.001
kn ⟶ UK kn		÷ 1	× 0.999
International knots (kn)			
Kilometres per hour (km/h)			
kn ⟶ km/h		× 2	× 1.852
km/h ⟶ kn		÷ 2	× 0.540
Miles per hour (mph)			
Feet per second (ft/s)			
mph ⟶ ft/s		× 1.5	× 1.467
ft/s ⟶ mph		÷ 1.5	× 0.682
Kilometres per hour (km/h)			
Metres per second (m/s)			
km/h ⟶ m/s		÷ 3.5	× 0.278
m/s ⟶ km/h		× 3.5	× 3.599

Speed

Sample calculations

Miles per hour (mph) to kilometres per hour (km/h)

> e.g. 100 miles per hour =
> 100 x 1.609 = 160.9 km/h
> **100 mph = 160.9 km/h**

Kilometres per hour (km/h) to miles per hour (mph)

> e.g. 70 kilometres per hour =
> 70 x 0.621 = 43.47 mph
> **70 km/h = 43.47 mph.**

Yards per minute (ypm) to metres per minute (m/min)

> e.g. 100 yards per minute =
> 100 x 1.094 = 109.4 m/min
> **100 yd = 104.9 m/min**

Metres per minute (m/min) to yards per minute (ypm)

> e.g. 1500 metres per minute =
> 1500 x 0.914 = 1371 ypm
> **1500 m/min = 1371 ypm**

Feet per minute (m/min) to metres per minute (ft/min)

> e.g. 200 feet per minute =
> 200 x 3.281 = 656.2 m/min
> **200 ft/min = 656.2 m/min**

Metres per minute (m/min) to feet per minute (ft/min)

> e.g. 200 metres per minute =
> 200 x 0.305 = 61 ft/min
> **200 m/min = 61 ft/min**

Inches per second (in/s) to centimetres per second (cm/s)

> e.g. 24 inches per second =
> 24 x 2.54 = 60.96 cm/s
> **24 in/s = 60.96 cm/s**

Centimetres per second (cm/s) to inches per second (in/s)

> e.g. 50 centimetres per second =
> 50 x 0.394 = 19.7 in/s
> **50 cm/s = 19.7 in/s**

International knots (kn) to miles per hour (mph)

> e.g. 15 international knots =
> 15 x 1.151 = 17.265 mph
> **15 kn = 17.265 mph**

Miles per hour (mph) to international knots (kn)

> e.g. 70 miles per hour =
> 70 x 0.869 = 60.83 kn
> **70 mph = 60.83 kn**

British knots (UK kn) to international knots (kn)

> e.g. 12 British knots =
> 12 x 1.001 = 12.012 kn
> **12 UK kn = 12.012 kn**

International knots (kn) to British knots (UK kn)

> e.g. 15 international knots =
> 15 x 0.999 = 14.985 UK kn
> **15 kn = 14.985 UK kn**

Feet per second (ft/s) to miles per hour (mph)

> e.g. 10 feet per second =
> 10 x 0.682 = 6.82 mph
> **10 ft/s = 6.82 mph**

Miles per hour (mph) to feet per second (ft/s)

> e.g. 5 miles per hour =
> 5 x 1.467 = 7.335 ft/s
> **5 mph = 7.335 ft/s**

Kilometres per hour (km/h) to metres per second (m/s)

e.g. 50 kilometres per hour =
50 x 0.278 = 13.9 m/s
50 km/h = 13.9 m/s

Metres per second (m/s) to kilometres per hour (km/h)

e.g. 10 metres per second =
10 x 3.599 = 35.99 km/h
10 m/s = 35.99 km/h

International knots (kn) to kilometres per hour (km/h)

e.g. 20 international knots =
20 x 1.852 = 37.04 km/h
20 kn = 37.04 km/h

Conversion tables

The following tables can be used to convert units of speed from one measuring system to another, imperial to metric and vice versa:

- Miles per hour to Kilometres per hour
- Kilometres per hour to Miles per hour
- Yards per minute to Metres per minute
- Metres per minute to Yards per minute
- Feet per minute to Metres per minute
- Metres per minute to Feet per minute
- Inches per second to Centimetres per second
- Centimetres per second to Inches per second
- International knots to Miles per hour
- Miles per hour to International knots
- UK knots to International knots
- International knots to UK knots
- International knots to Kilometres per hour
- Kilometres per hour to International knots
- Miles per hour to Feet per second
- Feet per second to miles per hour
- Kilometres per hour to Feet per second
- Metres per second to Kilometres per hour

Speed

Miles per hour to Kilometres per hour		Kilometres per hour to Miles per hour		Yards per minute to Metres per minute	
mph	km/h	km/h	mph	ypm	m/min
1	1.609	1	0.621	1	0.914
2	3.219	2	1.242	2	1.829
3	4.828	3	1.864	3	2.743
4	6.437	4	2.485	4	3.658
5	8.047	5	3.106	5	4.572
6	9.656	6	3.728	6	5.486
7	11.265	7	4.349	7	6.401
8	12.875	8	4.970	8	7.315
9	14.484	9	5.592	9	8.230
10	16.093	10	6.213	10	9.144
20	32.187	20	12.427	20	18.288
30	48.280	30	18.641	30	27.432
40	64.374	40	24.854	40	36.576
50	80.467	50	31.068	50	45.720
60	96.561	60	37.282	60	54.864
70	112.654	70	43.495	70	64.008
80	128.748	80	49.709	80	73.152
90	144.841	90	55.923	90	82.296
100	160.934	100	62.137	100	91.440

Metres per minute to Yards per minute		Feet per minute to Metres per minute		Metres per minute to Feet per minute	
m/min	ypm	ft/min	m/min	m/min	ft/min
1	1.094	1	0.305	1	3.281
2	2.187	2	0.610	2	6.562
3	3.281	3	0.914	3	9.842
4	4.374	4	1.219	4	13.123
5	5.468	5	1.524	5	16.404
6	6.562	6	1.829	6	19.685
7	7.655	7	2.134	7	22.966
8	8.749	8	2.438	8	26.246
9	9.842	9	2.743	9	29.527
10	10.936	10	3.048	10	32.808
20	21.872	20	6.096	20	65.616
30	32.808	30	9.144	30	98.424
40	43.744	40	12.192	40	131.232
50	54.680	50	15.240	50	164.040
60	65.616	60	18.288	60	196.848
70	76.552	70	21.336	70	229.656
80	87.488	80	24.384	80	262.464
90	98.424	90	27.432	90	295.272
100	109.360	100	30.480	100	328.080

Inches per second to Centimetres per second		Centimetres per second to Inches per second		International knots to Miles per hour	
in/s	cm/s	cm/s	in/s	kn	mph
1	2.54	1	0.394	1	1.151
2	5.08	2	0.787	2	2.302
3	7.62	3	1.181	3	3.452
4	10.16	4	1.579	4	4.603
5	12.70	5	1.969	5	5.753
6	15.24	6	2.362	6	6.905
7	17.78	7	2.760	7	8.055
8	20.32	8	3.150	8	9.206
9	22.86	9	3.543	9	10.357
10	25.40	10	3.937	10	11.508
20	50.80	20	7.874	20	23.016
30	76.20	30	11.811	30	34.523
40	101.60	40	15.748	40	46.031
50	127.00	50	19.685	50	57.540
60	152.40	60	23.622	60	69.047
70	177.80	70	27.559	70	80.555
80	203.20	80	31.496	80	92.062
90	228.60	90	35.433	90	103.570
100	254.00	100	39.370	100	115.078

Miles per hour to International knots		UK knots to International knots		International knots to UK knots	
mph	kn	UK kn	kn	kn	UK kn
1	0.869	1	1.001	1	0.999
2	1.738	2	2.001	2	1.999
3	2.607	3	3.002	3	2.998
4	3.476	4	4.003	4	3.997
5	4.345	5	5.003	5	4.997
6	5.214	6	6.004	6	5.996
7	6.083	7	7.004	7	6.996
8	6.952	8	8.005	8	7.995
9	7.821	9	9.006	9	8.994
10	8.690	10	10.006	10	9.994
20	17.380	20	20.013	20	19.987
30	26.069	30	30.019	30	29.981
40	34.759	40	40.026	40	39.974
50	43.449	50	50.032	50	49.968
60	52.139	60	60.038	60	59.962
70	60.828	70	70.045	70	69.955
80	69.518	80	80.051	80	79.949
90	78.208	90	90.058	90	89.942
100	86.898	100	100.064	100	99.936

Speed

International knots to Kilometres per hour		Kilometres per hour to International knots		Miles per hour to Feet per second	
kn	km/h	km/h	kn	mph	ft/s
1	1.852	1	0.540	1	1.467
2	3.704	2	1.08	2	2.933
3	5.556	3	1.62	3	4.400
4	7.408	4	2.16	4	5.867
5	9.260	5	2.70	5	7.334
6	11.112	6	3.23	6	8.800
7	12.964	7	3.77	7	10.267
8	14.816	8	4.31	8	11.734
9	16.668	9	4.85	9	13.203
10	18.520	10	5.30	10	14.667
20	37.040	20	10.78	20	29.334
30	55.560	30	16.17	30	44.001
40	74.080	40	21.56	40	58.668
50	92.600	50	26.95	50	73.335
60	111.120	60	32.34	60	88.002
70	129.640	70	37.73	70	102.669
80	148.160	80	43.12	80	117.336
90	166.680	90	48.51	90	132.003
100	185.200	100	53.90	100	146.670

Feet per second to Miles per hour	
ft/s	mph
1	0.682
2	1.364
3	2.046
4	2.728
5	3.410
6	4.092
7	4.774
8	5.456
9	6.138
10	6.820
20	13.640
30	20.460
40	27.280
50	34.100
60	40.920
70	47.740
80	54.560
90	61.380
100	68.200

Kilometres per hour to Feet per second	
km/h	m/s
1	0.278
2	0.556
3	0.834
4	1.111
5	1.389
6	1.669
7	1.945
8	2.222
9	2.500
10	2.778
20	5.556
30	8.334
40	11.112
50	13.890
60	16.668
70	19.446
80	22.224
90	25.002
100	27.780

Metres per second to Kilometres per hour	
m/s	km/h
1	3.599
2	7.198
3	10.797
4	14.396
5	17.995
6	21.594
7	25.193
8	28.792
9	32.391
10	35.990
20	71.980
30	107.970
40	143.960
50	179.950
60	215.940
70	251.930
80	287.920
90	323.910
100	359.900

Wind speeds

Wind is the movement of air across the surface of the Earth. Its direction is determined by a combination of factors: the Earth's rotation, land features such as mountains, and variations in the temperature and pressure of the atmosphere.

Beaufort scale

Wind speed is measured using the internationally recognized Beaufort scale, named after the 19th-century British admiral, Sir Francis Beaufort.

Page 166 lists the Beaufort wind force numbers and the range of speeds to which they apply. The brief official descriptions show the variety of wind speeds that are measured, and examples of their physical manifestations are given to illustrate the strengths of their relative forces.

The effect of wind speed on air temperature is tabled on page 133.

Number	Description	km/h	mph	Characteristics
0	Calm	Below 1	Below 1	Smoke goes straight up
1	Light air	1–5	1–3	Smoke blows in wind
2	Light breeze	6–12	4–7	Wind felt on face
3	Gentle breeze	13–20	8–12	Extends a light flag
4	Moderate breeze	21–29	13–18	Raises dust and loose paper
5	Fresh breeze	30–39	19–24	Small trees begin to sway
6	Strong breeze	40–50	25–31	Umbrellas hard to use
7	Moderate gale	51–61	32–38	Inconvenient to walk into
8	Fresh gale	62–74	39–46	Twigs broken off trees
9	Strong gale	75–87	47–54	Chimney pots and slates lost
10	Whole gale	88–102	55–63	Trees uprooted
11	Storm	103–120	64–75	Widespread damage
12–17	Hurricane	Over 120	Over 75	Extremely violent

Hurricane

Intense tropical revolving storms in the Atlantic and eastern Pacific are called hurricanes, from the Carib word *hurakán* meaning 'big wind'. Similar storms in the western Pacific are called typhoons, from the Chinese word *taifun*, also written *taai fung*, meaning 'great wind'.

Saffir-Simpson scale
Wind speed alone is inadequate to describe the destructive potential of a hurricane. The Saffir-Simpson scale was designed in the 1970s to provide a more complete picture by including the storm's impact on trees, buildings, signs, coastal roads, and boats in harbours, in addition to its maximum sustained wind speed, barometric pressure and storm-surge height.

Herbert Saffir is an engineer specializing in wind damage to buildings, and Robert Simpson is a former Director of the US National Hurricane Center.

Units
In the chart below, wind speeds are given in miles per hour, metres per second, and knots (nautical miles per hour). Surface pressure is given in millibars (1 mb = 0.029 inches or 0.750 mm of mercury). Storm-surge height is given in feet and metres above mean sea level.

Storm surge
The very low pressure at the heart of a hurricane causes sea level to rise. Also, the powerful winds of a hurricane cause the sea surface to pile up ahead of the storm. The two effects combined can cause disastrous flooding when the surge hits a low-lying coastal area or is funnelled into an estuary or bay.

Hurricane categories
Category on Saffir-Simpson scale

	1	2	3	4	5
Maximum sustained wind speed					
mph	74–96	97–111	112–131	132–155	Over 156
m/s	33–43	43–50	50–58	59–69	Over 70
kn	64–83	84–97	98–114	115–135	Over 136
Minimum surface pressure					
mb	Over 980	965–979	945–964	920–944	Below 920
Storm surge					
feet	3–5	6–8	9–12	13–18	Over 18
metres	1.0–1.5	1.8–2.4	2.7–3.7	3.9–5.5	Over 5.5

1O Geometry

Polygons

	Name of polygon	Number of sides	Each internal angle	Sum of internal angles
Triangle	Triangle	3	60°	180°
Square	Square	4	90°	360°
Pentagon	Pentagon	5	108°	540°
Hexagon	Hexagon	6	120°	720°
Heptagon	Heptagon	7	128.6°	900°
Octagon	Octagon	8	135°	1080°
Nonagon	Nonagon	9	140°	1260°
Decagon	Decagon	10	144°	1440°
Undecagon	Undecagon	11	147.3°	1620°
Dodecagon	Dodecagon	12	150°	1800°

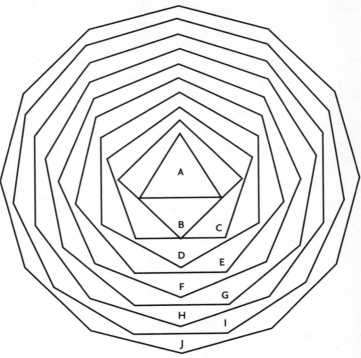

A Triangle
B Square
C Pentagon
D Hexagon

E Heptagon
F Octagon
G Nonagon
H Decagon

I Undecagon
J Dodecagon

Quadrilaterals

	Square	All the sides are the same length and all the angles are right angles.
	Rectangle	Opposite sides are the same length and all the angles are right angles.
	Rhombus	All the sides are the same length but none of the angles are right angles.
	Parallelogram	Opposite sides are parallel to each other and of the same length.
	Trapezium	One pair of the opposite sides is parallel.
	Kite	Adjacent sides are the same length and the diagonals intersect at right angles.

Triangles

	Equilateral	All the sides are the same length and all the angles are equal.
	Isosceles	Two sides are of the same length and two angles are of equal size.
	Scalene	All the sides are of different length and all the angles are of different sizes.
	Right angle	A triangle that contains one right angle.
	Obtuse angle	A triangle that contains one obtuse angle.
	Acute angle	A triangle with three acute angles.

The compass

The instrument that enables navigators to steer in any direction is called a magnetic compass. A compass also shows the direction of any visible object. It is divided into points, quarter points and degrees. North usually appears at the top.

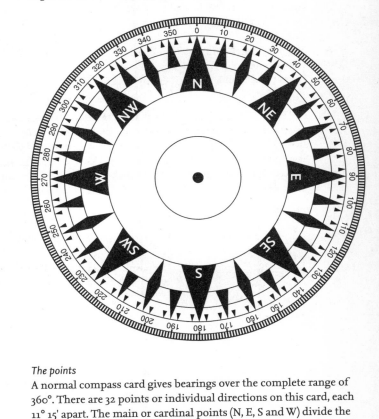

The points

A normal compass card gives bearings over the complete range of 360°. There are 32 points or individual directions on this card, each 11° 15' apart. The main or cardinal points (N, E, S and W) divide the card into four quadrants or quarters. Halfway between the cardinal points are NE, SE, SW and NW. They are called the quadrantal points. Halfway between the cardinal and quadrantal points are the intermediate points, which are named from the cardinal and quadrantal points between which they lie, the cardinal points being named first; NNE, ENE, ESE, SSE, SSW, WSW, WNW, NNW. Between all these points are 16 others (called 'by' points), named after the nearest cardinal and quadrantal points.

For example, in the first quadrant (between N and E) the points are:

The cardinal	N
The by-point next to it	N by E
The three-letter point halfway between N and E	NNE
The by-point next to the half cardinal	NE by N
The half cardinal	NE
The by-point	NE by E
The three-letter point between E and NE	ENE
The by-point	E by N
The cardinal point	E

Degrees

The compass circle is also divided into degrees. A course is usually given and steered in degrees (the Quadrantal Notation). The card is divided into 360°, but is marked 0° at North and South and 90° at East and West. NE would be given as N 45°E. Gyro compass cards are marked right round from North through 90° (East), 180° (South), 270° (West) and 360° (North). This is called Circular Notation.

Locating directions

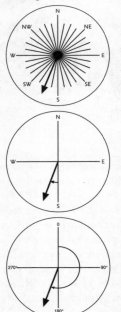

SSW bearing by points
The position is located by the compass points from North in a clockwise direction.

S22½°W bearing by degrees
The position is located by degrees from one of the four cardinal points, North, East, South or West.

202½° bearing by azimuth
The position is located from North in a clockwise direction 360° units.

Angles

The system of degrees is the most widely used system today. It was devised by the ancient Mesopotamians. The comparison of the three systems, all based on divisions of a circle, can be seen on this page. Modern mathematics favour the radian.

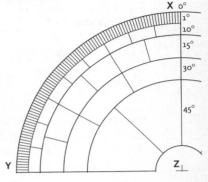

Degrees

The degree system divides the circle into 360 degrees (360°). If XY is a quarter of a circle, its angle XZY in degrees is 360 divided by four, that is 90° (known as a right angle). A semicircle has an angle of 180°.

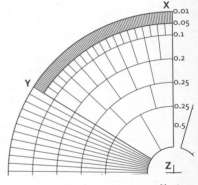

Radians

A radian is the angle at the centre of a circle that cuts off an arc on the circumference equal in length to the radius. If the arc XY equals the radii ZX and ZY, the angle XZY equals one radian (1 rad), and 1 rad equals 57.2958°.

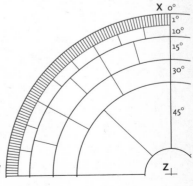

Grades

A grade, or gon, is one-hundredth of a right angle or quadrant. When XY is a quarter of the circumference, then the angle XZY is equal to 100 grades. Each circle contains 400 grades, and one grade is 0.9°.

Conversion tables

The tables below can be used to convert units of angle from one
measuring system to another. The tables show the conversion of:

- Degrees to Centrads
- Centrads to Degrees
- Degrees to Radians
- Radians to Degrees
- Radians to Grades

- Grades to Radians
- Degrees to Grades
- Grades to Degrees
- Centrads to Radians

Degrees to Centrads

°	centrad
1	1.7453
2	3.4907
3	5.2360
4	6.9813
5	8.7266
6	10.472
7	12.217
8	13.963
9	15.708
10	17.453
20	34.9065
30	52.3598
40	69.8131
50	87.2664
60	104.7197
70	122.1730
80	139.6263
90	157.0796
100	174.5328

Centrads to Degrees

centrad	°
1	0.5730
2	1.1459
3	1.7189
4	2.2918
5	2.8648
6	3.4378
7	4.0107
8	4.5837
9	5.1566
10	5.7296
20	11.4591
30	17.1887
40	22.9183
50	28.6478
60	34.3774
70	40.1070
80	45.8366
90	51.5662
100	57.2957

Degrees to Radians

°	rad
1	0.0174
2	0.0349
3	0.0523
4	0.0698
5	0.0872
6	0.1047
7	0.1221
8	0.1396
9	0.1570
10	0.1745
20	0.3490
30	0.5235
40	0.6981
50	0.8726
60	1.0471
70	1.2217
80	1.3962
90	1.5707
360	6.2830

Radians to Degrees

rad	°
1	57.2957
2	114.5915
3	171.8873
4	229.1831
5	286.4788
6	343.7746

Radians to Grades

rad	g
1	63.6619
2	127.3234
3	190.9859
4	254.6479
5	318.3098
6	381.9718

Grades to Radians

g	rad
1	0.0157
50	0.7853
100	1.5707
200	3.1412
300	4.7119
400	6.2824

Degrees to Grades

°	g
1	1.1111
2	2.2222
3	3.3333
4	4.4444
5	5.5555
6	6.6666
7	7.7777
8	8.8888
9	10
10	11.111
20	22.222
30	33.3333
40	44.4444
50	55.5555
60	66.6666
70	77.7777
80	88.8888
90	100
100	111.11

Grades to Degrees

g	°
1	0.9
2	1.8
3	2.7
4	3.6
5	4.5
6	5.4
7	6.3
8	7.2
9	8.1
10	9
20	18
30	27
40	36
50	45
60	54
70	63
80	72
90	81
100	90
400	360

Centrads to Radians

centrad	rad
1	0.01
2	0.02
3	0.03
4	0.04
5	0.05
6	0.06
7	0.07
8	0.08
9	0.09
10	0.1
20	0.2
30	0.3
40	0.4
50	0.5
60	0.6
70	0.7
80	0.8
90	0.9
100	1

11 Numbers

Standard UK paper sizes

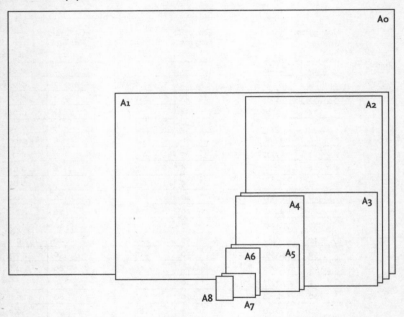

A0	841 × 1189 mm	33.11 × 46.81 in	**A5**	148 × 210 mm	5.83 × 8.27 in
A1	594 × 841 mm	23.39 × 33.11 in	**A6**	105 × 148 mm	4.13 × 5.83 in
A2	420 × 594 mm	16.54 × 23.39 in	**A7**	74 × 105 mm	2.91 × 4.13 in
A3	297 × 420 mm	11.69 × 16.54 in	**A8**	52 × 74 mm	2.05 × 2.91 in
A4	210 × 297 mm	8.27 × 11.69 in			

A	B5	176 × 250 mm	6.93 × 9.84 in
B	B4	250 × 353 mm	9.84 × 13.90 in
C	Foolscap	343 × 432 mm	13.50 × 17.00 in
D	Crown	381 × 508 mm	15.00 × 20.00 in
E	Large post	419 × 533 mm	16.50 × 21.00 in
F	Demy	445 × 572 mm	17.50 × 22.50 in
G	Medium	457 × 584 mm	18.00 × 23.00 in
H	Royal	508 × 635 mm	20.00 × 25.00 in
I	Elephant	508 × 686 mm	20.00 × 27.00 in
J	Imperial	559 × 762 mm	22.00 × 30.00 in

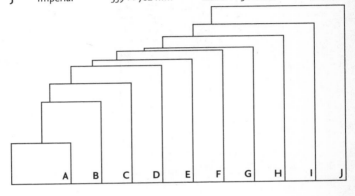

Envelope sizes and styles

Three of the most popular envelope styles are illustrated on page 178. Each style has many variations.

The primary envelope sizes are illustrated on page 177 (r); the table on page 178 gives dimensions and the styles in which each is available.

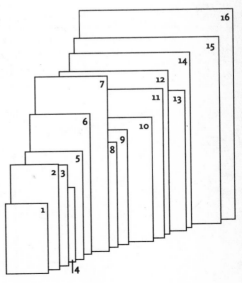

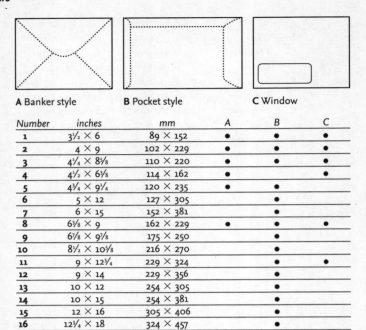

A Banker style   **B** Pocket style   **C** Window

Number	inches	mm	A	B	C
1	$3\frac{1}{2} \times 6$	89 × 152	●	●	●
2	4 × 9	102 × 229	●	●	●
3	$4\frac{1}{4} \times 8\frac{1}{8}$	110 × 220	●	●	●
4	$4\frac{1}{2} \times 6\frac{3}{8}$	114 × 162	●		●
5	$4\frac{3}{4} \times 9\frac{1}{4}$	120 × 235	●	●	
6	5 × 12	127 × 305		●	
7	6 × 15	152 × 381		●	
8	$6\frac{3}{8} \times 9$	162 × 229	●	●	●
9	$6\frac{7}{8} \times 9\frac{7}{8}$	175 × 250		●	
10	$8\frac{1}{2} \times 10\frac{5}{8}$	216 × 270		●	
11	$9 \times 12\frac{3}{4}$	229 × 324		●	●
12	9 × 14	229 × 356		●	
13	10 × 12	254 × 305		●	
14	10 × 15	254 × 381		●	
15	12 × 16	305 × 406		●	
16	$12\frac{3}{4} \times 18$	324 × 457		●	

Clothing sizes

UK clothing sizes are equal to US sizes for some items, such as children's shoes; for others, the two vary slightly. The European equivalents of UK and US clothing and shoe sizes are on pages 178 and 179. Remember also that sizes vary depending on the manufacturer.

Men's shoes

UK	USA	Europe
$6\frac{1}{2}$	7	39
7	$7\frac{1}{2}$	40
$7\frac{1}{2}$	8	41
8	$8\frac{1}{2}$	42
$8\frac{1}{2}$	9	43
9	$9\frac{1}{2}$	43
$9\frac{1}{2}$	10	44
10	$10\frac{1}{2}$	44
$10\frac{1}{2}$	11	45

Women's shoes

UK	USA	Europe
$3\frac{1}{2}$	5	36
$4\frac{1}{2}$	6	37
$5\frac{1}{2}$	7	38
$6\frac{1}{2}$	8	39
$7\frac{1}{2}$	9	40

Children's shoes

UK/USA	Europe
0	15
1	17
2	18
3	19
4	20
$4^1/_2$	21
5	22
6	23
7	24
8	25
$8^1/_2$	26
9	27
10	28
11	29
12	30
$12^1/_2$	31
13	32

Men's socks

UK/USA	Europe
9	38–39
10	39–40
$10^1/_2$	40–41
11	41–42
$11^1/_2$	42–43

Men's suits/overcoats

UK/USA	Europe
36	46
38	48
40	50
42	52
44	54
46	56

Men's shirts

UK/USA	Europe
12	30–31
$12^1/_2$	32
13	33
$13^1/_2$	34–35
14	36
$14^1/_2$	37
15	38
$15^1/_2$	39–40
16	41
$16^1/_2$	42
17	43
$17^1/_2$	44–45

Women's clothing

UK	USA	Europe
8	6	36
10	8	38
12	10	40
14	12	42
16	14	44
18	16	46
20	18	48
22	20	50
24	22	52

Children's clothing

UK	USA	Europe
16–18	2	40–45
20–22	4	50–55
24–26	6	60–65
28–30	7	70–75
32–34	8	80–85
36–38	9	90–95

Body measurements

The standard body measurements shown in the diagram below are those needed for garment fitting. Below are a few tips on taking some of these measurements.

Neck Measure at the fullest part.

Chest/bust Measure at the fullest part of the bust or chest and straight across the back.

Waist Tie a string around the thinnest part of your body (the waist) and leave it there as a point of reference for other measurements.

Hips There are two places to measure hips, depending on the garment: one is 2–4 inches below the waist, at the top of the hipbones; the other is at the fullest part, usually 7–9 inches below.

Arm Measure at the fullest part, usually about 1 inch below the armpit.

Arm length Start at the shoulder bone and continue past the elbow to the wrist, with the arm slightly bent.

Back Measure from the prominent bone in the back of the neck down the centre to the waist string.

a height
b head
c neck
d chest/bust
e waist
f hips
g thigh
h calf
i arm
j wrist
k arm length
l armpit to hip
m outside leg
n inside leg
o back

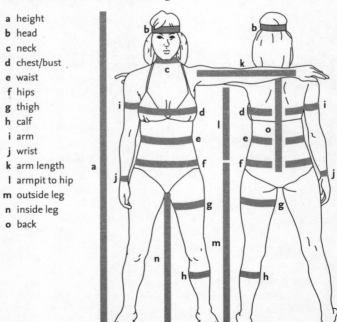

Gun gauge

A shotgun bore (diameter) is expressed in terms of gauge. Gauge was originally determined by the number of round lead balls – each the size of the shotgun bore – in a pound. For example, a 10-gauge shotgun was one that used balls that were 10 to the pound. The exception is the 410 bore, which is measured in inches: 410 in diameter, using 67.5 gauge. The most common size today is the 12-gauge.

The table below shows gauge and equivalent bore size.

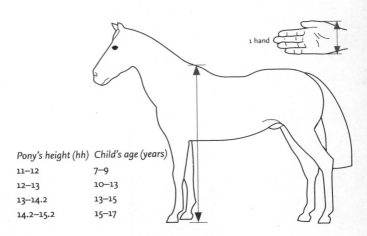

	A	B	C	D	E	F
Gauge	6	10	12	14	16	20
Bore (mm)	23.34	19.67	18.52	17.60	16.81	15.90

Horse measurements

The height of a horse or pony is measured to its withers (on the highest point of its back at the base of the neck), as shown below. Height is expressed in 'hands high' (hh). One hand is 4 in (10 cm), the average width of a person's hand. Height is given to the nearest inch – a pony measuring 50 in (127 cm) is said to measure 12.2 hands. The table below shows recommended heights of ponies for young riders.

1 hand

Pony's height (hh)	Child's age (years)
11–12	7–9
12–13	10–13
13–14.2	13–15
14.2–15.2	15–17

Numbers

Named numbers

Many numbers have names. Some names for specialized numbers have the same prefix. The prefix indicates the number to which the name refers, and is usually derived from the Latin or Greek word for that number.

Everyday use

¹⁄₁₀	Tithe	12	Dozen	50	Half century
2	Pair, couple, brace	13	Baker's dozen	100	Century
6	Half a dozen	20	Score	144	Gross

Musicians

1	Soloist	4	Quartet	7	Septet
2	Duo	5	Quintet	8	Octet
3	Trio	6	Sextet		

Multiple births

2	Twins	4	Quadruplets	5	Quintuplets (quins)
3	Triplets		(quads)	6	Sextuplets

Slang for money

£25	Pony	£500	Monkey
£100	Century	£1000	Grand

Numerical prefixes

Prefixes in numerical order

¹⁄₁₀	Deci-	4	Tetr-, tessera-, quadr-	9	Non-, ennea-
½	Semi-, hemi-, demi-	5	Pent-, quin-	10	Dec-
1	Uni-	6	Sex-, hex-	11	Hendeca-, undec-,
2	Bi-, di-	7	Hept-, sept-	12	Dodeca-
3	Tri-, ter-	8	Oct-	15	Quindeca-
				20	Icos-

Prefixes in alphabetical order

Bi-	2	Hex-	6	Sept-	7
Dec-, deca-	10	Icos-	20	Sex-	6
Deci-	¹⁄₁₀	Non-	9	Ter-	3
Demi-	½	Oct-	8	Tessera-	4
Di-	2	Pent-	5	Tetr-	4
Dodeca-	12	Quadr-	4	Tri-	3
Ennea-	9	Quindeca-	15	Undec-	11
Hemi-	½	Quinqu-	5	Uni-	1
Hendeca-	11	Quint-	5		
Hept-	7	Semi-	½		

Prefixes in order of value

*Atto-	0.000 000 000 000 000 001
*Femto-	0.000 000 000 000 001
*Pico-	0.000 000 000 001
*Nano-	0.000 000 001
*Micro-	0.000 001
*Milli-	0.001
*Centi-	0.01
*Deci-	0.1
Semi-, hemi-, demi-	0.5
Uni-	1
Bi-, di-	2
Tri-, ter-	3
Tetr-, tessera-, quadr-	4
Pent-, quin-	5
Sex-, hex-	6
Hept-, sept-	7
Oct-	8
Non-, ennea-	9
Dec-	10
Hendeca-, undec-	11
Dodeca-	12
Quindeca-	15
Icos-	20
Hect-	100
*Kilo-	1000
Myria-	10 000
*Mega-	1 000 000
*Giga-	1 000 000 000
*Tera-	1 000 000 000 000

* Approved for use with the SI system.

Roman numerals

The Roman number system a method of notation in which the capitals are modelled on ancient Roman inscriptions. The numerals are represented by seven capital letters of the alphabet:

I	one	L	fifty	M	one thousand
V	five	C	one hundred		
X	ten	D	five hundred		

These letters are the foundation of the system; they are combined in order to form all numbers. If a letter is preceded by another of lesser value (e.g. IX), the value of the combined form is the difference between the values of each letter (e.g. IX = X (10) – I (1) = 9).

To determine the value of a string of Roman numbers (letters), find the pairs in the string (those beginning with a lower value) and determine their values, then add these to the values of the other letters in the string:

MCMXCI
= M + CM + XC + I
= 1000 + 900 + 90 + 1 = 1991

A dash over a letter multiplies the value by 1000 (e.g. $\bar{V}$ = 5000).

1	I	12	XII	35	XXXV	100	C
2	II	13	XIII	40	XL	200	CC
3	III	14	XIV	45	XLV	300	CCC
4	IV or IIII	15	XV	50	L	400	CD
5	V	16	XVI	55	LV	500	D
6	VI	17	XVII	60	LX	600	DC
7	VII	18	XVIII	65	LXV	700	DCC
8	VIII	19	XIX	70	LXX	800	DCCC
9	IX	20	XX	75	LXXV	900	CM
10	X	25	XXV	80	LXXX	1000	M
11	XI	30	XXX	90	XC	2000	MM

Prime numbers

Prime numbers are whole numbers that have only two factors – the number itself and the number 1. The only even prime number is 2: all other prime numbers are odd. There are an infinite number of prime numbers. The first 126 are given below. The largest number found and proved to date (2004) has over 7 million digits. It is a Mersenne prime, and there have now only been 41 of this sort found.

2	47	109	191	269	353	439	523	617
3	53	113	193	271	359	443	541	619
5	59	127	197	277	367	449	547	631
7	61	131	199	281	373	457	557	641
11	67	137	211	283	379	461	563	643
13	71	139	223	293	383	463	569	647
17	73	149	227	307	389	467	571	653
19	79	151	229	311	397	479	577	659
23	83	157	233	313	401	487	587	661
29	89	163	239	317	409	491	593	673
31	97	167	241	331	419	499	599	677
37	101	173	251	337	421	503	601	683
41	103	179	257	347	431	509	607	691
43	107	181	263	349	433	521	613	701

Fibonacci sequence

Each number in a Fibonacci sequence is the sum of the two numbers preceding it. The sequence can therefore be built using simple addition. Below is an example of a Fibonacci sequence.

$$0 + 1 = 1$$
$$1 + 1 = 2$$
$$2 + 1 = 3$$
$$3 + 2 = 5$$
$$5 + 3 = 8$$
$$8 + 5 = 13$$
$$13 + 8 = 21$$
$$21 + 13 = 34$$
$$34 + 21 = 55$$
$$55 + 34 = 89$$
$$89 + 55 = 144$$
$$144 + 89 = 233$$
$$233 + 144 = 377$$
$$377 + 233 = 610$$
$$610 + 377 = 987$$

$$987 + 610 = 1597$$
$$1597 + 987 = 2584$$
$$2584 + 1597 = 4181$$
$$4181 + 2584 = 6765$$
$$6765 + 4181 = 10\ 946$$
$$10\ 946 + 6765 = 17\ 711$$
$$17\ 711 + 10\ 946 = 28\ 657$$
$$28\ 657 + 17\ 711 = 46\ 368$$
$$46\ 368 + 28\ 657 = 75\ 025$$
$$75\ 025 + 46\ 368 = 121\ 393$$
$$121\ 393 + 75\ 025. = 196\ 418$$
$$196\ 418 + 121\ 39 = 317\ 811$$
$$317\ 811 + 196\ 418 = 514\ 229$$
$$514\ 229 + 317\ 811 = 832\ 040$$
$$832\ 040 + 514\ 229 = 1\ 346\ 269$$

Numbers

Fractions, decimals and percentages

Fraction	Decimal	Percentage
1/9	0.111 111	11.11%
1/7	0.142 857	14.29%
1/6	0.166 667	16.67%
1/5	0.2	20.00%
2/9	0.222 222	22.22%
2/7	0.285 714	28.58%
3/9 2/6 1/3	0.333 333	33.33%
2/5	0.4	40.00%
3/7	0.428 571	42.86%
4/9	0.444 444	44.44%
5/9	0.555 555	55.56%
4/7	0.571 429	57.14%
3/5	0.6	60.00%
6/9 4/6 2/3	0.666 666	66.67%
5/7	0.714 286	71.43%
7/9	0.777 778	77.78%
4/5	0.8	80.00%
5/6	0.833 333	83.33%
6/7	0.857 143	85.71%
8/9	0.888 889	88.89%
9/9 7/7 6/6 5/5 3/3	1	100.00%
1/64	0.015 625	1.56%
2/64 1/32	0.031 25	3.13%
3/64	0.046 875	4.69%
4/64 2/32 1/16	0.062 5	6.25%
5/64	0.078 125	7.81%
6/64 3/32	0.093 75	9.38%
7/64	0.109 375	10.94%
8/64 4/32 2/16 1/8	0.125	12.50%

Fraction	Decimal	Percentage
9/64	0.140 625	14.06%
10/64 5/32	0.156 25	15.63%
11/64	0.171 875	17.19%
12/64 6/32 3/16	0.187 5	18.75%
13/64	0.203 125	20.31%
14/64 7/32	0.218 75	21.88%
15/64	0.234 375	23.44%
16/64 8/32 4/16 2/8 1/4	0.25	25.00%
17/64	0.265 625	26.56%
18/64 9/32	0.281 25	28.13%
19/64	0.296 875	29.69%
20/64 10/32 5/16	0.312 5	31.25%
21/64	0.328 125	32.81%
22/64 11/32	0.343 75	34.38%
24/64 12/32 6/16 3/8	0.375	37.50%
25/64	0.390 625	39.06%
26/64 13/32	0.406 25	40.63%
27/64	0.421 875	42.19%
28/64 14/32 7/16	0.437 5	43.75%
29/64	0.453 125	45.31%
30/64 15/32	0.468 75	46.88%
31/64	0.484 375	48.44%
32/64 16/32 8/16 4/8 2/4 1/2	0.5	50.00%
33/64	0.515 625	51.56%
34/64 17/32	0.531 25	53.13%
35/64	0.546 875	54.69%
36/64 18/32 9/16	0.562 5	56.25%
37/64	0.578 125	57.81%

Fraction	Decimal	Percentage
$\frac{38}{64}$ $\frac{19}{32}$	0.593 75	59.37%
$\frac{39}{64}$	0.609 375	60.94%
$\frac{40}{64}$ $\frac{20}{32}$ $\frac{10}{16}$		
$\frac{5}{8}$	0.625	62.50%
$\frac{41}{64}$	0.640 625	64.06%
$\frac{42}{64}$ $\frac{21}{32}$	0.656 25	65.63%
$\frac{43}{64}$	0.671 875	67.19%
$\frac{44}{64}$ $\frac{22}{32}$ $\frac{11}{16}$	0.687 5	68.75%
$\frac{45}{64}$	0.703 125	70.31%
$\frac{46}{64}$ $\frac{23}{32}$	0.718 75	71.88%
$\frac{47}{64}$	0.734 375	73.44%
$\frac{48}{64}$ $\frac{24}{32}$ $\frac{12}{16}$		
$\frac{6}{8}$ $\frac{3}{4}$	0.75	75.00%
$\frac{49}{64}$	0.765 625	76.56%
$\frac{50}{64}$ $\frac{25}{32}$	0.781 25	78.13%
$\frac{51}{64}$	0.796 875	79.69%

Fraction	Decimal	Percentage
$\frac{52}{64}$ $\frac{26}{32}$ $\frac{13}{16}$	0.812 5	81.25%
$\frac{53}{64}$	0.828 125	82.81%
$\frac{54}{64}$ $\frac{27}{32}$	0.843 75	84.38%
$\frac{55}{64}$	0.859 375	85.94%
$\frac{56}{64}$ $\frac{28}{32}$ $\frac{14}{16}$		
$\frac{7}{8}$	0.875	87.50%
$\frac{57}{64}$	0.890 625	89.06%
$\frac{58}{64}$ $\frac{29}{32}$	0.906 25	90.63%
$\frac{59}{64}$	0.921 875	92.19%
$\frac{60}{64}$ $\frac{30}{32}$ $\frac{15}{16}$	0.937 5	93.75%
$\frac{61}{64}$	0.953 125	95.31%
$\frac{62}{64}$ $\frac{31}{32}$	0.968 75	96.88%
$\frac{63}{64}$	0.984 375	98.44%
$\frac{64}{64}$ $\frac{32}{32}$ $\frac{16}{16}$		
$\frac{8}{8}$ $\frac{4}{4}$ $\frac{2}{2}$	1	100.00%

Square and cube roots*

Square and cube roots of 1 to 34

	$\sqrt{}$	$\sqrt[3]{}$
1	1.000	1.000
2	1.414	1.259
3	1.732	1.442
4	2.000	1.587
5	2.236	1.709
6	2.449	1.817
7	2.645	1.912
8	2.828	2.000
9	3.000	2.080
10	3.162	2.154
11	3.316	2.223
12	3.464	2.289
13	3.605	2.351
14	3.741	2.410
15	3.873	2.466
16	4.000	2.519
17	4.123	2.571
18	4.242	2.620
19	4.358	2.668
20	4.472	2.714
21	4.582	2.758
22	4.690	2.802
23	4.795	2.843
24	4.899	2.884
25	5.000	2.924
26	5.099	2.962
27	5.196	3.000
28	5.291	3.036
29	5.385	3.072
30	5.477	3.107
31	5.567	3.141
32	5.656	3.174
33	5.744	3.207
34	5.831	3.239

Square and cube roots of 35 to 68

	$\sqrt{}$	$\sqrt[3]{}$
35	5.916	3.271
36	6.000	3.301
37	6.082	3.332
38	6.164	3.361
39	6.245	3.391
40	6.324	3.419
41	6.403	3.448
42	6.480	3.476
43	6.557	3.503
44	6.633	3.530
45	6.708	3.556
46	6.782	3.583
47	6.855	3.608
48	6.928	3.634
49	7.000	3.659
50	7.071	3.684
51	7.141	3.708
52	7.211	3.732
53	7.280	3.756
54	7.348	3.779
55	7.416	3.802
56	7.483	3.825
57	7.549	3.848
58	7.615	3.870
59	7.681	3.893
60	7.746	3.913
61	7.810	3.936
62	7.874	3.957
63	7.937	3.979
64	8.000	4.000
65	8.062	4.020
66	8.124	4.041
67	8.185	4.061
68	8.246	4.081

Square and cube roots of 69 to 100

	$\sqrt{}$	$\sqrt[3]{}$
69	8.306	4.101
70	8.366	4.121
71	8.426	4.140
72	8.485	4.160
73	8.544	4.179
74	8.602	4.198
75	8.660	4.217
76	8.717	4.235
77	8.775	4.254
78	8.831	4.272
79	8.888	4.290
80	8.944	4.308
81	9.000	4.326
82	9.055	4.344
83	9.110	4.362
84	9.165	4.379
85	9.219	4.396
86	9.273	4.414
87	9.327	4.431
88	9.380	4.447
89	9.434	4.464
90	9.486	4.481
91	9.539	4.497
92	9.591	4.514
93	9.643	4.530
94	9.695	4.546
95	9.746	4.562
96	9.798	4.578
97	9.848	4.594
98	9.899	4.610
99	9.949	4.626
100	10.000	4.641

*Accurate to 3 decimal places.

Multiplication tables

x 2	
1	2
2	4
3	6
4	8
5	10
6	12
7	14
8	16
9	18
10	20
11	22
12	24
13	26
14	28
15	30
16	32
17	34
18	36
19	38
25	50
35	70
45	90
55	110
65	130
75	150
85	170
95	190

x 3	
1	3
2	6
3	9
4	12
5	15
6	18
7	21
8	24
9	27
10	30
11	33
12	36
13	39
14	42
15	45
16	48
17	51
18	54
19	57
25	75
35	105
45	135
55	165
65	195
75	225
85	255
95	285

x 4	
1	4
2	8
3	12
4	16
5	20
6	24
7	28
8	32
9	36
10	40
11	44
12	48
13	52
14	56
15	60
16	64
17	68
18	72
19	76
25	100
35	140
45	180
55	220
65	260
75	300
85	340
95	380

Numbers

Multiplication tables (continued)

x 5	
1	5
2	10
3	15
4	20
5	25
6	30
7	35
8	40
9	45
10	50
11	55
12	60
13	65
14	70
15	75
16	80
17	85
18	90
19	95
25	125
35	175
45	225
55	275
65	325
75	375
85	425
95	475

x 6	
1	6
2	12
3	18
4	24
5	30
6	36
7	42
8	48
9	54
10	60
11	66
12	72
13	78
14	84
15	90
16	96
17	102
18	108
19	114
25	150
35	210
45	270
55	330
65	390
75	450
85	510
95	570

x 7	
1	7
2	14
3	21
4	28
5	35
6	42
7	49
8	56
9	63
10	70
11	77
12	84
13	91
14	98
15	105
16	112
17	119
18	126
19	133
25	175
35	245
45	315
55	385
65	455
75	525
85	595
95	665

x 8	
1	8
2	16
3	24
4	32
5	40
6	48
7	56
8	64
9	72
10	80
11	88
12	96
13	104
14	112
15	120
16	128
17	136
18	144
19	152
25	200
35	280
45	360
55	440
65	520
75	600
85	680
95	760

x 9	
1	9
2	18
3	27
4	36
5	45
6	54
7	63
8	72
9	81
10	90
11	99
12	108
13	117
14	126
15	135
16	144
17	153
18	162
19	171
25	225
35	315
45	405
55	495
65	585
75	675
85	765
95	855

x 10	
1	10
2	20
3	30
4	40
5	50
6	60
7	70
8	80
9	90
10	100
11	110
12	120
13	130
14	140
15	150
16	160
17	170
18	180
19	190
25	250
35	350
45	450
55	550
65	650
75	750
85	850
95	950

Multiplication tables (continued)

X 11		X 12		X 13	
1	11	1	12	1	13
2	22	2	24	2	26
3	33	3	36	3	39
4	44	4	48	4	52
5	55	5	60	5	65
6	66	6	72	6	78
7	77	7	84	7	91
8	88	8	96	8	104
9	99	9	108	9	117
10	110	10	120	10	130
11	121	11	132	11	143
12	132	12	144	12	156
13	143	13	156	13	169
14	154	14	168	14	182
15	165	15	180	15	195
16	176	16	192	16	208
17	187	17	204	17	221
18	198	18	216	18	234
19	209	19	228	19	247
25	275	25	300	25	325
35	385	35	420	35	455
45	495	45	540	45	585
55	605	55	660	55	715
65	715	65	780	65	845
75	825	75	900	75	975
85	935	85	1020	85	1105
95	1045	95	1140	95	1235

	x 14
1	14
2	28
3	42
4	56
5	70
6	84
7	98
8	112
9	126
10	140
11	154
12	168
13	182
14	196
15	210
16	224
17	238
18	252
19	266
25	350
35	490
45	630
55	770
65	910
75	1050
85	1190
95	1330

	x 15
1	15
2	30
3	45
4	60
5	75
6	90
7	105
8	120
9	135
10	150
11	165
12	180
13	195
14	210
15	225
16	240
17	255
18	270
19	285
25	375
35	525
45	675
55	825
65	975
75	1125
85	1275
95	1425

	x 16
1	16
2	32
3	48
4	64
5	80
6	96
7	112
8	128
9	144
10	160
11	176
12	192
13	208
14	224
15	240
16	256
17	272
18	288
19	304
25	400
35	560
45	720
55	880
65	1040
75	1200
85	1360
95	1520

Multiplication tables (continued)

x 17		x 18		x 19	
1	17	1	18	1	9
2	34	2	36	2	38
3	51	3	54	3	57
4	68	4	72	4	76
5	85	5	90	5	95
6	102	6	108	6	114
7	119	7	126	7	133
8	136	8	144	8	152
9	153	9	162	9	171
10	170	10	180	10	190
11	187	11	198	11	209
12	204	12	216	12	228
13	221	13	234	13	247
14	238	14	252	14	266
15	255	15	270	15	285
16	272	16	288	16	304
17	289	17	306	17	323
18	306	18	324	18	342
19	323	19	342	19	361
25	425	25	450	25	475
35	595	35	630	35	665
45	765	45	810	45	855
55	935	55	990	55	1045
65	1105	65	1170	65	1235
75	1275	75	1350	75	1425
85	1445	85	1530	85	1615
95	1615	95	1710	95	1805

Multiplication grid

Below is a quick-reference grid giving products and quotients. It can be used for multiplication or for division.

	Column											
Row	**1**	**2**	**3**	**4**	**5**	**6**	**7**	**8**	**9**	**10**	**11**	**12**
1	1	2	3	4	5	6	7	8	9	10	11	12
2	2	4	6	8	10	12	14	16	18	20	22	24
3	3	6	9	12	15	18	21	24	27	30	33	36
4	4	8	12	16	20	24	28	32	36	40	44	48
5	5	10	15	20	25	30	35	40	45	50	55	60
6	6	12	18	24	30	36	42	48	54	60	66	72
7	7	14	21	28	35	42	49	56	63	70	77	84
8	8	16	24	32	40	48	56	64	72	80	88	96
9	9	18	27	36	45	54	63	72	81	90	99	108
10	10	20	30	40	50	60	70	80	90	100	110	120
11	11	22	33	44	55	66	77	88	99	110	121	132
12	12	24	36	48	60	72	84	96	108	120	132	144

Multiplication

To multiply 6 by 9, for example, scan down column six until you reach row nine. The number in the square where column six intersects row nine is the product, 54.

Division

To divide 56 by 8, scan down column eight to find 56 (the dividend) then scan across to find the row number. This is the quotient, 7.

Mathematical symbols

$+$	plus or positive		$\geqslant$	greater than or equal to
$-$	minus or negative		$\leqslant$	less than or equal to
$\pm$	plus or minus, positive or negative		$\gg$	much greater than
$\times$	multiplied by		$\ll$	much less than
$\div$	divided by		$\sqrt{}$	square root
$=$	equal to		∞	infinity
$\equiv$	identically equal to		$\propto$	proportional to
$\neq$	not equal to		$\sum$	sum of
$\not\equiv$	not identically equal to		$\prod$	product of
$\approx$	approximately equal to		Δ	difference
$\sim$	of the order of or similar to		$\therefore$	therefore
$>$	greater than		$\angle$	angle
$<$	less than		$\parallel$	parallel to
$\not>$	not greater than		$\perp$	perpendicular to
$\not<$	not less than		$:$	is to

Arithmetic operations

The four basic arithmetic operations are addition, subtraction, multiplication and division. Each part of an arithmetic operation has a specific name.

Addition

29 Addend
+6 Addend
---
35 Sum

Subtraction

74 Minuend
-16 Subtrahend
---
58 Difference

Multiplication

46 Multiplicand
x9 Multiplier
---
414 Product

Division

```
       ___ Divisor
       3     Quotient
   ___
13) 44      Dividend
   39
   ___
    5     Remainder
```

Fraction

$5/8$ $\dfrac{5}{8}$ Numerator
Denominator

Simple (or vulgar) fraction

$9/7$ $\dfrac{9}{7}$ Numerator
Denominator

Astronomy

Planetary features

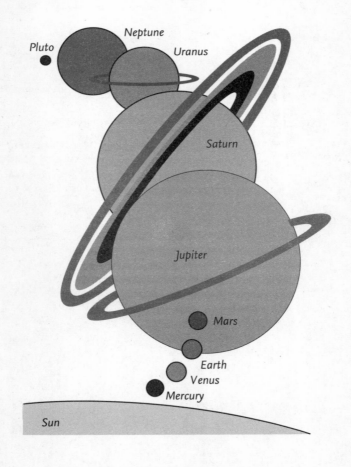

Pluto

Neptune

Uranus

Saturn

Jupiter

Mars

Earth

Venus

Mercury

Sun

Diameter at equator

Planet	km	mi
Mercury	4878	2926.8
Venus	12 104	7262.4
Earth	12 756	7653.6
Mars	6795	4077.0
Jupiter	142 800	85 680.0
Saturn	120 000	72 000.0
Uranus	50 800	30 480.0
Neptune	48 500	29 100.0
Pluto	3000	1800.0

Rotation period

Mercury	58 days	15 hr	
Venus	243 days		
Earth		23 hr	56 min
Mars		24 hr	37 min
Jupiter		9 hr	50 min
Saturn		10 hr	14 min
Uranus		16 hr	10 min
Neptune		18 hr	26 min
Pluto	6 days	9 hr	

Average surface temperatures

Solid surface

Mercury	350 °C (day)
	−170 °C (night)
Venus	480 °C
Earth	22 °C
Mars	−23 °C

Cloud surface

Jupiter	−150 °C
Saturn	−180 °C
Uranus	−210 °C
Neptune	−220 °C
Pluto	−230 °C

Planetary distances

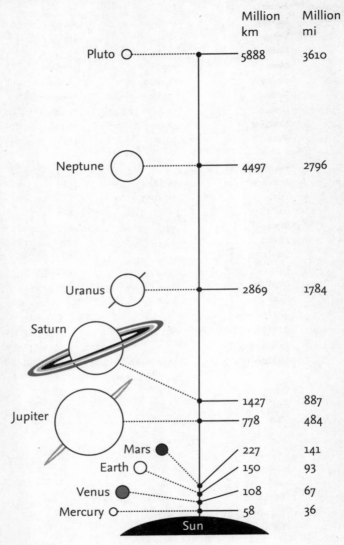

	Million km	Million mi
Pluto	5888	3610
Neptune	4497	2796
Uranus	2869	1784
Saturn	1427	887
Jupiter	778	484
Mars	227	141
Earth	150	93
Venus	108	67
Mercury	58	36
Sun		

Mean distance from the Sun

Planet	km	mi
Mercury	58 000 000	36 000 000
Venus	108 000 000	67 000 000
Earth	150 000 000	93 000 000
Mars	227 000 000	141 000 000
Jupiter	778 000 000	484 000 000
Saturn	1 427 000 000	887 000 000
Uranus	2 869 000 000	1 784 000 000
Neptune	4 497 000 000	2 796 000 000
Pluto	5 888 000 000	3 661 000 000

Closest distance to the Earth

Planet	km	mi
Mercury	80 800 000	50 000 000
Venus	40 400 000	25 000 000
Mars	56 800 000	35 000 000
Jupiter	591 000 000	367 000 000
Saturn	1 198 000 000	744 000 000
Uranus	2 585 000 000	1 607 000 000
Pluto	4 297 000 000	2 670 000 000
Neptune	4 308 000 000	2 678 000 000

All of the planets have eliptical orbits which means that their distances
from the Sun vary. Pluto has the most eccentric orbit. For about 20
years of each of its 248-year orbits it is closer to the Sun than Neptune.

Sidereal period

Sidereal period is the time it takes a planet to orbit the Sun. Planets' orbital speeds vary, as does the distance of each from the Sun, so the sidereal period is different for each planet. The diagram opposite shows how far each planet travels in its orbit during the time it takes the Earth to complete one orbit (approximately 1 year).

		Sidereal period	*Average orbital speed*
A	Mercury	88.0 days	47.9 km/s
B	Venus	224.7 days	35.0 km/s
C	Earth	365.3 days	29.8 km/s
D	Mars	687.0 days	24.1 km/s
E	Jupiter	11.86 years	13.1 km/s
F	Saturn	29.46 years	9.6 km/s
G	Uranus	84.01 years	6.8 km/s
H	Neptune	164.8 years	5.4 km/s
I	Pluto	247.7 years	4.7 km/s

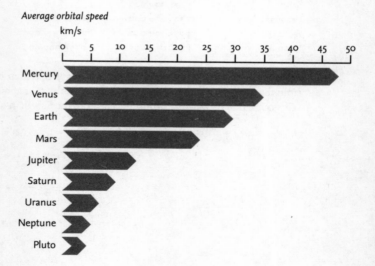

The solar system: orbits and rotations

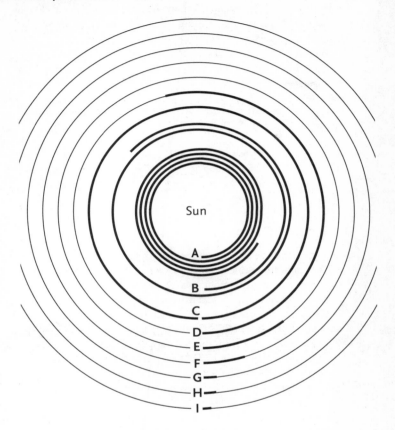

The above diagram shows planet Mercury (A) doing more than four orbits of the Sun to Earth's one (C). The most distant planet, Pluto (I), does about 0.004 orbits of the Sun to Earth's one.

Light years

The table below lists standard abbreviations and equivalents for the units used in measuring astronomical distances. These are very large units and are related to the Earth's orbit.

A light year (ly) is the distance light travels – at its speed of 299 792.458 km/s – through space over a tropical year (see page 137).

An astronomical unit (AU) is the mean distance between the Earth and the Sun.

A parsec (pc) is the distance at which a baseline of 1 au in length subtends an angle of 1 second.

1 AU	=	149 600 000 km	=	93 000 000 mi
1 ly	=	9 460 500 000 000 km	=	5 878 000 000 000 mi
1 pc	=	30 857 200 000 000 km	=	19 174 000 000 000 mi
1 ly	=	63 240 AU		
1 pc	=	206 265 AU	=	3.262 ly

Stellar magnitudes

Stellar magnitude is a measure of the brightness of a star.

The magnitude scale has no units. It simply assigns a number to a star. The greater the number, the fainter the star.

The magnitude scale is logarithmic. Most logarithmic scales, such as the Richter scale for measuring earthquakes, step up in factors of ten so that a measure of 5 is ten times greater than a measure of 4. The magnitude scale steps down in factors of about 2.5, so that a magnitude 5 star is 2.5 times dimmer than a magnitude 4 star.

The brightest stars in the sky have negative magnitudes.

Apparent magnitude is a measure of how bright a star appears when observed from Earth.

Absolute magnitude is a measure of how bright a star would appear if it were observed from a distance of 10 parsecs (32.6 light years).

A star with a high apparent magnitude may have a low absolute magnitude. Its brightness in the night sky is due more to its proximity than its inherent luminosity.

The ten nearest stars

	Name	Constellation	Apparent magnitude
1	Proxima Centauri	Centaurus	+11.1
2	Alpha Centauri	Centaurus	-0.01
3	Barnard's Star	Ophiuchus	+9.5
4	Wolf 358	Leo	+13.6
5	Lalande 21185	Ursa Major	+7.7
6	Luyten 726-8	Cetus	+12.3
7	Sirius	Canis Major	-1.44
8	Ross 154	Sagittarius	+10.5
9	Ross 248	Andromeda	+12.2
10	Epsilon Eridani	Eridanus	+3.7

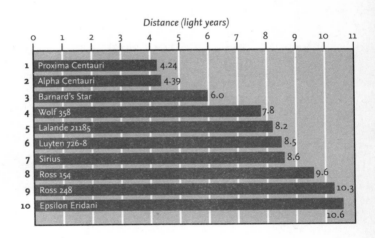

Distance (light years)

		Distance (light years)
1	Proxima Centauri	4.24
2	Alpha Centauri	4.39
3	Barnard's Star	6.0
4	Wolf 358	7.8
5	Lalande 21185	8.2
6	Luyten 726-8	8.5
7	Sirius	8.6
8	Ross 154	9.6
9	Ross 248	10.3
10	Epsilon Eridani	10.6

13 Food

Cooking measurements

The tables below give cup and spoonful measures with UK imperial, US imperial and metric unit equivalents. *See also* Cooking measures in the Volume chapter on page 106.

UK cups and spoonfuls

Cups/spoonfuls		UK imperial		Metric
2 cups	=	1 pint	=	568 ml
1 cup	=	10 fl oz	=	284 ml
½ cup	=	1 gill or 5 fl oz	=	142 ml
	=	10 tablespoons		
1 tablespoon	=	½ fl oz	=	15 ml
	=	3 teaspoons		
1 teaspoon	=	⅙ fl oz	=	5 ml

US cups and spoonfuls

Cups/spoonfuls		US imperial		Metric
2 cups	=	1 pint	=	473 ml
1 cup	=	8 fl oz	=	237 ml
½ cup	=	1 gill or 4 fl oz	=	118 ml
	=	8 tablespoons		
1 tablespoon	=	½ fl oz	=	15 ml
	=	3 teaspoons		
1 teaspoon	=	⅙ fl oz	=	5 ml

Spoonful equivalents for ingredients

The table below gives the number of level tablespoons needed to measure approximately 30 g or 1 oz of various ingredients.

Common ingredients measured in spoonfuls
Tablespoons (tbsp) needed for 30 g or 1 oz (UK imperial) of an ingredient

Breadcrumbs	dried	3 tbsp
	fresh	7 tbsp
Butter		2 tbsp
Cheese	(grated cheddar)	3 tbsp
	(grated parmesan)	4 tbsp
Cocoa		4 tbsp
Coffee	ground	4½ tbsp
	instant	6½ tbsp
Cornflour		2¾ tbsp
Custard powder		2¾ tbsp
Flour	(unsifted)	3 tbsp
Gelatine	(powdered)	3 tbsp
Honey		1 tbsp
Lard		2 tbsp
Margarine		2 tbsp
Milk	(powdered, dried, skimmed)	5 tbsp
Parsley	(freshly chopped)	10 tbsp
Rice	uncooked	2 tbsp
Suet	shredded	3 tbsp
Sugar	(caster, demerara, granulated)	2 tbsp
Sugar	icing	3 tbsp
Syrup		1 tbsp
Yeast (dried)		2 tbsp

Kitchen weights

UK imperial to metric conversions

The imperial pound (lb) equals 16 ounces (oz), which is equal to 0.454 kilograms (kg) – slightly less than ½ kilogram (500 g).

1 lb or 16 oz	=	0.454 kg or 454 g
½ lb or 8 oz	=	0.227 kg or 227 g
¼ lb or 4 oz	=	0.113 kg or 113 g
1 oz	=	28 g

Approximate conversions for kitchen use

Imperial	Metric	Imperial	Metric
1 oz	30 g	13 oz	370 g
2 oz	60 g	14 oz	400 g
3 oz	85 g	15 oz	425 g
4 oz	110 g	(1 lb) 16 oz	450 g
5 oz	140 g	1½ lb	680 g
6 oz	170 g	2 lb	910 g
7 oz	200 g	2½ lb	1.1 kg
(½ lb) 8 oz	225 g	3 lb	1.4 kg
9 oz	255 g	3½ lb	1.6 kg
10 oz	280 g	4 lb	1.8 kg
11 oz	310 g	4½ lb	2 kg
12 oz	340 g	5 lb	2.3 kg

Accurate conversions

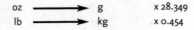

oz ⟶ g   x 28.349
lb ⟶ kg   x 0.454

Metric to UK imperial conversions
The metric kilogram (kg) equals 1000 grams (g), which is equal to
2.205 pounds (lb) – just over 35 ounces (oz).

1 kg or 1000 g	=	2.205 lb or 35.27 oz
½ kg or 500 g	=	1.102 lb or 17.63 oz
100 g	=	3.527 oz
10 g	=	0.353 oz

Approximate conversions for kitchen use

Metric	Imperial	Metric	Imperial
15 g	½ oz	910 g	2 lb
30 g	1 oz	1 kg	2¼ lb
60 g	2 oz	1.5 kg	3¼ lb
100 g	3½ oz	2 kg	4½ lb
200 g	7 oz	2.5 kg	5½ lb
300 g	10½ oz	3 kg	6½ lb
400 g	14 oz	3.5 kg	7¾ lb
500 g	17½ oz	4 kg	8¾ lb
600 g	21 oz	4.5 kg	10 lb
700 g	25 oz	5 kg	11 lb
800 g	28 oz		

Accurate conversions

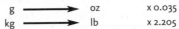

g ⟶ oz	x 0.035
kg ⟶ lb	x 2.205

Note: UK imperial weight measures are equivalent to US customary weight
measures.

Food and energy

Calories and joules

Food provides our bodies with energy. The metric unit of energy is the joule. In nutrition, the energy derived from food is measured in kilojoules (kJ).

1 kilojoule (kJ) = 1000 joules.

Although the kilojoule has officially replaced the kilocalorie, many people still talk in terms of calories. A calorie is defined as the amount of energy needed to raise the temperature of 1 cubic centimetre of water by 1 °C. The energy derived from food is usually referred to in terms of kilocalories (kcal).

1 kilocalorie (kcal) = 1000 calories.

The factor used for conversion between kilocalories and kilojoules is:

1 kilocalorie (kcal) = 4.19 kilojoules (kJ).

Conversion

kcal $\longrightarrow$ kJ   x 4.19

Energy in different foods

Different nutrients provide us with different amounts of energy. For example, a gram of carbohydrate provides 17 kJ but a gram of fat provides 38 kJ. Replacing fats with carbohydrates in the diet is a good way to reduce calorie intake.

Energy yields of foods

Food	Energy yield	
	kJ per g/ml	kcal per g/ml
Fats	38	9
Carbohydrates	17	4
Proteins	17	4
Vitamins	0	0
Minerals	0	0
Water	0	0
Fibre	0	0

Food and drink calorie table

(energy per 100 g / 100 ml of edible portion)

Food/drink	Energy per 100 g / 100 ml	
Alcoholic drinks	kJ	kcal
Beer, bitter	130	31
Cider, dry	151	36
Lager, bottled	122	29
Spirits, 40% volume	930	222
Wine, white, medium	314	75
Wine, red	285	68
Beverages	kJ	kcal
Cocoa powder	1307	312
Coffee, infusion 5 minutes	8	2
Coffee, instant powder	419	100
Drinking chocolate powder	1534	366
Tea, without milk	0	0
Breads	kJ	kcal
Brown bread	913	218
White bread	985	235
White bread with added fibre	964	230
Wholemeal bread	901	215
Cereals	kJ	kcal
Corn flakes	1508	360
Flour, plain, white	1428	341
Flour, wholemeal	1299	310
Muesli	1521	363
Oats, porridge, raw	1571	375
Rice, brown, boiled	591	141
Rice, white, boiled	578	138
Spaghetti, white, boiled	436	104
Cheese	kJ	kcal
Brie	1336	319
Cheddar	1726	412
Cheese spread	1156	276
Cottage cheese	411	98
Fromage frais, fruit added	549	131
Eggs	kJ	kcal
Eggs, hens', boiled	616	147
Eggs, hens', fried	750	179

| Food/drink | Energy per 100 g / 100 ml | |
Fats and oils	kJ	kcal
Butter	3088	737
Low-fat spread	1634	390
Margerine, polyunsaturated	3096	739
Sunflower seed oil	3767	899

Fish and fish products	kJ	kcal
Cod in batter, fried in vegetable oil	834	199
Fish fingers, grilled	897	214
Haddock, steamed	411	98
Herring, grilled	834	199
Mackerel, fried	788	188
Pilchards, canned in tomato sauce	528	126
Prawns, boiled	448	107
Sardines, canned in oil, drained	909	217
Tuna, canned in brine, drained	448	107

Fruit	kJ	kcal
Apples, eating, raw	197	47
Apricots, raw	117	28
Apricots, stewed with sugar	251	60
Avocado	796	190
Bananas	398	95
Blackcurrants, stewed with sugar	247	59
Cherries, raw, weighed without stones	201	48
Dates, dried, weighed without stones	1131	270
Figs, dried	876	209
Gooseberries, stewed with sugar	210	50
Grapefruit, raw	126	30
Grapes	252	60
Kiwi fruit	205	49
Mangoes, ripe	239	57
Melon, honeydew	117	28
Oranges	155	37
Peaches, canned in syrup	272	65
Peaches, raw	138	33
Pears, raw	168	40
Pineapple, canned in juice	222	53
Plums, raw	151	36
Prunes	591	141
Raspberries, raw	105	25

Food/drink	Energy per 100 g / 100 ml	
Fruit (continued)	kJ	kcal
Rhubarb, stewed with sugar	189	45
Strawberries, raw	113	27
Sultanas	1048	250

Meat	kJ	kcal
Bacon, back rasher, fried	1948	465
Bacon, back rasher, grilled	1697	405
Beef, lean, roast	821	196
Beef, mince, stewed	960	229
Beefburgers, frozen, fried	1106	264
Chicken boiled, no skin	767	183
Chicken roast, meat and skin	905	216
Chicken roast, no skin	620	148
Corned beef, canned	909	217
Kidney, pig, stewed	641	153
Lamb, chops, grilled	930	222
Lamb, roast, no skin	1115	266
Liver, chicken, fried	813	194
Liver, lamb, fried	972	232
Pate, liver	1324	316
Pork chops, loin, lean only, grilled	947	226
Pork, roast, lean and fat	1198	286
Salami	2057	491
Sausages, beef, grilled	1110	265
Sausage, low fat, grilled	960	229
Sausages, pork, grilled	1332	318
Steak and kidney pie, individual	1353	323
Turkey, roast, meat and skin	716	171

Milk and milk products	kJ	kcal
Cream, fresh, single	830	198
Dried skimmed milk	210	50
Evaporated milk	270	64
Semi-skimmed milk	193	46
Skimmed milk	138	33
Whole milk	277	66
Yoghurt, low fat	197	47
Yoghurt, whole milk, fruit	440	105
Yoghurt, whole milk, plain	331	79

Food/drink	Energy per 100 g / 100 ml	
Nuts	kJ	kcal
Almonds	2564	612
Coconut, desiccated	2531	604
Peanut butter (smooth)	2610	623
Peanuts, roasted and salted	2522	602
Potatoes and potato products	kJ	kcal
Chips, fried in vegetable oil	792	189
Oven chips, frozen, baked	679	162
Potato crisps	2288	546
Potatoes, new, boiled	318	76
Potatoes, old, baked, flesh and skin	356	85
Potatoes, old, boiled	335	80
Potatoes, old, mashed	499	119
Potatoes, old, roasted in vegetable oil	624	149
Soft drinks and juices	kJ	kcal
Cola	163	39
Lemonade, bottled	88	21
Orange drink, undiluted	448	107
Orange juice, unsweetened	151	36
Pineapple juice, unsweetened	172	41
Sugars and preserves	kJ	kcal
Honey	1207	288
Jam, fruit	1094	261
Maple syrup	1048	250
Marmalade	1094	261
Peppermints	1642	392
Sugar, white	1651	394
Syrup, golden	1249	298
Bread pudding	1244	297
Cheesecake, frozen	1014	242
Chocolate biscuits	2196	524
Chocolate, milk	2221	530
Currant buns	1240	296
Custard made with whole milk	490	117
Digestive biscuits, plain	1973	471
Fruit cake, rich	1429	341
Fruit pie	1089	260
Jam tarts	1542	368
Rice pudding, canned	373	89

Food/drink	Energy per 100 g / 100 ml	
Sugars and preserves (continued)	kJ	kcal
Swiss roll, individual	1412	337
Trifle	670	160

Vegetables	kJ	kcal
Aubergine, raw	63	15
Beans, baked, canned, tomato sauce	352	84
Beans, red kidney, canned, drained	419	100
Beans, runner, boiled	75	18
Beetroot, boiled	193	46
Brussels sprouts	147	35
Cabbage, boiled	38	19
Cabbage, raw	109	26
Carrots, old, boiled	101	24
Cauliflower, boiled	117	28
Celery, raw	29	7
Courgette, raw	75	18
Cucumber	42	10
Lentils, red, boiled	419	100
Lettuce	59	14
Mushrooms, raw	54	13
Onions, raw	151	36
Parsnips, boiled	277	66
Peas, frozen, boiled	289	69
Peppers, green, raw	63	15
Plantin, boiled	469	112
Processed peas, canned, re-heated	415	99
Spinach, frozen, boiled	88	21
Sweetcorn, canned, re-heated	511	122
Sweet potato, boiled	352	84
Tofu (soya bean curd), steamed	306	73
Tomatoes, raw	71	17
Turnip, boiled	50	12
Watercress	92	22
Yam, boiled	557	133

Note: Calorific values for cooked foods are for 100 g of food weighed after cooking.

14 Computers and the internet

Binary numbers

The binary system is formulated on a base of 2, or on a sum of powers of 2. For example, the number 101011 is equal to $2^5 + 0 + 2^3 + 0 + 2^1 + 2^0$; in the decimal system, this number equals 43. The system is used frequently in computer applications.

Decimal	Binary	Decimal	Binary
1	1	21	10101
2	10	30	11110
3	11	40	101000
4	100	50	110010
5	101	60	111100
6	110	90	1011010
7	111	100	1100100
8	1000	200	11001000
9	1001	300	100101100
10	1010	400	110010000
11	1011	500	111110100
12	1100	600	1001011000
13	1101	900	1110000100
14	1110	1 000	1111101000
15	1111	2 000	11111010000
16	10000	4 000	111110100000
17	10001	5 000	1001110001000
18	10010	10 000	10011100010000
19	10011	20 000	100111000100000
20	10100	100 000	11000011010100000

Data storage

As hardware capacity has increased, the standard units for measuring data storage have changed, from hard drives measured in megabytes to DVDs measured in gigabytes.

bit(s)	= 1 unit	bit(s)	= 1 unit
1	bit	5830656	floppy disk
4	nibble		(3.5 in, DD)
8	byte	11661312	floppy disk
16	word		(3.5 in, HD)
32	double-word	23322624	floppy disk
64	quadruple-word		(3.5 in, ED)
1024	kilobit	2915328	floppy disk,
4096	block		(5.25 in, DD)
8000	kilobyte	9711616	floppy disk
8192	kilobyte		(5.25 in, HD)
1048576	megabit	803454976	Zip 100
8388608	megabyte	2008637440	Zip 250
8000000	megabyte	8589934592	Jaz 1GB
1073741824	gigabit	17179869184	Jaz 2GB
8000000000	gigabyte	5448466432	CD (74 minute)
8589934592	gigabyte	5890233976	CD (80 minute)
$1.09951162778 \times 10^{12}$	terabit	40372692582.4	DVD (1 layer,
$8.79609302221 \times 10^{12}$	terabyte		1 side)
8×10^{12}	terabyte	73014444032	DVD (2 layers,
$1.12589990684 \times 10^{15}$	petabit		1 side)
$9.00719925474 \times 10^{15}$	petabyte	80745385164.8	DVD (1 layer,
8×10^{15}	petabyte		2 sides)
$1.15292150461 \times 10^{18}$	exabit	146028888064	DVD (2 layers,
$9.22337203685 \times 10^{18}$	exabyte		2 sides)
8×10^{18}	exabyte		

Data transfer rates

As hardware efficiency has improved, ever greater speeds of data transfer have been achieved. The table below lists different units of rates of transfer expressed in bits per second.

bit(s)/second	= 1 unit/second	bit(s)/second	= 1 unit/second
1	bit/sec	128×10^7	SCSI (LVD Ultra160)
8	byte/sec	256×10^7	SCSI (LVD Ultra320)
1000	kilobit/sec (SI)	336×10^5	IDE (DMA mode 0)
8000	kilobyte/sec (SI)	1064×10^5	IDE (DMA mode 1)
1024	kilobit/sec	1328×10^5	IDE (DMA mode 2)
8192	kilobyte/sec	1328×10^5	IDE (UDMA mode 0)
1×10^6	megabit/sec (SI)	2×10^8	IDE (UDMA mode 1)
8×10^6	megabyte/sec (SI)	264×10^6	IDE (UDMA mode 2)
1048576	megabit/sec	4×10^8	IDE (UDMA mode 3)
8388608	megabyte/sec	528×10^6	IDE (UDMA mode 4)
1×10^9	gigabit/sec (SI)	8×10^8	IDE (UDMA mode 5)
8×10^9	gigabyte/sec (SI)	1066666666.67	IDE (UDMA mode 6)
1073741824	gigabit/sec	264×10^6	IDE (UDMA-33)
8589934592	gigabyte/sec	528×10^6	IDE (UDMA-66)
1×10^{12}	terabit/sec (SI)	8×10^8	IDE (UDMA-100)
8×10^{12}	terabyte/sec (SI)	1066666666.67	IDE (UDMA-133)
1.0995×10^{12}	terabit/sec	12×10^6	USB
8.7961×10^{12}	terabyte/sec	48×10^7	USB 2.0
1×10^7	ethernet	4×10^8	firewire (IEEE-1394)
1×10^8	ethernet (fast)	12×10^5	CD-ROM 1X
1×10^9	ethernet (gigabit)	24×10^5	CD-ROM 2X
1×10^{10}	ethernet (10 gigabit)	36×10^5	CD-ROM 3X
64000	ISDN (single channel)	48×10^5	CD-ROM 4X
128000	ISDN (dual channel)	72×10^5	CD-ROM 6X
9600	modem (9600)	96×10^5	CD-ROM 8X
14400	modem (14.4k)	144×10^5	CD-ROM 12X
28800	modem (28.8k)	192×10^5	CD-ROM 16X
33600	modem (33.6k)	288×10^5	CD-ROM 24X
56000	modem (56k)	384×10^5	CD-ROM 32X
12×10^6	SCSI (Async)	48×10^6	CD-ROM 40X
4×10^7	SCSI (Sync)	576×10^5	CD-ROM 48X
8×10^7	SCSI (Fast)	624×10^5	CD-ROM 52X
16×10^7	SCSI (Fast Ultra)	102×10^5	DVD-ROM 1X
16×10^7	SCSI (Fast Wide)	204×10^5	DVD-ROM 2X
32×10^7	SCSI (Fast Ultra Wide)	306×10^5	DVD-ROM 3X
64×10^7	SCSI (Ultra-2)	408×10^5	DVD-ROM 4X
128×10^7	SCSI (Ultra-3)	612×10^5	DVD-ROM 6X
64×10^7	SCSI (LVD Ultra80)	816×10^5	DVD-ROM 8X

Computer coding systems: ASCII

ASCII (American Standard Code for Information Interchange) is an international coding system of character representation. Its codes represent computer commands and letters of the alphabet. Hexadecimal is a system of numbering based on 16 digits (as opposed to 10 in the decimal system): 1 to 9 and A to F.

Binary, ASCII and hexadecimal systems are used in computer programming.

The table below shows character equivalents in decimal, hexadecimal and ASCII systems.

Dec	Hex	ASCII	Dec	Hex	ASCII
000	00	NUL	031	1F	US
001	01	SOH	032	20	SPACE
002	02	STX	033	21	!
003	03	ETX	034	22	"
004	04	EOT	035	23	#
005	05	ENQ	036	24	$
006	06	ACK	037	25	%
007	07	BEL	038	26	&
008	08	BS	039	27	'
009	09	HT	040	28	(
010	0A	LF	041	29	)
011	0B	VT	042	2A	*
012	0C	FF	043	2B	+
013	0D	CR	044	2C	,
014	0E	SO	045	2D	–
015	0F	SI	046	2E	.
016	10	DLE	047	2F	/
017	11	DC1	048	30	0
018	12	DC2	049	31	1
019	13	DC3	050	32	2
020	14	DC4	051	33	3
021	15	NAK	052	34	4
022	16	SYN	053	35	5
023	17	ETB	054	36	6
024	18	CAN	055	37	7
025	19	EM	056	38	8
026	1A	SUB	057	39	9
027	1B	ESCAPE	058	3A	:
028	1C	FS	059	3B	;
029	1D	GS	060	3C	<
030	1E	RS	061	3D	=

Computer coding systems (cont.)

Dec	Hex	ASCII	Dec	Hex	ASCII
062	3E	>	101	65	e
063	3F	?	102	66	f
064	40	@	103	67	g
065	41	A	104	68	h
066	42	B	105	69	i
067	43	C	106	6A	j
068	44	D	107	6B	k
069	45	E	108	6C	l
070	46	F	109	6D	m
071	47	G	110	6E	n
072	48	H	111	6F	o
073	49	I	112	70	p
074	4A	J	113	71	q
075	4B	K	114	72	r
076	4C	L	115	73	s
077	4D	M	116	74	t
078	4E	N	117	75	u
079	4F	O	118	76	v
080	50	P	119	77	w
081	51	Q	120	78	x
082	52	R	121	79	y
083	53	S	122	7A	z
084	54	T	123	7B	{
085	55	U	124	7C	|
086	56	V	125	7D	}
087	57	W	126	7E	~
088	58	X	127	7F	DEL
089	59	Y			
090	5A	Z			
091	5B	[			
092	5C	\			
093	5D	]			
094	5E	^			
095	5F	_			
096	60	`			
097	61	a			
098	62	b			
099	63	c			
100	64	d			

Computer coding systems: Unicode™

The adoption of the Unicode™ Standard has massively increased the number of characters available to programmers since the advent of ASCII in the 1960s. The following tables give codes for the most common characters in the Latin, Greek and Cyrillic alphabets. Further Latin diacritics and characters from other scripts are available in the Unicode® Consortium's online charts at www.unicode.org.

Basic Latin

0020		Space
0021	!	Exclamation mark
0022	"	Quotation mark
0023	#	Number sign
0024	$	Dollar sign
0025	%	Percent sign
0026	&	Ampersand
0027	'	Apostrophe
0028	(	Left parenthesis
0029	)	Right parenthesis
002A	*	Asterisk
002B	+	Plus sign
002C	,	Comma
002D	-	Hyphen (minus)
002E	.	Full stop
002F	/	Solidus
0030	0	Digit zero
0031	1	Digit one
0032	2	Digit two
0033	3	Digit three
0034	4	Digit four
0035	5	Digit five
0036	6	Digit six
0037	7	Digit seven
0038	8	Digit eight
0039	9	Digit nine
003A	:	Colon
003B	;	Semicolon
003C	<	Less-than sign
003D	=	Equals sign
003E	>	Greater-than sign

Basic Latin

003F	?	Question mark
0040	@	Commercial at
0041	A	A (u.c.)
0042	B	B (u.c.)
0043	C	C (u.c.)
0044	D	D (u.c.)
0045	E	E (u.c.)
0046	F	F (u.c.)
0047	G	G (u.c.)
0048	H	H (u.c.)
0049	I	I (u.c.)
004A	J	J (u.c.)
004B	K	K (u.c.)
004C	L	L (u.c.)
004D	M	M (u.c.)
004E	N	N (u.c.)
004F	O	O (u.c.)
0050	P	P (u.c.)
0051	Q	Q (u.c.)
0052	R	R (u.c.)
0053	S	S (u.c.)
0054	T	T (u.c.)
0055	U	U (u.c.)
0056	V	V (u.c.)
0057	W	W (u.c.)
0058	X	X (u.c.)
0059	Y	Y (u.c.)
005A	Z	Z (u.c.)
005B	[	Left square bracket
005C	\	Reverse solidus
005D	]	Right square bracket

l.c. Lower case u.c. Upper case

Basic Latin

005E	^	Circumflex accent
005F	_	Low line
0060	`	Grave accent
0061	**a**	a (l.c.)
0062	**b**	b (l.c.)
0063	**c**	c (l.c.)
0064	**d**	d (l.c.)
0065	**e**	e (l.c.)
0066	**f**	f (l.c.)
0067	**g**	g (l.c.)
0068	**h**	h (l.c.)
0069	**i**	i (l.c.)
006A	**j**	j (l.c.)
006B	**k**	k (l.c.)
006C	**l**	l (l.c.)
006D	**m**	m (l.c.)
006E	**n**	n (l.c.)
006F	**o**	o (l.c.)
0070	**p**	p (l.c.)
0071	**q**	q (l.c.)
0072	**r**	r (l.c.)
0073	**s**	s (l.c.)
0074	**t**	t (l.c.)
0075	**u**	u (l.c.)
0076	**v**	v (l.c.)
0077	**w**	w (l.c.)
0078	**x**	x (l.c.)
0079	**y**	y (l.c.)
007A	**z**	z (l.c.)
007B	{	Left curly bracket
007C	|	Vertical line
007D	}	Right curly bracket
007E	~	Tilde

Latin-1 Supplement

00A1	¡	Inverted exclamation (Sp)
00A2	¢	Cent sign
00A3	£	Pound sterling sign
00A4	¤	Currency sign
00A5	¥	Yen sign
00A6	¦	Broken vertical bar
00A7	§	Section sign
00A8	¨	Diaeresis
00A9	©	Copyright sign
00AA	ª	Feminine ordinal (Sp)
00AB	«	Left guillemet (Fr)
00AC	¬	Not sign (maths)
00AD	-	Soft hyphen
00AE	®	Registered sign
00AF	¯	Macron
00B0	°	Degree sign
00B1	±	Plus-minus sign
00B2	²	Superscript two
00B3	³	Superscript three
00B4	´	Acute accent
00B5	µ	Micro sign
00B6	¶	Pilcrow; paragraph sign
00B7	•	Middle dot
00B8	¸	Cedilla
00B9	¹	Superscript one
00BA	º	Masculine ordinal (Sp)
00BB	»	Right guillemet (Fr)
00BC	¼	Vulgar fraction one quarter
00BD	½	Vulgar fraction one half
00BE	¾	Vulgar fraction three quarters
00BF	¿	Inverted question mark (Sp)
00C0	À	Latin A grave (u.c.)
00C1	Á	Latin A acute (u.c.)
00C2	Â	Latin A circumflex (u.c.)
00C3	Ã	Latin A tilde (u.c.)

Danish French German Icelandic Italian Norwegian Old English Portuguese Spanish Swedish l.c. lower case u.c. upper case

Latin-1 Supplement

00C4	Ä	Latin A diaeresis (u.c.)
00C5	Å	Latin A ring (Da, No, Sw) (u.c.)
00C6	Æ	Latin AE ligature (u.c.)
00C7	Ç	Latin C cedilla (u.c.)
00C8	È	Latin E grave (u.c.)
00C9	É	Latin E acute (u.c.)
00CA	Ê	Latin E circumflex (u.c.)
00CB	Ë	Latin E diaeresis (u.c.)
00CC	Ì	Latin I grave (u.c.)
00CD	Í	Latin I acute (u.c.)
00CE	Î	Latin I circumflex (u.c.)
00CF	Ï	Latin I diaeresis (u.c.)
00D0	Ð	Latin eth (u.c.)
00D1	Ñ	Latin N tilde (u.c.)
00D2	Ò	Latin O grave (u.c.)
00D3	Ó	Latin O acute (u.c.)
00D4	Ô	Latin O circumflex (u.c.)
00D5	Õ	Latin O tilde (u.c.)
00D6	Ö	Latin O diaeresis (u.c.)
00D7	×	Multiplication sign (maths)
00D8	Ø	Latin O slash (Da, No) (u.c.)
00D9	Ù	Latin U grave (u.c.)
00DA	Ú	Latin U acute (u.c.)
00DB	Û	Latin U circumflex (u.c.)
00DC	Ü	Latin U diaeresis (u.c.)
00DD	Ý	Latin Y acute (u.c.)
00DE	Þ	Latin thorn (OE, Ic) (u.c.)
00DF	ß	Latin Eszett (Ger) (l.c. only)
00E0	à	Latin a grave (l.c.)
00E1	á	Latin a acute (l.c.)
00E2	â	Latin a circumflex (l.c.)
00E3	ã	Latin a tilde (Port) (l.c.)
00E4	ä	Latin a diaeresis (l.c.)

Latin-1 Supplement

00E5	å	Latin a ring (Da, No, Sw) (l.c.)
00E6	æ	Latin ae ligature (Da, Ic, No, Faroese, Fr); ash (OE) (l.c.)
00E7	ç	Latin c cedilla (l.c.)
00E8	è	Latin e grave (l.c.)
00E9	é	Latin e acute (l.c.)
00EA	ê	Latin e circumflex (l.c.)
00EB	ë	Latin e diaeresis (l.c.)
00EC	ì	Latin i grave (It) (l.c.)
00ED	í	Latin i acute (l.c.)
00EE	î	Latin i circumflex (l.c.)
00EF	ï	Latin i diaeresis (l.c.)
00F0	ð	Latin eth (Ic, Faroese, OE) (l.c.)
00F1	ñ	Latin n tilde; enya (Sp) (l.c.)
00F2	ò	Latin o grave (l.c.)
00F3	ó	Latin o acute (l.c.)
00F4	ô	Latin o circumflex (l.c.)
00F5	õ	Latin o tilde (Port) (l.c.)
00F6	ö	Latin o diaeresis (l.c.)
00F7	÷	Division sign (maths)
00F8	ø	Latin o slash (Da, No) (l.c.)
00F9	ù	Latin u grave (Fr, It) (l.c.)
00FA	ú	Latin u acute (l.c.)
00FB	û	Latin u circumflex (l.c.)
00FC	ü	Latin u diaeresis (l.c.)
00FD	ý	Latin y acute (l.c.) (Czech, Slovak, Ic, Faroese, Welsh)
00FE	þ	Latin thorn (Ic, OE, from Runic script) (l.c.)
00FF	ÿ	Latin y diaeresis (Fr) (l.c.)

Danish French German Icelandic Italian Norwegian Old English Portuguese Spanish Swedish l.c. lower case u.c. upper case

Greek			Greek		
0391	A	Alpha (u.c.)	03C1	ρ	Rho (l.c.)
0392	B	Beta (u.c.)	03C2	v	Final sigma (l.c.)
0393	G	Gamma (u.c.)	03C3	s	Sigma (l.c.)
0394	D	Delta (u.c.)	03C4	t	Tau (l.c.)
0395	E	Epsilon (u.c.)	03C5	u	Upsilon (l.c.)
0396	Z	Zeta (u.c.)	03C6	f	Phi (l.c.)
0397	H	Eta (u.c.)	03C7	c	Chi (l.c.)
0398	Q	Theta (u.c.)	03C8	y	Psi (l.c.)
0399	I	Iota (u.c.)	03C9	w	Omega (l.c.)
039A	K	Kappa (u.c.)			
039B	L	Lamda (u.c.)			
039C	M	Mu (u.c.)			
039D	N	Nu (u.c.)			
039E	X	Xi (u.c.)			
039F	O	Omicron (u.c.)			
03A0	P	Pi (u.c.)			
03A1	R	Rho (u.c.)			
03A3	S	Sigma (u.c.)			
03A4	T	Tau (u.c.)			
03A5	U	Upsilon (u.c.)			
03A6	F	Phi (u.c.)			
03A7	C	Chi (u.c.)			
03A8	Y	Psi (u.c.)			
03A9	W	Omega (u.c.)			
03B1	a	Alpha (l.c.)			
03B2	b	Beta (l.c.)			
03B3	g	Gamma (l.c.)			
03B4	d	Delta (l.c.)			
03B5	e	Epsilon (l.c.)			
03B6	z	Zeta (l.c.)			
03B7	h	Eta (l.c.)			
03B8	j	Theta (l.c.)			
03B9	i	Iota (l.c.)			
03BA	κ	Kappa (l.c.)			
03BB	l	Lamda (l.c.)			
03BC	m	Mu (l.c.)			
03BD	n	Nu (l.c.)			
03BE	x	Xi (l.c.)			
03BF	o	Omicron (l.c.)			
03C0	p	Pi (l.c.)			

l.c. Lower case   u.c. Upper case

Cyrillic				Cyrillic		
`0410	А	A (u.c.)		0438	и	I (l.c.)
0411	Б	Be (u.c.)		0439	й	Short i (l.c.)
0412	В	Ve (u.c.)		043A	к	Ka (l.c.)
0413	Г	Ghe (u.c.)		043B	л	El (l.c.)
0414	Д	De (u.c.)		043C	м	Em (l.c.)
0415	Е	Ie (u.c.)		043D	н	En (l.c.)
0416	Ж	Zhe (u.c.)		043E	о	O (l.c.)
0417	З	Ze (u.c.)		043F	п	Pe (l.c.)
0418	И	I (u.c.)		0440	р	Er (l.c.)
0419	Й	Short i (u.c.)		0441	с	Es (l.c.)
041A	К	Ka (u.c.)		0442	т	Te (l.c.)
041B	Л	El (u.c.)		0443	у	U (l.c.)
041C	М	Em (u.c.)		0444	ф	Ef (l.c.)
041D	Н	En (u.c.)		0445	х	Ha (l.c.)
041E	О	O (u.c.)		0446	ц	Tse (l.c.)
041F	П	Pe (u.c.)		0447	ч	Che (l.c.)
0420`	Р	Er (u.c.)		0448``	ш	Sha (l.c.)
0421	С	Es (u.c.)		0449`	щ	Shcha (l.c.)
0422	Т	Te (u.c.)		044A`	ъ	Hard sign (l.c.)
0423	У	U (u.c.)		044B	ы	Yeru (l.c.)
0424	Ф	Ef (u.c.)		044C	ь	Soft sign (l.c.)
0425	Х	Ha (u.c.)		044D	э	E (l.c.)
0426	Ц	Tse (u.c.)		044E	ю	Yu (l.c.)
0427	Ч	Che (u.c.)		044F	я	Ya (l.c.)
0428	Ш	Sha (u.c.)		0450	è	Ie with grave (l.c.)
0429	Щ	Shcha (u.c.)		0451	ё	Io (l.c.)
042A	Ъ	Hard sign (u.c.)				
042B	Ы	Yeru (u.c.)				
042C	Ь	Soft sign (u.c.)				
042D	Э	E (u.c.)				
042E	Ю	Yu (u.c.)				
042F	Я	Ya (u.c.)				
0430	а	A (l.c.)				
0431	б	Be (l.c.)				
0432	в	Ve (l.c.)				
0433	г	Ghe (l.c.)				
0434	д	De (l.c.)				
0435	е	Ie (l.c.)				
0436	ж	Zhe (l.c.)				
0437	з	Ze (l.c.)				

l.c. Lower case u.c. Upper case

Common HTML codes

HyperText Markup Language (HTML) is the basic coding language of the World Wide Web, the highly graphical international network of computers that most people now regard as the internet. HTML was developed in 1989 by Sir Tim Berners-Lee at the CERN in Geneva.

The tags below are some of the most basic codes that convert plain text to formatted HTML text for use on the web. For further information visit the World Wide Web Consortium at www.w3.org.

<a href="#NAME"></a> Links to a target location on a page

<a href="mailto:EMAIL"></a> Creates an email

<a href="URL"></a> Creates a hyperlink

<a name="NAME"></a> Creates a target location on a page

<b></b> Displays enclosed text as bold

<blockquote> </blockquote> Indent text from left and right

<body alink=?> Specifies the colour of links on click

<body bgcolor=?> Specifies the background colour

<body link=?> Specifies the colour of links

<body text=?> Specifies the text colour

<body vlink=?> Specifies the colour of followed links

<body></body> Encloses the main visible part of the page

**
** Inserts a line break

<cite></cite> Marks text as a citation

<dd> Marks each definition in a list

<div align=?> Aligns sections of HTML to the left, right or centre

<dl></dl> Creates a definition list

<dt> Marks each term to be defined in a list

<em></em> Emphasizes text with italic type

<font color=?></font> Specifies font colour

<font size=?></font> Specifies font size

<form></form> Creates a form

<frame name="name"> Names a frame

<frame noresize> Prevents users resizing the frame

<frame src="URL"> Specifies the page to be displayed in a frame

<frame> Defines a frame

<frameset></frameset> Defines a frameset and replaces the <body> tag in a page with frames

<head></head> Creates the head section of an HTML page, which – apart from the title – is invisible

<h1></h1> to <h6></h6> Creates headers in diminishing order of size, where <h1> is the largest and <h6> the smallest

<hr noshade> Creates an unshaded horizontal rule

<hr size=?> Specifies the size (height) of a horizontal rule

<hr width=?> Specifies the width of a horizontal rule

<hr> Creates a horizontal rule

<html></html> Identifies enclosed text as HTML

<i></i> Displays enclosed text as italic

<img src="name" align=?> Aligns an image to the left, right, centre, bottom, top or middle

<img src="name" border=?> Specifies the size of a border around an image

<img src="name"> Inserts an image from the URL specified

<input type="checkbox" name="NAME"> Creates a checkbox on a form

<input type="image" border=o name="NAME" src="name.gif"> Creates a button on a form using an image

<input type="reset"> Creates a Reset button on a form

<input type="submit" value="NAME"> Creates a Submit button on a form

<li></li> Creates a list item

<noframes></noframes> Defines an alternative for users with browsers that don't support frames

<ol></ol> Creates an ordered list, using either numbers or symbols

<option> Defines menu items on a form

<p align=?> Aligns a paragraph to the left, right or centre

<p></p> Creates a new paragraph

<pre></pre> Displays preformatted text

<select name="NAME"></select> Creates a pulldown menu on a form

<strong></strong> Emphasizes enclosed text in bold

<table border=#> Specifies the width of a table's border

<table cellpadding=#> Specifies the space between a cell's contents and borders

<table cellspacing=#> Specifies the space between table cells

<table width=# or %> Specifies the width of a table – in pixels or as a percentage of the page's total width

<table></table> Creates a table

<td></td> Creates standard cells in a table

<th></th> Creates header cells in a table

<title></title> Creates the name of the page to display in the title bar

<tr align=?> Aligns a table row left, right or centre

<tr valign=?> Sets the vertical alignment of a table row to top, middle or bottom

<tr></tr> Creates rows in a table

<tt></tt> Displays text in a monospaced (typewriter-style) font

<u></u> Displays enclosed text as underlined

<ul></ul> Creates an unordered (bulleted) list

Internet addresses

An internet address (or Uniform Resource Locator, URL) usually consists of at least the following parts:

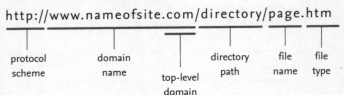

There are 14 top-level domains, each intended to demarcate different areas of the web. The top-level domains are:

.aero	aviation industry
.biz	commercial businesses
.com	companies
.coop	co-operative associations
.edu	US educational institutions
.gov	US government
.info	information
.int	international treaty organisations
.mil	US military
.museum	museums
.name	individuals
.net	networks
.org	non-commercial organizations
.pro	professional associations

The top level of a geographically located domain name is usually the country code, for example .uk for the United Kingdom. These can then be further categorized into, for instance, .ac.uk, .org.uk and .co.uk, for academic, non-commercial and commercial domains respectively. The following table lists the top-level codes for every country in the world.

Internet country codes

.ad	Andorra	**.am**	Armenia
.ae	United Arab Emirates	**.an**	Netherlands Antilles
.af	Afghanistan	**.ao**	Angola
.ag	Antigua and Barbuda	**.aq**	Antarctica
.ai	Anguilla	**.ar**	Argentina
.al	Albania	**.as**	American Samoa

Internet country codes (continued)

.at	Austria		.cv	Cape Verde
.au	Australia		.cx	Christmas Island
.aw	Aruba		.cy	Cyprus
.ax	Åland Islands		.cz	Czech Republic
.az	Azerbaijan		.de	Germany
.ba	Bosnia and Herzegovina		.dj	Djibouti
.bb	Barbados		.dk	Denmark
.bd	Bangladesh		.dm	Dominica
.be	Belgium		.do	Dominican Republic
.bf	Burkina Faso		.dz	Algeria
.bg	Bulgaria		.ec	Ecuador
.bh	Bahrain		.ee	Estonia
.bi	Burundi		.eg	Egypt
.bj	Benin		.eh	Western Sahara
.bm	Bermuda		.er	Eritrea
.bn	Brunei Darussalam		.es	Spain
.bo	Bolivia		.et	Ethiopia
.br	Brazil		.fi	Finland
.bs	Bahamas		.fj	Fiji
.bt	Bhutan		.fk	Falkland Islands
.bv	Bouvet Island		.fm	Micronesia, Federated States
.bw	Botswana		.fo	Faroe Islands
.by	Belarus		.fr	France
.bz	Belize		.ga	Gabon
.ca	Canada		.gd	Grenada
.cc	Cocos (Keeling) Islands		.ge	Georgia
.cd	Congo, The Democratic Republic of the		.gf	French Guiana
.cf	Central African Republic		.gh	Ghana
.cg	Congo		.gi	Gibraltar
.ch	Switzerland		.gl	Greenland
.ci	Côte d'Ivoire		.gm	Gambia
.ck	Cook Islands		.gn	Guinea
.cl	Chile		.gp	Guadeloupe
.cm	Cameroon		.gq	Equatorial Guinea
.cn	China		.gr	Greece
.co	Colombia		.gs	South Georgia and the South Sandwich Islands
.cr	Costa Rica		.gt	Guatemala
.cs	Serbia and Montenegro		.gu	Guam
.cu	Cuba		.gw	Guinea-Bissau

Internet country codes (continued)

.gy	Guyana	.lt	Lithuania
.hk	Hong Kong	.lu	Luxembourg
.hm	Heard Island and McDonald Islands	.lv	Latvia
		.ly	Libyan Arab Jamahiriya
.hn	Honduras	.ma	Morocco
.hr	Croatia	.mc	Monaco
.ht	Haiti	.md	Moldova, Republic of
.hu	Hungary	.mg	Madagascar
.id	Indonesia	.mh	Marshall Islands
.ie	Ireland	.mk	Macedonia, The Former Yugoslav Republic of
.il	Israel		
.in	India	.ml	Mali
.io	British Indian Ocean Territory	.mm	Myanmar
.iq	Iraq	.mn	Mongolia
.ir	Iran, Islamic Republic Of	.mo	Macao
.is	Iceland	.mp	Northern Mariana Islands
.it	Italy	.mq	Martinique
.jm	Jamaica	.mr	Mauritania
.jo	Jordan	.ms	Montserrat
.jp	Japan	.mt	Malta
.ke	Kenya	.mu	Mauritius
.kg	Kyrgyzstan	.mv	Maldives
.kh	Cambodia	.mw	Malawi
.ki	Kiribati	.mx	Mexico
.km	Comoros	.my	Malaysia
.kn	Saint Kitts and Nevis	.mz	Mozambique
.kp	Korea, Democratic People's Republic Of (North)	.na	Namibia
		.nc	New Caledonia
.kr	Korea, Republic Of (South)	.ne	Niger
.kw	Kuwait	.nf	Norfolk Island
.ky	Cayman Islands	.ng	Nigeria
.kz	Kazakhstan	.ni	Nicaragua
.la	Lao People's Democratic Republic	.nl	Netherlands
		.no	Norway
.lb	Lebanon	.np	Nepal
.lc	Saint Lucia	.nr	Nauru
.li	Liechtenstein	.nu	Niue
.lk	Sri Lanka	.nz	New Zealand
.lr	Liberia	.om	Oman
.ls	Lesotho	.pa	Panama

Internet country codes (continued)

.pe	Peru		.tg	Togo
.pf	French Polynesia		.th	Thailand
.pg	Papua New Guinea		.tj	Tajikistan
.ph	Philippines		.tk	Tokelau
.pk	Pakistan		.tl	Timor-Leste
.pl	Poland		.tm	Turkmenistan
.pm	Saint Pierre and Miquelon		.tn	Tunisia
.pn	Pitcairn		.to	Tonga
.pr	Puerto Rico		.tr	Turkey
.ps	Palestinian Territory		.tt	Trinidad and Tobago
.pt	Portugal		.tv	Tuvalu
.pw	Palau		.tw	Taiwan
.py	Paraguay		.tz	Tanzania, United Republic of
.qa	Qatar		.ua	Ukraine
.re	Réunion		.ug	Uganda
.ro	Romania		.uk	United Kingdom
.ru	Russian Federation		.um	US Minor Outlying Islands
.rw	Rwanda		.us	United States
.sa	Saudi Arabia		.uy	Uruguay
.sb	Solomon Islands		.uz	Uzbekistan
.sc	Seychelles		.va	Vatican City State
.sd	Sudan		.vc	Saint Vincent and the Grenadines
.se	Sweden			
.sg	Singapore		.ve	Venezuela
.sh	Saint Helena		.vg	Virgin Islands, British
.si	Slovenia		.vi	Virgin Islands, US
.sj	Svalbard and Jan Mayen		.vn	Vietnam
.sk	Slovakia		.vu	Vanuatu
.sl	Sierra Leone		.wf	Wallis and Futuna
.sm	San Marino		.ws	Samoa
.sn	Senegal		.ye	Yemen
.so	Somalia		.yt	Mayotte
.sr	Suriname		.za	South Africa
.st	Sao Tome and Principe		.zm	Zambia
.sv	El Salvador		.zw	Zimbabwe
.sy	Syrian Arab Republic			
.sz	Swaziland			
.tc	Turks and Caicos Islands			
.td	Chad			
.tf	French Southern Territories			

INDEX

abampere 22
abbreviations, glossary
  14–18
abcoulomb 22
abfarad 22
abhenry 22
absolute zero 22
absorptiometer 22
absorption hygrometer 23
abvolt 23
acceleration 23
accelerometer 23
acidity 23
acre 23
acute angle 24
aeon, eon 24
altazimuth 24
altimeter 24
altitude 24
alto- 24
amagat 24
ammeter 25
ampere (A) 25
ampere hour 25
ampere turn 25
Ampère, André Marie 25
amu 25
anemometer 25
aneroid barometer 26
angles 26, 173
ångström (Å) 26
Ångström, Anders Jonas
  26
anomalistic month 26
anomalistic year 26
apothecaries' system 27
are (a) 27
area rod 27
arithmetic operations 197
astrolabe 27

astronomical distances 27
astronomical
  measurements 69
astronomical unit (AU) 27
atmosphere 27
atomic clock 27
atomic mass 113
atomic mass unit (amu)
  28, 113
atto- 28
Avogadro, Amedeo 28
Avogadro's number 28
avoirdupois system 28
baker's dozen 28
balance 29
barleycorn 29
barograph 29
barometer 29
baud 29
becquerel (Bq) 29
Becquerel, Antoine Henri
  30
Beaufort, Sir Francis 30
bel (B) 30
beverage measures 108
billion (bil) 30
binary numbers 216
binary system 30
bit 30
body measurements 180
bolt 31
boutylka 31
British thermal unit (Btu)
  31
Bourdon gauge 31
bushel (bu) 31
byte 31
calendar, perpetual 142–57
calendar, types of 141–42
calibre 31
caliper 31
calorie (cal) 32

candela 32
carat 32
Celsius, Anders 32
Celsius scale 32
centi- 32
centigrade 32
centilitre 32
centimetre 33
centimetre-gram-second
  (cgs) system 33
centrad 33
century 33
chain 33
chaldron 33
circular inch 33
circular mil 33
clock 34
clothes sizes 34, 178–79
common HTML codes
  226-27
compass 171
computer coding systems
  219-20
conductance 34
conversion formulae, area
  78–79
conversion formulae,
  energy 120–21
conversion formulae,
  length 69–70
conversion formulae,
  speed 158–59
conversion formulae,
  temperature 129
conversion formulae,
  volume 90–92
conversion formulae,
  weight 110–11
conversion tables, angles
  174–75
conversion tables, area
  81–84

conversion tables, energy 122

conversion tables, length 72–76

conversion tables, speed 161-64

conversion tables, temperature 129–31

conversion formulae, time 135

conversion tables, volume 96–103

conversion tables, weight 114–17

cooking measures 106, 206

cord 34

coulomb (C) 34

counting stick 34

crore 34

cubic units (cu or 3) 34

cubit 35

cup 35

curie (Ci) 35

Curie, Marie 35

customary units 35

cycle 36

data storage 217

data transfer rates 218

day 36

deca- 36

decade 36

deci- 36

decibel (dB) 37

decimals 186–87

decimal system 37

degree (°) 37

digit 37

digitizer 37

dioptre (D) 37

douzième 38

dozen 38

drachm 38

dram (dr) 38

dry 38

dry quart (dry qt) 38

dynamometer 38

dyne 38

early units 39

EDM (Electronic-distance-measuring equipment) 39

electromagnetic spectrum 124

electromagnetic waves 123

EMU (electromagnetic units) 39

electronvolt (eV) 39

ESU (electrostatic units) 39

engineer's chain 39

envelope sizes and styles 177–78

erg 39

exa- 39

Fahrenheit, Daniel Gabriel 40

farad (F) 40

faraday 40

Faraday, Michael 40

fathom (fm) 40

feet per minute 40

femto- 40

Fibonacci sequence 185

firkin 40

fluid 41

fluid dram 41

fluid ounce 41

food and drink calorie table 211–15

food and energy 210

foot (ft) 41

force pound 41

fractions 186–87

furlong (fur) 41

gallon (gal) 41

galvanometer 41

gauge 41

Geiger counter 41

geological timescale 140

geometric degree 42

geometric minute 42

geometry of area, formulae 86–87

geometry of surface area, formulae 88–89

geometry of volume, formulae 104–05

giga- 42

gill 42

global positioning system 42

grade (g) 42

gradient 42

gradienter 42

gradiometer 43

grain (gr) 43

gram (g) 43

gross 43

gun gauge 181

Gunter's chain 43

Gyrocompass 43

Gyroscope 43

half life 43

hand 44

hardness 44

hectare 44

hecto- 44

henry (H) 44

hertz (Hz) 44

Hertz, Heinrich Rudolf 44

horse measurements 181

horsepower (hp) 44

hour (hr) 44

hundredweight (cwt) 45

hurricane 166–67

hydrometer 45
hygrometer 45
inch (in) 45
inches per second 45
interferometer 45
internet addresses 228
internet country codes
    228–31
joule (J) 46
Joule, James Prescott 46
keg 46
kelvin (k) 46
kilo- 46
kilocalorie (kcal or cal) 46
kilometre (km) 46
kiloparsec 46
kilowatt (kW) 46
kilowatt-hour (kWh) 47
kitchen weights 208–09
knot (kn) 47
lakh 47
lambda 47
league 47
length rod 47
light year 47, 204
litre (l) 47
long distances 47
long (UK) hundredweight
    (cwt) 47
lumen (lm) 48
lunar month 48
lux (lx) 48
magnum 48
Mach, Ernst 48
manometer 48
maser 48
mass quarter 48
mathematical symbols
    196
mean solar day 49
mega- 49
measurement systems,

early 68
measuring earthquakes
    124–25
measuring large distances
    69
measuring small
    distances 68
measuring sound 126–127
measuring tapes 49
measuring time 137
Mercalli, Giuseppe 49
meridian 49
metre (m) 49
metres per minute
    (m/min) 50
metric horsepower 50
metric ounce 50
metric system 50
metric ton 50
metric units 50
mho 51
micro- 51
micrometre 51
micron (μm) 51
microscopic lengths 51
mile (mi) 51
miles per hour (mph) 51
millennium 51
milli- 52
Milne, John 52
Minim 52
minute (m or min) 52
Mohs' scale (of hardness)
    52
Mohs, Friedrich 52
Mole (mol) 53
Morley, Edward Williams
    53
month 53
multiplication grid 195
multiplication tables
    189–94

nano- 53
Napier, John 53
named numbers 182
nautical chain 53
nautical mile (n mi) 53
newton (N) 53
Newton, Isaac 54
numerical prefixes 182
Ohm (Ω) 54
Ohm, Georg Simon 54
orbital second 54
ounce (oz) 54
ounce troy 54
pace 54
palm 55
paper sizes, standard UK
    176
parsec (pc) 55
pascal (Pa) 55
Pascal, Blaise 55
peck (pk) 55
pennyweight (dwt) 55
perch 55
percentages 186–87
perigee 55
peta- 55
pi (π) 55
pica 56
pico- 56
pint (pt) 56
pixel 56
planetary distances
    200–01
planetary features 198
point 56
pole 56
polygons 168–70
pound (lb) 56
poundal 56
prefixes in order of value
    183
prime numbers 185

protractor 56
PSI 57
Pythagoras 57
quadrilaterals 170
quart (qt) 57
quarter (qr) 57
quarter troy (qr tr) 57
quintal (q) 57
quipu 57
rad 57
radar 57
Rankine scale of
    temperature 58
Rankine, William John
    MacQuorn 58
ream 58
Réaumur 58
reputed quart 58
Richter, Charles Francis
    58
Richter scale 58
r.m.s. value 59
rod 59
Roman mile 59
Roman numerals 184
röntgen 59
Röntgen, Wilhelm Conrad
    59
rood 60
roots, cube 188
roots, square 188
rulers 60
score 60
scales of hardness 118–19
scruple 60
sea mile 60
second 60
short (US) hundredweight
    60
sidereal day 60
sidereal month 60
sidereal period 202

sidereal second 60
sidereal year 61
siemens (S) 61
Siemens, William 61
Solar system 203
specialist units 61
spoonful equivalents for
    ingredients 207
square chain 61
square units 61
stars, nearest 205
stellar magnitudes 204
steradian 61
stère 61
stone 62
synodic month 62
systems of measurement,
    temperature 128
system of units,
    international 19
tablespoon (tbsp) 62
teaspoon (tsp) 62
tera- 62
tesla (T) 62
Tesla, Nikola 62
theodolite 63
thermograph 63
thermometer 63
Thomson, William Kelvin
    63
time zones of the world
    138–39
ton 63
tonne (t) 63
tonne of coal equivalent
    63
ton troy (ton tr) 63
trillion 64
triple point 64
Torricelli, Evangelista 64
total station 64
transit 64

triangles 170
tropical month 64
tropical year 64
troy pound (lb tr) 65
troy system 65
Unicode™ conversion
    charts 221-25
unit conversion index
    12–13
units, imperial 20
units, capacity 93
units, metric 20, 50
units, time 134
useful temperatures 132
vernier scale 65
volume quarter 65
volt (V) 65
Volta, Alessandro
    Giuseppe Anastasi 65
volt-ampere 65
voltmeter 65
watt (W) 66
Watt, James 66
weber (W) 66
Weber, Wilhelm Eduard
    66
Winchester quart 66
wind-chill temperature
    133
wind speeds 166
X-unit (x or XU) 66
yard (yd) 66
yards per minute (ypm) 67
yardstick 67
year 67
yocto- 67
yotta- 67
zepto- 67
zetta- 67